The Perils of International Regime Complexity in Shadow Banking

The Perils of International Regime Complexity in Shadow Banking

LUCIA QUAGLIA

OXFORD
UNIVERSITY PRESS

OXFORD
UNIVERSITY PRESS

Great Clarendon Street, Oxford, OX2 6DP,
United Kingdom

Oxford University Press is a department of the University of Oxford. It furthers the University's objective of excellence in research, scholarship, and education by publishing worldwide. Oxford is a registered trade mark of Oxford University Press in the UK and in certain other countries

Impression: 1

Published in the United States of America by Oxford University Press
198 Madison Avenue, New York, NY 10016, United States of America

British Library Cataloguing in Publication Data
Data available

Library of Congress Control Number: 2021970081

ISBN 978–0–19–286652–3

DOI: 10.1093/oso/9780192866523.001.0001

Printed and bound by
CPI Group (UK) Ltd, Croydon, CR0 4YY

Preface

Shadow banking is an umbrella term used to describe a variety of entities and activities outside the 'traditional' banking sector. Indeed, the definition of what exactly is shadow banking, which entities and activities fall within its scope, and the very use of the term— which is seen as having some negative connotations—have been contested. Shadow banking massively increased in the decades before the 2008 international financial crisis and substantially contributed to it. After a setback in the wake of that crisis, the growth of the shadow banking system gradually resumed, at least for some entities and activities, and became a significant concern in the context of the covid-related economic crisis in 2020–1. Despite its massive size, its cross-border nature, and the risks it entails for financial stability, the international post-crisis reforms concerning the governance of shadow banking were limited and regulation remained overall rather feeble. Why?

Whereas most academic research has examined post-crisis domestic regulatory changes, especially in the main jurisdictions, namely the United States, the European Union, and China, this book discusses the international governance of shadow banking by examining the post-crisis reforms that involved a multitude of organizations and committees that monitor and regulate various aspects of global shadow banking. Furthermore, several international standards (or 'soft laws') were jointly issued by two (or more) bodies. This resulted in an international 'regime complex' in which states, regulators, and private actors engaged in a 'game of shadows' concerning the definition, monitoring, and regulation of global shadow banking. The aim of this research is to investigate these processes and their outcomes by providing a theoretically informed and empirically grounded account of post-crisis reforms at the international level.

While writing this book, there were several challenges. First, the international governance of shadow banking is a moving target, hence the content of the book had to be updated over time and parts of it remain work in progress. Yet, most of the post-2008 crisis regulatory reforms concerning shadow banking have been set in place by now. Second, there is a trade-off between the scope of the research and the depth of analysis, including its level of detail.

I opted for a broad coverage and, therefore, I had to be selective about the material included (or not) in each chapter. Since this book is about international governance, the domestic level is examined only in so far as this is useful to shed light on the international standard-setting process. Third, I wanted to write a book that could be of interest and accessible to political scientists, political economists, and public policy scholars. Thus, I adopted a similar structure for each empirical chapter. In each chapter, I discuss the main issues at stake regarding a specific aspect (or 'elemental regime') of shadow banking and the international standard-setting process. I, then, assess the explanatory power of the analytical framework put forward in Chapter 2 against the empirical record. The penultimate chapter carries out a comparative assessment across shadow banking elemental regimes.

Since I started my research, several academics have generously given me their advice and commented on parts of the book, conference papers, and other academic publications in which some of the findings of my research were presented. In particular, I would like to thank, Elena Baracani, Shawn Donnelly, Sandra Eckert, Scott James, Daniela Gabor, David Howarth, Peter Knaack, Matthias Kranke, Antonio Marcacci, Giuseppe Montalbano, Manuela Moschella, Elliot Posner, Bernardo Rangoni, Aneta Spendzharova, Mark Thatcher, Matthias Thiemann, who commented on parts of my manuscript. I am also grateful to the anonymous reviewers of my book manuscript for their constructive comments. I have further benefited from a range of comments offered by participants at conferences organised by the International Studies Association (ISA) and the European Consortium for Political Research (ECPR) as well as research seminars organsied by the Foundation of Law and Finance at the University of Frankfurt, the Department of Economics and Political Science at the University of St Gallen and the Department of Political Science at the University of York . Part of Chapter 5 on shadow banking entities draws on my joint article with Scott James, published in *Regulation & Governance* (2022) and part of Chapter 7 on securitization draws on an article I have published in the *Journal of Common Market Studies* (2021).

Last but surely not least, I wish to thank the OUP series editor, Dominic Byatt, for his prompt interest in and unfaltering commitment to this project, as well as Celine Louasli, the project editor

Bologna, October 2021

Contents

List of Figures

List of Tables

List of Abbreviations

BCBS	Basel Committee on Banking Supervision
BIS	Bank for International Settlements
ECB	European Central Bank
EBA	European Banking Authority
ESMA	European Securities and Markets Authority
ESRB	European Systemic Risk Board
EU	European Union
FSB	Financial Stability Board
G-SIFI	globally systemically important financial institution
G20	Group of Twenty
FSOC	Financial Stability Oversight Council
IAIS	International Association of Insurance Supervisors
IASB	International Accounting Standards Board
IMF	International Monetary Fund
IOSCO	International Organization of Securities Commissions
MMF	money market fund
MUNFI	Monitoring universe of non-bank financial intermediation
NAV	Net asset value
NBFI	Non-bank financial intermediation
OECD	Organization for Economic Co-operation and Development
OFI	Other Financial Intermediary
OIF	Other Investment Fund
SEC	Securities and Exchange Commission
UK	United Kingdom
US	United States

1
Introduction
Shadow Banking

Shadow banking, which constitutes a huge part of the global financial system, played a crucial role in the building up and amplification of the international financial crisis of 2008 because it turbo charged that sequence of events, and it was where the financial 'weapons of mass destruction' were mostly located (Group of Thirty 2009; De Larosière et al. 2009; Financial Services Authority 2009). Despite the acknowledgement of the risks posed by shadow banking, post-crisis regulatory reforms were feeble and piecemeal. At the international level, the political leaders of the jurisdictions of the Group of Twenty (G20) (2010) tasked financial regulators gathered in the Financial Stability Board (FSB) and other international standard-setting bodies to 'strengthen the oversight and regulation of the shadow banking system' and regulators worked on this matter for several years. Yet, the results were underwhelming and the international governance of shadow banking remained weak. Indeed, in the context of the Covid-19 economic crisis, there are growing concerns about this important part of the financial sector.

This book argues that the main reason for this disappointing outcome is the international architecture for shadow banking governance, which is a 'regime complex' characterized by the presence of multiple institutions and elemental regimes governing a set of related issues (Alter and Meunier 2009; Keohane and Victor 2011; Johnson and Urpelainen 2012; Pratt 2018, 2019). Indeed, shadow banking is a quintessential case for demonstrating the perils of international regime complexity,[1] which compounds problems that arise in 'silos-like' regimes, while splintering solutions. This research goes further than the existing literature in showing the negative effects of international regime complexity, explaining why it is a problem and what could be done about it. The crux of the argument is that regime complexity magnifies problems

[1] I borrowed this expression from Drezner (2009) and Alter (2022).

The Perils of International Regime Complexity in Shadow Banking. Lucia Quaglia, Oxford University Press.
 DOI: 10.1093/oso/9780192866523.003.0001

that are endemic in governing global finance—namely, interstate competition, disagreement between technocratic bodies, and the power of the financial industry—while splintering solutions, due to the fragmentation of regulatory authority. As illustrated in this book, the interplay of states, regulators, and private actors produced a 'game of shadows' concerning the definition, monitoring, and regulation of shadow banking. The playing out of such a game was facilitated by international regime complexity, which produced a multi-dimensional chessboard.

There is not a universally agreed definition of shadow banking and even the term 'shadow banking' is contested and is often accompanied by an explanatory footnote, as discussed in Chapter 3. By and large, shadow banking refers to the system of credit intermediation that involves *entities* and *activities* outside the traditional banking system. It includes entities that raise funding with deposit-like characteristics; perform maturity and/or liquidity transformation; engage in credit risk transfer; and use direct or indirect leverage (FSB 2011a, b). These entities include: money market funds (MMFs);[2] investment funds that provide credit or are leveraged, such as hedge funds[3] and private equity funds;[4] securitization[5] vehicles, such as special purpose vehicles,[6] structured investment vehicles,[7] and conduits.[8] A member of the Federal Reserve Board, Daniel Tarullo (2016a), noted that the integration of traditional bank lending and capital markets is most clearly in evidence in shadow banking, albeit in different ways.

The shadow banking system grew considerably in the run-up to the international financial crisis of 2008 also due to its competitive advantages over the traditional banking system. In fact, before the crisis, shadow banking was for the most part outside the perimeter of public regulation and oversight, although there was variation across countries (Thiemann 2018, 2014). The

[2] MMFs are a type of mutual funds that invest in high-quality, short-term debt instruments.

[3] Hedge funds are highly leveraged funds that pool investors' funds and engage in complex portfolio-construction, using high risk—high return strategies.

[4] Private equity funds resemble venture capital firms because they invest directly in companies. Once they acquire or control a company, private equity funds restructure it with the goal of selling the company for a profit.

[5] Securitization is the process whereby certain types of assets (such as mortgages, or credit card obligations) are pooled so that they can be repackaged into interest-bearing securities (Jobst 2008; for further details see Chapter 7).

[6] A special purpose vehicle, also referred to as special purpose entity, is a bankruptcy-remote subsidiary of a company that may be used as a holding company for the securitization of debt.

[7] A structured investment vehicle is a pool of investment assets that seeks to profit from credit spreads between short-term debt and long-term structured finance products, such as asset-backed securities.

[8] Conduits involve the use of special purpose vehicles by banks and other financial institutions to raise short-term funding.

shadow banking system was one of the main culprits of the crisis and some commentators considered the international financial crisis as a bank run on shadow banks (Krugman 2009), or a bank run through the back door (Engelen 2018), especially in the repo market (Gorton 2010; Gorton and Metrick 2009, 2010). Thus, from 2009 onwards, there was a concerted effort to monitor and regulate various aspects of shadow banking. At the international level, the reform of financial regulation, including shadow banking, was discussed by the political authorities (i.e. national governments) in the G20 (Viola 2014, 2015). It was followed by 'soft laws' (Brummer 2015; Zaring 2020), that is to say, international standards[9] issued by various transgovernmental fora of domestic financial regulators (Bach and Newman 2010, 2014; Newman and Posner 2018). A vast array of international financial standard-setting bodies as well as non-financial standard setters, such as the International Accounting Standards Board (IASB), were involved in the post-crisis regulation of shadow banking (see Figure 1.1) and several standards were jointly issued by these bodies, as elaborated in the following chapters.

The result was an over-crowded regulatory space and an international regime complex, whereby international standards were issued concerning shadow banking entities, activities as well as traditional banks that interacted with shadow banks (see Figure 1.1). These standards were part of elemental regimes, partly 'nested', partly 'parallel', partly 'interlinked', which are not hierarchically ordered, as elaborated in Chapter 3. Regime complexity, which has become a prominent phenomenon in world politics and the global economy

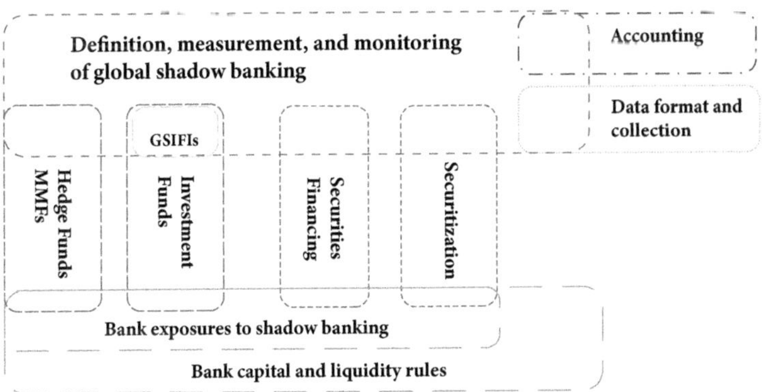

Fig. 1.1 Overview of the post-2008 crisis international shadow banking regime complex

[9] According to the FSB (2018a), international standards set out 'principles, practices, or guidelines in a given area'.

(Henning 2017; Pratt 2018), increased considerably in finance after the crisis of 2008, in particular in areas that previously were not subject to regulation and dealt with several cross-cutting issues, such as shadow banking.

Research Questions and Research Design

The magnitude of financial assets in the shadow banking system, its relatively loose regulation and oversight (especially if compared to the 'traditional' banking system), and its interconnectedness with the banking system contribute to systemic risk. Whereas other parts of the financial sector, such as banking and derivatives, were subject to significant international and domestic regulatory reforms after the international financial crisis of 2008, the governance of shadow banking remained feeble, especially at the international level, and became somewhat less stringent as time passed by, as documented in the following chapters. This is rather puzzling, given the vast size of the shadow banking system, its cross-border nature, the danger of regulatory arbitrage, and the risks it poses for financial stability. Such risk can go undetected and unmanaged in shadow banking.

Shadow banking grew dramatically in the run-up to the financial crisis of 2008—it even briefly overtook the traditional banking system in the United States (US) (Financial Crisis Inquiry Commission 2011)—and began to grow again, especially in Europe and in large emerging economies (first and foremost, China), a few years after the crisis. According to the most recent data, the 'narrow measure' of global shadow banking (for various definitions and measurements of shadow banking, see Chapter 4) is estimated at $51 trillion, around 75% of the gross domestic product of all jurisdictions of the G20, including the euro area as a whole (FSB 2019a). Furthermore, shadow banking, like derivatives (which also played a major role in the building up of the 2008 crisis), has a strong cross-border dimension, which would have called for robust international governance to safeguard the 'common good' of financial stability as well as the 'levelled playing field' across jurisdictions (Kapstein 1989; Singer 2007). Yet, this was not the case. Why?

Theoretically, this book brings together the literatures on the regulation of finance in international political economy and regime complexity in international relations. From the literature on international standard-setting in finance, this research teases out three sets of actors—states, regulators, and private actors—and several pathways through which they influenced the governance of shadow banking after the 2008 crisis. From the literature on regime complexity, this research takes the perspective of analysing the making of several international standards concerning various aspects of shadow banking at the same time, examining how they interact with one another, rather than looking at each of them in isolation, and spelling out the governance challenges in a regime complex.

Methodologically, this research is operationalized, first, by distinguishing various elemental regimes concerning different aspects of shadow banking, namely: international standards for defining, measuring, and monitoring global shadow banking; international standards for shadow banking entities, including MMFs, hedge funds, and investment funds; international standards for shadow banking activities, such as securitization, securities lending, and repos; international standards for bank capital exposures to shadow banking. For each elemental regime, this book investigates the international standard-setting processes, teasing out the key issues at stake, the preferences of states, regulators, and private actors as well as the pathways through which they exerted influence. Furthermore, the elemental regimes and their dynamics are compared and contrasted in the penultimate chapter. Overall, the book discusses the making of more than a dozen standards (principles, guidelines, etc.) from the peak of the international financial crisis in late 2008 to the present (see Figure 3.1). To do so, it relies on a variety of sources, including a systematic survey of press coverage, policy documents, responses to consultations, and confidential semi-structured elite interviews.

Overall Argument

This book identifies a 'game of shadows', which unfolded in consecutive and recursive steps concerning the definition, monitoring, and regulation of shadow banking internationally (see Figure 1.2). In a real-life game of shadows, the casting of selective light in different directions also moves the shadows in different ways, failing to illuminate the entire picture.[10] Likewise, states, regulators, and private actors tended to cast light away from various parts of the shadow banking system—which was portrayed as 'something else', 'somewhere else' (Palan and Nesvetailova 2014). Thus, shadow banking was (re)fined

[10] In one of her novels, the science-fiction writer Ursula K. Le Guin wrote that 'When you light a candle, you also cast a shadow', a metaphor used by Greene and Broomfield (2013) with reference to shadow banking.

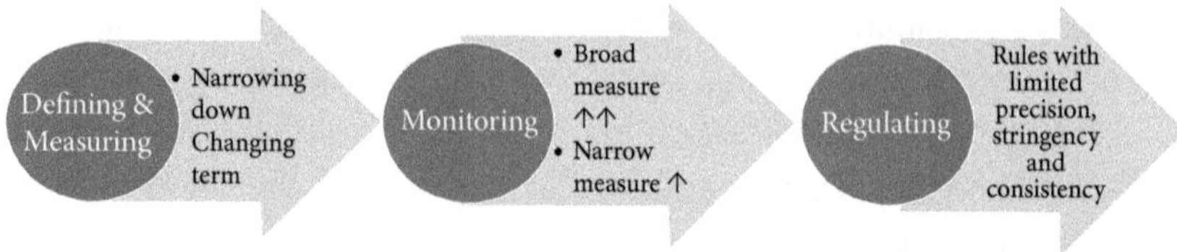

Fig. 1.2 International shadow banking governance and the game of shadows

over time, its measurement was narrowed down, lessening the (perceived) need for regulation.

The first step in the game of shadow concerned the *definition* of shadow banking, which was narrowed down over time, several entities and activities fell outside its scope, and eventually, the very term disappeared and was replaced by non-bank financial intermediation and market-based finance (which had fewer negative connotations). This had implications for the second step in the game of shadow, namely, the *measuring* and *monitoring* of global shadow banking, whereby the broad measure was complemented and, eventually, supplanted by a narrow measure. Whereas the broad measure increased considerably over time in the post-crisis period, the narrow measure did not increase to the same extent, underestimating the potential risks that shadow banking entailed and, thus, the need for regulation. In turn, the definition and monitoring had implications for the third step, the *regulation* of shadow banking, which was selective—international rules did not focus on entities and activities that were considered outside the scope or at the margins of shadow banking; and remained rather 'thin'—international rules were partly hollowed out or watered down over time, whereas important issues remained off the agenda. Overall, the post-crisis international governance of shadow banking was rather feeble because international standards for shadow banking entities and activities had limited precision, stringency, and consistency, even though there was variation across elemental regimes.

The playing out of the game of shadow by states, regulators, and private actors was facilitated by international regime complexity, which produced a multi-dimensional chessboard. Regime complexity compounded problems that are endemic in regulating global finance: interstate competition (that is, conflicts among jurisdictions); competition between financial regulatory bodies (that is, conflicts among technocrats), and the power of the financial industry, which mobilizes across multiple levels and venues. At the same time, it hindered problem-solving and the quest for policy solutions due to the fragmentation of regulatory authority across elemental regimes, meaning that no actor was in the driving seat, several of them worked at cross purposes, whereas a focal coordinating institution was missing in the complex. The analysis of the international governance of shadow banking through the prism of regime complexity has considerable value-added because it allows us to consider the interplay of a variety of actors in an international institutional architecture characterized by the lack of hierarchy, the multiplicity of regulatory venues, combined with gaps, overlaps, and interlinkages across elemental regimes. Moreover, since the key players—states, regulators, private actors—participate in all the elemental regimes of the complex at the same time, their influence can be gauged only by looking at the complex as a whole, as well as its individual components.

Structure and Content of the Book

The structure of the book is as follows. Chapter 2 discusses the state of the art, the research design, and the methodology, outlining the scope of the research, the timeframe, and the empirical coverage. Chapter 3 examines the international shadow banking regime complex, delineating the institutional architecture for the governance of shadow banking and the elemental regimes of the complex. Chapter 4 provides several definitions and measurements of shadow banking and maps the evolution of its global monitoring after the international financial crisis of 2008.

Chapters 5, 6, 7, and 8 examine the post-crisis regulation of shadow banking entities and activities, as well as the link between traditional banking and shadow banking. These chapters follow a similar structure, whereby each chapter begins by discussing the key issues at stake in the regulation of a given aspect of shadow banking (e.g. investment funds, securities financing, securitization) and then explains the influence of states, regulators, and private actors in the international standard-setting process and the regulatory outcomes. Specifically, Chapter 5 examines the international standards for shadow banking entities: MMFs, hedge funds, and investment funds. Chapter 6 examines international standards for securities lending and repos. Chapter 7 examines international standards for securitization. Chapter 8 examines international standards for bank exposures to shadow banking. The penultimate chapter engages in a comparative cross-cutting assessment of various elemental regimes in the shadow banking complex, spelling out the perils of regime complexity and putting forward some policy recommendations. The concluding chapter summarizes the main findings, discusses how they contribute to the literature, and teases out some open issues concerning shadow banking.

The empirical chapters offer a complete picture of the post-crisis regime complex on shadow banking, rather than examining only certain parts, which would only provide a piecemeal view of the regulatory reforms undertaken. However, there is a trade-off between the broad scope of the research and the limited amount of detail that can be examined on specific issues. For this reason, although international standards produce domestic changes, feedback effects (Newman and Posner 2018, 2016a, b) and compliance problems (Chey 2006, 2007, 2014; Mosley 2003, 2010; Quaglia 2019; Walter 2008), these are beyond the scope of this research.

2

Understanding the Politics of Regulating Global Finance

The first part of this chapter reviews several bodies of scholarly works that are relevant to this research, which brings together the international political economy literature on regulating global finance, and the international relations literature on regime complexity. Building on the first body of works, this chapter discusses the main actors—states, regulators, and private actors—that affect the governance of global finance, teasing out the pathways through which they exert their influence. Then, building on the second body of works, regime complexity is considered as a contextual factor that affects global governance in a given policy area, in this case, shadow banking, by compounding problems, while splintering solutions. The second part of the chapter spells out the research design, the methodology, and the sources used. It also clarifies the scope of the research, the empirical coverage, and the timeframe.

The International Political Economy Literature on Financial Regulation

The political science and political economy literatures have discussed extensively the regulatory reforms undertaken after the international financial crisis of 2008 at the international, regional (EU), and national levels. However, relatively few works have focused on shadow banking (for some notable exceptions, see Ban and Gabor 2016; Nesvatailova 2018). Those that have done so have either discussed the reforms undertaken in the main jurisdictions, notably, the US (Ziegler and Woolley 2016; Ryan and Ziegler 2015), the EU (Gabor 2016b; Gabor and Vestergaard 2018), and China (Gruin and Knaack 2020; Knaack and Gruin 2020), or they have examined specific international standards (for example, those on the repo market, see Gabor 2016a, or MMFs, see Woyames Dreher 2019). Relatively recently, scholarship has

The Perils of International Regime Complexity in Shadow Banking. Lucia Quaglia, Oxford University Press.
 DOI: 10.1093/oso/9780192866523.003.0002

paid attention to shifting alliances between central bankers and academic economists (Thiemann et al. 2020) and the 'performative understanding' of systemic risk by international institutions (Kranke and Yarrow 2019). By and large, these studies have regarded the post-crisis changes in shadow banking regulation as rather incremental (Rixen 2013; Engelen 2018; Gabor and Ban 2016; Gabor 2016a), feeding into a broader stream of literature that has stressed the persistence of the status quo in finance (Bieling 2014; Engelen et al. 2011; Helleiner 2014; Underhill 2015; Tsingou 2015b).

Particularly intriguing is the game of shadows that involves three consecutive and recursive steps concerning the definition, monitoring, and regulation of global shadow banking. The first step concerns the definition of shadow banking, which has implications for the second step, namely, the measuring and monitoring of global shadow banking—the narrower the definition, the smaller the size of the shadow banking sector and, hence, the 'scale' of the potential problem to be tackled. In turn, definition and monitoring have implications for the third step, the regulation of shadow banking, because entities and activities that are excluded from the definition of shadow banking fall outside the perimeter of the potential regulation of shadow banking. Moreover, the smaller the (measured) size of the sub-sectors of specific shadow banking entities and activities (e.g. MMFs, hedge funds, securities financing transactions), the lesser the (potential) problem to address via regulation. Finally, even for entities and activities that fall squarely within the definition, there is a tendency to downplay the financial stability risks they pose.

The literature on the politics and political economy of regulating global finance has pointed out several *actors* and *pathways*[1] that can account for the playing out of the game of shadow in shadow banking. A first strand of literature has focused on the interests and power of *states* in regulating global finance. These works examined the market power (Simmons 2001; Drezner 2007; Helleiner 2014), regulatory capacity (Posner 2009, 2010; Quaglia 2014a), and domestic politics (Singer 2007; Gravelle and Pagliari 2018) of the main jurisdictions, first and foremost, the US (Oatley 2015). The argument, in brief, is that the great powers (Drezner 2007) have the ability to set international standards due to the size of their domestic market and advanced regulatory capacity. These jurisdictions engage in *pace-setting* by promoting international rules, if it is in their interest to do so to limit negative externalities (such financial instability or international competitive disadvantages), or balance

[1] For the purpose of this research, pathways are conceptualized as links between the explanatory factors and the outcomes of interest—they are 'processes by which a certain effect is produced or a purpose is accomplished' (Gerring 2008: 178; see also Falleti and Lynch 2009).

business and electoral pressures at home (Singer 2004, 2007; Rixen 2013; James and Quaglia 2020). Instead, states engage in *foot-dragging* by resisting international rules if these rules produce high domestic adjustment costs and negative externalities are limited (Quaglia and Spendzharova 2017). In a regime complex, states can be pace-setters and foot-draggers at the same time in different parts of the complex, working at cross purposes and weakening their influence.

Furthermore, states sometimes engage in issue-linkage by simultaneously discussing two or more matters for joint settlement to avoid protracted deadlocks in international negotiations (Davis 2004; Farrell and Newman 2018). They can also adopt the opposite strategy, that is, issue de-linkage by separating the more controversial issues from the less controversial ones to further agreement (Quaglia and Spendzharova 2021a). Yet, both these strategies assume that states have an overall view of the issues at stake and act as unitary actors in international negotiations that take place in various venues. This is less likely in a regime complex, where different domestic authorities are involved in different elemental regimes. The absence of *pace-setting* jurisdictions, the presence of *foot-dragging* jurisdictions, and the limited opportunities for issue-linkage (or de-linkage) are likely to result in 'thin' international standards.

A second strand of literature has focused on the role of transgovernmental networks of *domestic regulators* (Ahdieh 2015; Bach and Newman 2010, 2014; Bach, De Francesco, Maggetti and Ruffing 2016a, b; Coen and Thatcher 2008; Jordana 2017; Turk 2014; Verdier 2009), arguing that international standard-setting no longer belongs to the realm of intergovernmental negotiations, but falls within the responsibility of a 'transnational policy community of experts actors' (Tsingou 2008, 2015a) that have common professional and educational backgrounds and share similar epistemological views (Chwieroth 2015; Kapstein 1992). Of particular interest are transgovernmental networks of regulators that have the following core features: they meet in multilateral bodies that are not established pursuant to treaties; their membership consists of domestic regulatory agencies; they work by consensus; and they issue (non-legally binding) soft law (Barr and Miller 2006; Brummer 2015, 2010a,b; Pauwelyn, Wessel and Wouters 2012; Verdier 2009).

The autonomous role of transgovernmental networks that are gathered in international standard-setting bodies is often downplayed by state-centric accounts because these bodies are considered as 'empty vessels', where national interests play out and negotiations among different jurisdictions take place. Alternatively, these fora are considered by business power accounts as targets for the lobbying activity of the financial industry, which might result in regulatory capture (Lall 2012; cf. Young 2012). On the one hand, transgovernmental networks of regulators are more than the sum of their members because the sharing of the same body of technical knowledge and similar epistemic views are important 'glues' for transgovernamental networks (Ban, Seabrooke, and Freitas 2016; Djelic and Quack 2010; Seabrooke and Henriksen 2017; Tsingou 2015a).[2] On the other hand, the development of consensual knowledge is more difficult if there is a considerable level of uncertainty concerning a certain policy area, which, in turn, is more likely if a variety of sectoral regulators with distinct mandates, competences, and regulatory outlooks are involved (Broome and Seabrooke 2015; Mügge and Stellinga 2015; Broome, Homolar, and Kranke 2018; Mügge and Perry 2014), as it is often the case in a regime complex. In these instances, there can be considerable *puzzling* about problem-definition and problem-solving (Thiemann, Birk, and Friedrich 2018) as well as *turf fighting* among regulators seeking to fulfil their mandates and protect their competences (Busuioc 2016; Woyames Dreher 2019).

A third strand of literature has focused on the role of the business community, arguing that international standards tend to reflect the interests of private actors (Baker 2010; Baker and Wigan 2017; Bell and Hindmoor 2014, 2015, 2016; Macartney, Howarth, and James 2020; Mügge 2010; Underhill and Zhang 2008), that is to say, the rules that the financial industry finds more advantageous (or less burdensome), on the basis of the distributional implications of the new rules. This literature has examined the structural and instrumental power of the *financial industry* (Culpepper and Reinke 2014; James, Pagliari, and Young 2021; Pagliari 2012; Woll 2013, 2014, 2016), which, sometimes, also has infrastructural power because central banks operate in and through the financial markets (Braun 2020; Braun and Gabor 2020; Gabor and Ban 2016).

To limit adverse regulatory changes, private financial actors engage in *lobbying* as well as *venue shopping* by targeting a variety of regulatory venues at multiple levels of governance (James, Pagliari, and Young 2021; Lall 2012, 2014; Young 2014). Venue shopping is the idea that in seeking to maximize their influence over policy, actors—like financial industry lobbyists—seek out policy venues that are the most amenable to their preferences and goals (Baumgartner and Jones 2009; Beyers and Kerremans 2012; Mahoney and Baumgartner 2008). Regime complexes offer several opportunities to deploy this strategy because they encompass multiple venues. The private financial

[2] A related scholarship has highlighted the origins of financial regulation in professional 'ecologies' (Seabrooke and Tsingou 2014), as well as 'boundary work', whereby international organizations claim specific expertise in certain domains (Kranke 2020).

actors that are better placed to engage in venue shopping are transnational associations (Cerny 2010; McKeen-Edwards and Porter 2013), such as the Institute of International Finance (IIF) (Newman and Posner 2016b), or the International Swaps and Derivatives Association (ISDA) (Newman and Bach 2014), as well as the largest domestic players. At times, the financial industry is also able to form broad coalitions with actors in the real economy (see Pagliari and Young 2014; Young and Pagliari 2015).

The International Relations Literature on Regime Complexity

In the international relations literature, the presence of multiple institutions governing a single issue or a set of related issues is referred to as an international regime complex (Alter and Meunier 2009, 2006; Alter and Raustiala 2018; Breen, Hodson, and Moschella 2020; Heldt and Schmidtke 2019; Henning 2017; Keohane and Victor 2011; Raustiala and Victor 2004). Regime complexes are marked by the existence of several sets of rules—also referred to as 'elemental regimes'—that are created and maintained in distinct fora with the participation of different sets of actors (Orsini, Morin, and Young 2013; Morin and Orsini 2014). Thus, there can be 'nested' regimes, where institutions are embedded within each other in concentric circles, like Russian dolls; 'overlapping' regimes, where multiple institutions have authority over an issue, but agreements are not mutually exclusive or subsidiary to another; and 'parallel' regimes, where there is no formal or direct substantive overlap (Alter and Meunier 2009; Orsini, Morin, and Young 2013). Besides, elemental regimes can be 'interlinked', whereby the rules in a given elemental regime have direct implications for other regimes (Quaglia 2020).

In the literature, there are two contrasting views about the effects of regime complexity on the international governance of a given policy area.[3] Some scholars argue that it brings distinct advantages over 'traditional' silos-like regimes. Thus, regime complexes are more flexible and adaptable (Keohane and Victor 2011); they can foster a sensible division of work among international standard-setting bodies (Gehring and Faude 2014), which allows the efficient use of their respective expertise (Quaglia and Spendzharova 2021a,b), for example, via institutional deference (Pratt 2018); they can reinforce the comparative advantage of individual institutions (Lesage and Van de

[3] The literature on regime complexity in international relations has several points in common with the third wave theorizing in international political economy (Oatley 2011), in particular, the concept of complex interdependence (Oatley 2011, 2019).

Graaf 2013); and they can facilitate actions that might otherwise be blocked (Kelley 2009).

A handful of authors emphasize the role of states in managing effectively regime complexity, arguing that countries that are multiple members of various elemental regimes value the collective goods produced by these regimes and operate as rational actors, whereby, when determining their actions in one regime, they take into account the implications that this will have on other elemental regimes within the complex (Gehring and Faude 2014).[4] This is more likely if there are negative spillovers across elemental regimes, whereby 'cooperation in one issue area undermines the pursuit of objectives in another issue area' (Johnson and Urpelainen 2012). On the one hand, these scholars assume that states act as rational unitary actors with complete information. On the other hand, that is often not the case, especially in finance, where a variety of semi-independent domestic regulatory agencies are involved and uncertainty looms large. Other authors argue that a focal institution might emerge (e.g. the OECD on taxation, see Lesage and Van de Graaf 2013), taking the lead in promoting coordination in the international regime complex, or that like-minded professional networks might perform this function, for instance, in global tax policy (Seabrooke and Wigan 2016, 2017). Yet, it is difficult for technocratic actors and professional networks to play a coordinating role in a regime complex that includes different, often competing, sectoral regulators and their networks (Mügge and Perry 2014), as in the case of shadow banking.

In contrast to the positive view on international regime complexity just outlined, other scholars consider it as a 'pathology' (cf Abbott, Genschel, Snidal, and Zangl 2015: 7) that undermines governance effectiveness for three reasons. First, there is an inefficient duplication of rules and institutions (Pratt 2019), which is costly for states as well as for private actors. More generally, regime complexes are laden with legal inconsistencies because the rules in one regime are rarely coordinated closely with overlapping rules in related regimes (Breen, Hodson, and Moschella 2020). Second, there can be negative spillovers, if cooperation in one area of the complex undermines the pursuit of objectives in another area (Johnson and Urpelainen 2012). Third, regime complexity can foster regulatory arbitrage, whereby interested parties (mainly states, but also interest groups) engage in forum shopping (Busch 2007), regime shifting (Helfer 2009), or competitive multilateralism (Morse and Keohane 2014).

[4] Thus, countries that are members of multiple elemental regimes are likely to promote institutional adaptation via 'complementary processes', even if their interests diverge (Gehring and Faude 2014).

There can also be turf fighting and epistemic disagreements among different sectoral regulators (Thiemann, Birk, and Friedrich 2018).

In addition to the shortcomings that have just been mentioned and have already been explored by the literature, this research investigates an important overlooked downside of international regime complexity, namely: it combines and magnifies problems that are present in traditional silos-like regimes, whereas problem-solving is hampered by the fragmentation of regulatory authority across elemental regimes. The governance of several policy areas is often bedevilled by distributional and ideational conflicts. In a regime complex, these conflicts pile up, while their resolution is made more difficult by the institutional architecture, which creates a multi-dimensional chessboard, where there are various players, none of which is in control and several of which work at cross purposes and have de facto veto powers.

As spelled out in the previous section, the governance of global finance is laden with conflicts, notably about who wins and who loses in regulating (or not) certain entities and activities in certain ways. In a regime complex, these conflicts are compounded, while no actor (states, regulators, private actors) has the resources to steer the policy process successfully nor the ability to coordinate effectively across different parts of the regime (Alter and Raustiala 2018). It is difficult for the 'great powers' (even, for the 'hegemon', see Simmons 2001) to promote stringent, precise, and consistent rules across elemental regimes, while sectoral regulators are often unable to iron out interstate controversies because technocrats disagree on consequential matters. In turn, private actors exploit these divisions and use venue shopping to water down rules and promote regulatory arbitrage, while the forging of coalitions in favour of regulatory reforms is hampered by the archipelago architecture of the regime. Thus, international regime complexity is an important factor to consider in order to explain how the policy actors discussed in the previous section affect the governance of global finance.

Research Design and Operationalization

In this research, the *explanandum* is the post-crisis international governance of shadow banking, namely, the definition, monitoring, and regulation of various aspects of shadow banking. Of particular interest are the precision, stringency, and consistency of the standards issued across the elemental regimes on shadow banking. The *explanans* are three sets of actors—namely, states, regulators, and private actors—that influence international shadow banking governance through a variety of pathways. Regime complexity is a contextual factor that mediates the effects of states, regulators, and private actors on the outcome, that is, shadow banking governance and, specifically, the definition, monitoring, and regulation of various aspects of shadow banking. This research design is operationalized as follows.

Beginning with *states*, the research teases out the policy preferences of the main jurisdictions by outlining their domestic market structures and regulatory frameworks with reference to shadow banking entities and activities. It then discusses the role of the US, the UK, the EU, and, where relevant, China, in the international policy debate on various aspects of shadow banking. The specific pathways investigated are *pace-setting* and *foot-dragging* and have to do with the interests and ability of states to promote (or resist) precise, stringent, and consistent international rules in a given policy domain. The lack of a pace-setter and/or the presence of foot-draggers are likely to result in weak rules, especially in a regime complex, where issue-linkage and the avoidance of negative spillovers is more difficult because states are engaged in a multidimensional game, partly played by semi-independent domestic regulatory agencies.

Second, this research investigates the role of financial regulators, which are technocrats at the interface between the domestic and international levels. In a regime complex, a variety of sectoral regulatory agencies with different regulatory outlooks, mandates, and competences are involved. Thus, this research teases out the preferences of sectoral regulators and then considers the pathways through which they affect the regulatory outcome. Specifically, *bureaucratic turf fighting*, whereby sectoral regulators might be eager to regulate entities and activities outside their purview, clashing with the competences and mandates of other regulators; and *puzzling*, which has to do with problem-definition and problem-solving, bringing to the fore epistemic agreements and disagreements among regulators that might not share the same body of technical knowledge if they deal with different parts of the financial sector. Bureaucratic tugs of war and epistemic dissonance, which are investigated by looking at speeches and policy documents of regulatory agencies, are more likely in a regime complex that involves different technocratic bodies, each with its own mandate, competence, and regulatory outlook.

Third, this research examines the preferences and mobilization of the financial industry. In general, but not always, financial interest groups are likely to lobby against precise and stringent rules that would constrain their discretion and increase their compliance costs. Furthermore, individual actors are likely to seek exemptions from certain rules, or to extend them to their competitors.

Private actors mobilize in a variety of venues, seeking to move policy discussions to the international fora that are more likely to be sympathetic to the views of the industry (Chalmers 2015; De Bièvre, Poletti, Thomann 2014; Eckhardt and De Bievre 2015) as well as forge coalition with other private actors within and without finance. *Lobbying cum venue shopping*, which is more likely in a regime complex where a variety of venues are available, is investigated by outlining the expected costs and benefits of the new international rules for various parts of the financial industry and by tracing the interventions of private actors in the regulatory debate (for an overview, see Figure 2.1).

International regime complexity is operationalized by distinguishing various elemental regimes concerning shadow banking entities and activities, as well as the link between traditional banking and shadow banking. Specifically, there are international standards for global shadow banking measurement and monitoring; international standards for shadow banking entities, namely, MMFs, hedge funds, and investment funds; international standards for securities lending and repos; international standards for securitization; international standards for bank exposures to shadow banking. For each elemental regime (or set of standards), the book investigates the international standard-setting processes, teasing out the main issues at stake, the preferences and influence of the main jurisdictions, regulators, and private financial actors. Then, the main dynamics of each elemental regime are compared and contrasted in the penultimate chapter, which also teases out the drawbacks of regime complexity.

Fig. 2.1 Analytical framework: actors and pathways

The empirical research covers all the main international standards concerning various aspects of post-crisis shadow banking regulation, whereby the new sets of rules (such as standards on securitization, or capital requirements for bank exposures to shadow banks) are the units of analysis. In line with the FSB (2018a), we adopt a broad definition of international standards, which include: 'policy frameworks', which are usually set out in a general and encompassing way (e.g. the FSB's 'Policy Framework for Strengthening Oversight and Regulation of Shadow Banking Entities' in 2011); 'recommendations', which are usually rather general, but concern a specific topic (e.g. the FSB's 'Policy Recommendations to Address Structural Vulnerabilities from Asset Management Activities' in 2017); 'guidelines', which provide detailed guidance on the requirements to be met (for example, the FSB's 'Reporting Guidelines on Securities Financing Transactions' in 2018); and reports, whenever they outline various regulatory options for jurisdictions to follow. As far as the time frame is concerned, the research analyses the standard-setting that took place after the international financial crisis of 2008. Data-gathering was carried out by making use of a wealth of primary sources. To begin with, there are documents issued by international standard-setting bodies, such as the FSB, the IOSCO, the Basel Committee on Banking Supervision (BCBS) as well as by the national and regional (EU) authorities. Second, there are policy papers, press statements, and responses to consultations issued by international, regional, and national financial associations, large individual companies as well as think tanks. Third, a set of confidential interviews with policy-makers and stakeholders in various jurisdictions were drawn upon, together with a systematic survey of press coverage.

Conclusion

By combining the bodies of scholarly works on the governance of global finance in international political economy and regime complexity in international relations, this chapter has taken stock of the existing literature, outlining the theoretical framework and the research design of the book. It has identified the key players—states, regulators, private actors—and the pathways through which they affect the game of shadows in shadow banking governance. This book has opted for what Sil and Katzenstein (2010a: 10) call 'analytical eclecticism', which they define as any approach that integrates analytic elements—concepts, pathways—of different theories that address related aspects of substantive problems that have academic and practical significance.

Analytical eclecticism refuses to 'carve out complex social phenomena for the sole purpose of making them more tractable' (Sil and Katzenstein 2010a: 3). By spotting the connections and interactions among a range of factors normally analysed in isolation with one another, analytical eclecticism encourages a conversation between different causal forces as part of a complex but usable analytical framework (Sil and Katzenstein 2010a: 11).

The 'eclectic' or 'holistic' or analytical framework adopted in this book has strengths and weaknesses. On the one hand, it adds value to academic and policy debates by integrating different strands of scholarship and making intellectual and practical connections among clusters of analyses that are substantially related, but normally formulated in different theoretical approaches. It allows richer explanations, avoiding simplifications based on a single theoretical lens, which often involves trade-offs and can produce enduring blind spots (Sil and Katzenstein 2010a: 3). It has the potential to reduce the gap between the research produced by academics (often criticized for their 'flight from reality', Shapiro 2005: 2) and the practical knowledge required by policy makers and practitioners in the real world (Sil and Katzenstein 2010a: 13). On the other hand, the use of this approach rules out a neat, linear, parsimonious explanation and its different components need to be carefully combined. There is also the potential danger of theoretical incoherence if the approaches used are incommensurable (Sil and Katzenstein 2010b), which is not the case for those used in this research.

The next chapter outlines the international institutional architecture for the governance of shadow banking and the vast array of post-crisis international standards issued. The fourth chapter discusses the first and second steps in the game of shadows, namely, the definition and monitoring of global shadow banking. The subsequent empirical chapters deal with the third step in the game of shadows by examining the main elemental regimes concerning shadow banking entities and activities.

3

The International Architecture for Shadow Banking Governance

This chapter sets the context for the rest of the book—after explaining what is shadow banking, it outlines the shadow banking regime complex and the multi-dimensional chessboard it generates. Three institutional features of the complex have profound implications for the global governance of shadow banking. First, a variety of international standard-setting bodies that have different memberships, remits, tasks, and epistemic views are involved in the definition, monitoring, and regulation of shadow banking entities and activities. Second, there is not a focal institution in the shadow banking regime complex—the FSB sought to play such a role, with limited success. Third, international bodies bring together domestic regulators that oversee different parts of the financial sector and have distinctive mandates, competences and regulatory outlooks. These domestic regulatory agencies have considerable degrees of autonomy, which makes it difficult for states to act as rational unitary actors in international standard-setting concerning various aspects of shadow banking and provides a multiplicity of access points for the financial industry. Moreover, occasionally, domestic bureaucratic and epistemic conflicts between sectoral regulatory agencies get transmitted to the international level and vice versa.

The material in this chapter is organized as follows. The first section provides different definitions of shadow banking, in particular distinguishing between entities and activities. The second section discusses the post-2008 crisis international institutional architecture for the governance of shadow banking, and identifies the main international bodies that issued non-legally binding soft law on this matter. The third section outlines the post-2008 international regulatory reforms concerning the governance of shadow banking, which will be discussed in detail in the following chapters. It is argued that the various elemental regimes concerning various aspects of shadow banking have limited stringency, precision, and consistency (bar some exceptions).

The Perils of International Regime Complexity in Shadow Banking. Lucia Quaglia, Oxford University Press.
 DOI: 10.1093/oso/9780192866523.003.0003

What Is Shadow Banking?

The term shadow bank was coined by the economist Paul McCulley in 2007[1] with reference to mainly to non-bank financial institutions that engaged in maturity transformation in the US. The term was then used by policy-makers (see, for example, Tucker 2010) and the first articles on shadow banking were published by Pozsar (2008) and Adrian and Shin (2009). Afterward, considerable effort went into the definition of shadow banking (see Engelen 2018 for a critical review). The most authoritative source for the definition of shadow banking is the FSB, which, however, slightly modified its terminology over time. Indeed, the definition and measurement of global shadow banking were some of the most contested issues dealt with by the FSB.

From the outset, the FSB (2011a) explained in a footnote that 'it is important to note that the use of the term "shadow banking" is not intended to cast a pejorative tone on this system of credit intermediation… Alternative terms used by some authorities or market participants include "market-based financing" or "market-based credit intermediation"… The FSB has chosen to use the term "shadow banking" as this is most commonly employed and, in particular, has been used in the earlier G20 communications.' As Engelen (2018) points out, the FSB's footnote suggests that this body was aware of the negative connotations of the term shadow banking and considered the possibility of using more neutral synonyms (see also Ophele and D'Hoir 2018).

According to the initial definition of the FSB (2011a), shadow banking is 'the system of credit intermediation that involves entities and activities outside the regular banking system.' Thus, the FSB drew attention to credit intermediation (that is to say, taking money from savers and lending it to borrowers) that took place outside the perimeter of the regulation and supervision of the banking sector. More precisely, according to the FSB (2011a), 'this implies that credit intermediation takes place in an environment where prudential regulatory standards and supervisory oversight are either not applied, or are applied to a materially lesser or different degree than is the case for regular banks engaged in similar activities.'

While the FSB's initial approach cast a 'wide net'—incorporating, potentially, any entity or activity along the credit intermediation chain—it also

[1] McCully (2007) referred to the shadow banking system as 'the whole alphabet soup of levered up non-bank investment conduits, vehicles, and structures. Unlike regulated real banks …. unregulated shadow banks fund themselves with uninsured commercial paper, which may or may not be backstopped by liquidity lines from real banks. Thus, the shadow banking system is particularly vulnerable to runs.'

called for a narrower focus, highlighting activities involving four types of risks: *maturity transformation*, that is to say, obtaining short-term funds to invest in longer-term assets; *liquidity transformation*, which is a concept similar to maturity transformation and entails using cash-like liabilities to buy harder-to-sell assets; *leverage*, that is to say, the use of debt to buy assets to increase the potential profits on investment; and *credit risk transfer*, that is to say, taking the risk of a borrower's default and transferring it from the originator of the loan (or the issuer of a bond) to another party (FSB 2011b).

In its *Global Shadow Banking Monitoring Report*, the FSB (2013d: 1) made the first attempt to narrow down the broad measure of shadow banking by filtering out non-bank financial activities that had no direct relation to credit intermediation (e.g. equity investment funds), or that were already prudentially consolidated into banking groups. In particular, the FSB excluded other financial institutions that were consolidated into banking groups; on balance sheet securitization (i.e. securitization without credit risk transfer from the banking system), such as retained securitization; and equity funds, which did not contribute directly to credit intermediation (FSB 2013d). In the *Global Shadow Banking Monitoring Report* in 2015, the FSB (2015a) introduced a new activity-based measure of shadow banking by identifying five economic functions, discussed in Chapter 4. From 2018 onwards, the FSB replaced the term 'shadow banking' with the term 'non-bank financial intermediation'.

An alternative definition of shadow banking was given by Pozsar et al. (2010: 11), whereby shadow banking includes 'financial intermediaries that conduct maturity, credit, and liquidity transformation without access to central bank liquidity or public sector credit guarantees'. This definition focuses on the nature of the liabilities involved, whereby liabilities that are explicitly guaranteed by the official sector are not part of shadow banking. Moreover, if an uninsured liability is consolidated onto the balance sheet of an institution with access to the lender of last resort (the central bank), that uninsured liability is also not part of shadow banking. By contrast, uninsured liabilities are part of the shadow banking system. Shadow banking 'decomposes the simple process of deposit-funded, hold-to-maturity lending conducted by banks into a more complex, wholesale funded, securitization-based lending process' that involves a range of financial entities (Pozsar et al. 2010: 13). Thus, shadow banking is considered as part of the broader transformation of a bank-based financial system into market-based finance, discussed below.

Pozsar et al. (2010: 66) distinguish between internal, external, and parallel shadow banking. 'Internal' shadow banking is the transformation of banks from regular on balance credit intermediaries into highly leveraged financial entities that adopt an originate to distribute model through the securitization of loans and off-balance-sheet vehicles (special investment vehicles, special purpose vehicles, and conduits) to minimize funding costs and maximize profits. 'External' shadow banking comprises off-balance-sheet vehicles that are part of credit intermediation outside large banking groups and specialize in securitized corporate loans, often located in offshore financial centres. In both cases, these parts of the shadow banking system are controlled by banks, either large universal banks using retail loans (mortgages) in the case of internal shadow banking, or large investment banks using wholesale financial products (corporate loans and securitized assets) in the case of external shadow banking. By contrast, 'parallel' shadow banking includes MMFs, hedge funds,[2] finance companies,[3] mutual funds,[4] which are linked with one another through conduits, special investment vehicles, and special purpose vehicles (this paragraph draws on Pozsar et al. 2010).[5]

The definitions of shadow banking outlined above are complementary (Adrian, Ashcraft, Breuer, and Cetorelli 2019). The FSB's approach focuses on intermediation activities taking place outside banks, while Pozsar et al. (2010) focus on the funding of credit without official sector credit and liquidity support. Traditional banks engage in maturity transformation when they use deposits, which are normally short-term, to fund loans, which are longer-term. Likewise, shadow banks often borrow short-term funds and use them to buy assets with longer-term maturities. On the one hand, shadow banks are not subject to traditional bank regulation. On the other hand, unlike banks, they do not have access to emergency lending by the central bank and are not covered by deposit insurance schemes. Thus, they are in the 'shadows' (Kodres 2017).

Summing up the definitions discussed above, the shadow banking system includes: *entities* operating outside the regular banking system engaged in one of the following activities: (i) accepting funding with deposit-like characteristics; (ii) performing maturity and/or liquidity transformation; (iii) undergoing credit risk transfer; (iv) using direct or indirect financial leverage; and *activities,* such as securitization, securities lending, and repurchase transactions

[2] These are highly leveraged funds that engage in complex portfolio-management, using high risk and high return strategies.

[3] These are financial entities that sell commercial paper or other short-term obligations and use the earnings to provide credit to households.

[4] These are companies that pool money from many investors and invest in securities, such as stocks and bonds.

[5] Similarly, Adrian and Ashcraft (2012) distinguish between 'shadow' banking activities undertaken by banks off balance sheets and 'parallel' banking, that is to say, banking activities taking place outside banks and that do not benefit from lender of last resort and deposit guarantee schemes.

(repos), that could act as important sources of funding of non-bank entities. Thus, shadow banking can be defined on the basis of the entities that perform it, or the activities performed.

On the one hand, shadow banking offers alternative forms of investment with risk diversification, away from the banking system. It also provides alternative funding for the real economy, outside the traditional banking system. On the other hand, shadow banking can generate risks, due to the complexity of shadow banking entities and activities; their cross-border business; and, the interconnectedness of shadow banking with the regular banking system. These risks can be summarized as: 'runs' on deposit-like activities; the building-up of leverage; the circumvention of banking rules and, more generally, regulatory arbitrage (Kodres 2017). Shadow banking has also implications for systemic risk, macro-prudential regulation (Borio 2012; Rubio 2017; Gebauer and Mazelis 2019) as well as monetary policy, whereby shadow-banking liabilities are substitutes for high-powered money and therefore have implications for money supply (Chen, Ren, and Zha 2018).

Shadow banking is often conflated with market-based finance, and indeed, as time went by, a deliberate reframing of shadow banking as market-based finance took place in the policy-making discourse (Engelen 2018). According to Hardie and Howarth (2013), market-based finance includes not only the shadow banking system *strictu sensu*, but also parts of commercial banking that are dependent on the market to finance and hedge the assets on commercial banks' balance sheets. Thus, there are three possible forms of market-based finance (see Hardie and Howarth 2013). Non-market-based liabilities (i.e. deposits) can finance market-based assets. Alternatively, market-based liabilities finance non-market-based assets. Finally, market-based assets are financed by market-based liabilities.

Shadow banking can be considered as the less resilient version of market-based finance (Adrian 2017), which partly explains why shadow banking was strategically reframed by regulators and private financial actors as market-based finance. Several reasons account for the greater resilience of market-based finance in comparison to shadow banking. Whereas maturity and/or liquidity transformation characterize all types of credit intermediation, leverage, complexity, and opaqueness are prominent in shadow banking, while market-based finance generally involves less risk transformation, complexity, and opaqueness (Adrian and Jones 2018). Furthermore, risk transformation in shadow banking is often performed by a chain of specialized and interconnected intermediaries, and collateral is often reused, generating lengthy collateral chains. Finally, shadow banking often benefits from the implicit financial support provided by a bank. By contrast, the more resilient parts of market-based finance have self-supporting financing structures (Adrian and Jones 2018).

Since there are several different definitions of shadow banking, there are also several different ways of measuring it. At a first cut, two different measures can be used and have been used, for example, by the FSB (as elaborated in the following chapter): by entity, whereby a catch-all category of 'other financial intermediaries' (OFIs) (that is to say, financial intermediaries other than insurance corporations and pension funds) is used; and by 'function'. Furthermore, measuring the size of the global shadow banking system is particularly difficult because many entities and activities are outside the purview of regulators. Thus, data on certain entities and activities are missing. In addition, cross-country aggregation is difficult because the definitions of entities and activities vary across countries. A considerable part of international standard-setting on shadow banking concerned the development of harmonized rules for reporting and measuring, as well as data collection and analysis. As explained in the following chapter, the definition and monitoring of global shadow banking were some of the crucial policy issues to be dealt with internationally.

International Institutional Architecture for Shadow Banking Governance

After the international financial crisis, several international standard-setting bodies were involved in the regulation of various aspects of shadow banking, namely: the FSB, the IOSCO, and the BCBS. The Bank for International Settlements (BIS), the IMF were also involved in the policy debate, and so was the IASB (see Table 3.1 and Figure 1.1). The FSB, the IOSCO, and the BCBS are transgovernmental networks of domestic regulators that share some common features: they are multilateral bodies that are not established according to treaties; their membership consists of domestic regulatory agencies; they work by consensus; and they issue (not legally binding) soft laws (Ahdieh 2015; Brummer 2010a, b, 2015; Bach and Newman 2010, 2014; Gadinis 2015; Jordana 2017; Newman and Posner 2018; Slaughter and Zaring 2006; Turk 2014; Verdier 2009; Zaring 2013, 2020). The soft law issued by international standard-setters becomes legally binding only when it is incorporated into the domestic legal framework of the member jurisdictions. The expectation is that jurisdictions that sign up to the standards will do so. In fact, several authors pointed out the 'hardening of international soft law' in finance when it

Table 3.1 The international institutional architecture for shadow banking governance

International standard-setting body	Date of establishment	Membership/ composition	Functions concerning financial services regulation
FSB	2009	Central bankers, financial supervisors and treasury officials of G20 jurisdictions, plus officials from BCBS, IOSCO, CPMI, IAIS, IMF, BIS, OECD, World Bank	To assess and address the vulnerabilities of the financial system To coordinate the work of international standard-setters To issue standards on specific matters To monitor domestic compliance
(formerly Financial Stability Forum)	1999	(formerly, officials of G10 jurisdictions)	
IOSCO	1983	Securities markets regulators worldwide (more than 100 jurisdictions)	To set international standards in securities markets To promote exchange of information and supervisory cooperation
BCBS	1974	Central bankers and banking supervisors of 28 jurisdictions (formerly, central bankers and banking supervisors of G10 jurisdictions)	To set international standards in banking To promote cooperation in banking supervision To monitor domestic compliance
BIS	1930	Central banks of more than 60 countries	To foster monetary and financial stability, international cooperation, and to act as a bank for central banks
IMF	1945	About 180 countries	To foster the stability of the international system, monitor the global economy, and lend to ailing countries
IASB	2001	14 member experts with relevant experience	To set and promote the use of international financial reporting standards

is incorporated into domestic regulatory frameworks (Arner and Taylor 2009; Karmel and Kelly 2009; Newman and Bach 2014).

The FSB brings together central bankers, financial regulators, and treasury ministry officials of the G20 jurisdictions (Arner and Taylor 2009; Donnelly 2012; Gadinis 2014; Helleiner 2010, 2013; Pagliari 2013a). In the case of smaller G20 jurisdictions, only the national central bank is a member of the FSB. The FSB also includes representatives from all other international standard-setting bodies (the Committee on Payments and Market Infrastructures, the IOSCO, the BCBS, the International Association of Insurance Supervisors (IAIS)), as well as the BIS, the World Bank, the IMF, and the OECD. Given that the FSB includes treasury ministry officials, it is somewhat more intergovernmental and less 'technocratic' than other international standard-setting bodies, such as the BCBS, or the IOSCO. However, out of about seventy participants in the FSB, only twenty are finance ministry officials, all the others are technical regulators.

The FSB was established by the G20 in the wake of the international financial crisis in 2009, building on its predecessor, the Financial Stability Forum, to promote international financial stability by coordinating the actions of national financial authorities and international standard-setting bodies. The FSB was to act as a transmission mechanism between the G20 (the political level, see Viola 2014, 2015; Cooper and Thakur 2013; Kirton 2013) and international standard setters composed of domestic regulators (the technical level) (Pagliari 2013a). Its establishment was primarily sponsored by the US, with the support of the EU. With a hyperbole, it was described by US Treasury Minister Geithner as a novel 'fourth pillar' of the global economic architecture, alongside the IMF, the World Bank, and the World Trade Organization (Helleiner 2014). Daniel Tarullo (2011), a member of the Board of Governors of the Federal Reserve, stressed the 'coordinating and gap-filling strengths of the FSB...which can parcel out appropriate components of larger projects to standard-setting committees'.

The Charter of the FSB gave this body a specific mandate to 'promote and help coordinate the alignment of the activities' of international standard setters and to 'undertake joint strategic reviews' of their work to ensure it was 'timely, coordinated, focused on priorities and addressing gaps'. However, the FSB charter also stated that the reporting of international standard-setters to the FSB would be 'without prejudice to their existing reporting arrangements or their independence' (Helleiner 2010, 2013). Regarding shadow banking, the FSB was in the driving seat in coordinating the international regulatory efforts and took primary responsibility for monitoring the evolution of this sector and the domestic implementation of internationally agreed rules. Finally, the FSB was also directly involved in the international discussions concerning the regulation and oversight of other shadow banking entities and securities financing transactions, first and foremost, repos (which had implications for the conduct of monetary policy and the public debt market).

The international standard-setting body in securities markets is the IOSCO, whose membership includes more than one hundred jurisdictions. The IOSCO never developed the international status and expertise of its counterpart in banking (Kempthorne 2013; Marcacci 2012, 2014), and, in fact, it did not manage to issue capital requirements for investment firms (Singer 2004, 2007). Instead, the IOSCO focused on the development of bilateral and multilateral memoranda of understanding designed to facilitate information sharing and enforcement across jurisdictions (Bach and Newman 2010). It also developed standardized templates for securities trading (Kempthorne 2013; Underhill and Zhang 2008). Regarding shadow banking, securities market regulators mainly deal with rules on MMFs, hedge funds, investment funds, asset management, securities financing transactions, and securitization.

The US is represented in the IOSCO by the SEC and the Commodity Futures Trading Commission. Before the crisis, the SEC used to have a predominant role within the IOSCO (Bach and Newman 2010; Newman and Posner 2018). For example, most of the pre-crisis regulatory output of the IOSCO had been informed by US Securities Law, contributing to the 'spreading of a US-Like regulatory philosophy around the world' (Marcacci 2014: 759). As for the EU, before the crisis, there was no EU representative in the IOSCO. Afterward, the European Commission and the European Securities and Markets Authority (ESMA) became associate members. The securities market regulators of most EU member states are ordinary members of the IOSCO. China is represented in the IOSCO by the China Securities Regulatory Commission.

The international standard-setting body in banking is the BCBS, which was established in 1974. Before the reform introduced in 2009, the Committee's members came from Belgium, Canada, France, Germany, Italy, Japan, Luxembourg, the Netherlands, Spain, Sweden, Switzerland, the UK, and the US. After the 2008 financial crisis, the membership of the Committee was extended to all countries of the G20 because financial activity in emerging economies had become more important. Countries are represented in the Committee by their central bank and by the authority with formal responsibility for banking supervision, whenever this is not the central bank. The BCBS has recognized expertise in banking regulation (Goodhart 2011; Wood 2005), largely through the work carried out by its working groups of national regulators, which discuss the technical details of regulation and meet regularly. With reference to shadow banking, central bankers and banking regulators mainly deal with bank capital and liquidity requirements related to bank exposures to shadow banking, the functioning of repo markets (which is important also for the conduct of monetary policy), and securitization (in particular, capital standards for securitization).

The US is represented in the BCBS by multiple prudential regulators, which reflects the variety of regulatory agencies involved in banking regulation at the federal and state levels. Thus, the Board of Governors of the Federal Reserve, the Federal Reserve of New York, the Office of the Comptroller of the Currency, and the Federal Deposit Insurance Corporation sit in the BCBS. In the US, inter-agency competition in banking has been frequent (see, for example, Lavelle 2013, 2019) and also played out in the negotiations of the Basel accords (Wood 2005), which set capital requirements for internationally active banks. As for the EU, prior to the establishment of Banking Union, the European Commission and the European Central Bank (ECB) used to participate in the BCBS as observers. After the establishment of Banking Union, the ECB became a full member of the BCBS (Quaglia 2019). Moreover, several EU countries are directly represented in the Committee by their national central bank and the banking supervisory authority (if separated from the central bank). These countries are Belgium, France, Germany, Italy, Luxembourg, the Netherlands, Spain, Sweden, and the UK (before Brexit). China is represented in the BCBS by the central bank (the People's Bank of China) and the China Banking Regulatory Commission.

Outside the financial realm, another international standard-setting body involved in the post-crisis regulation of certain aspects of shadow banking was the IASB, which set accounting standards also for the financial sector (Botzem 2014b; Botzem and Quack 2009; Mügge and Stellinga 2015). The IASB has 16 members chosen on the basis of expertise in reporting standards and financial markets. It is the standard-setting body of the International Financial Reporting Standards Foundation (Büthe and Mattli 2011; Bengston 2011; Botzem 2013, 2014a; Leblond 2011; Mügge and Stellinga 2015; Posner 2010). The Foundation is an independent, not-for-profit private accounting organization. It has 22 trustees, 18 of whom represent the regions of North America, Europe, and Asia/Oceania (with six Trustees per region), one from Africa, one from South America, and two from the rest of the world. They represent various professions, including accountants, auditors, users (financial institutions and public authorities), and academics.

Finally, two international organizations were involved in the international policy debates on shadow banking. The BIS conducted several studies on this topic and contributed to international data harmonization, collection, and aggregation (see, for example, FSB–BIS 2018). Likewise, the IMF stressed the importance of closing data gaps in this respect (see, for instance, the IMF's *Global Financial Stability Report* in 2015). The IMF also envisaged several regulatory options to reduce shadow banking risks, including activity-based (as opposed to entity-based) regulation and the development of macroprudential tools for non-banks. For instance, the bi-annual *Global Financial Stability Report* of the IMF (2014) devoted an entire issue to shadow banking. Subsequent *Global Financial Stability Reports* of the IMF (e.g. IMF 2015, 2018) highlighted concerns about the liquidity of investment funds that could expose asset managers to fire-sale losses, with potential negative spillovers to other intermediaries.

Given the scope of the post-crisis regulatory efforts and various aspects of shadow banking to consider, a multitude of international standard-setting bodies and organizations was involved (see Table 3.1) and several standards were jointly issued by two or more bodies. On the one hand, the division of work on shadow was difficult because this was a new area that previously had not been subject to international regulation, thus there were no pre-defined standard-setting bodies. Some of the issues discussed were cross-sectoral—thus, it was unclear which specific regulatory body should take the lead—and they cropped up in the regulatory agenda in a non-linear way, and not necessarily in the most logical order. Policy-makers, especially those of the main jurisdictions that were actively involved in all international regulatory fora, were aware of this problem. As Daniel Tarullo (2011: 6), member of the Board of Governors of the Federal Reserve, noted:

> the overlapping, sometimes competing, activities of all the international committees and arrangements are completely understandable in light of the number of new and urgent issues to be tackled. Similarly, the involvement of political officials through the G20 was imperative to galvanize the legislative and regulatory processes of participating countries to undertake the breadth of needed reforms.... But we must rationalize the often confusing and duplicative process whereby the Basel Committee, the FSB, and some other BIS committees are all involved in the same subjects.

On the other hand, as the member of the Executive Board of the ECB, Vitor Constâncio (2012a), remarked 'it was clear from the outset the importance of pooling expertise and resources from several authorities, as a comprehensive assessment of all the financial sectors was needed to clearly understand the problem [posed by shadow banking]. This was possible thanks to the steering of the FSB'. However, the steering authority of the FSB was at times challenged both by other international standard-setting bodies—for instance, the IOSCO opposed the FSB's attempts to tighten up the regulation of investment funds, as explained in Chapter 5—as well as by jurisdictions, for instance, China contested the FSB's measurement of shadow banking, as explained in Chapter 4.

The work on shadow banking was divided as follows. The FSB established a system-wide monitoring framework to track developments in global non-bank financial intermediation with a view to identifying the build-up of systemic risks. The FSB also dealt with the regulation of shadow banking securities financing transactions, and repos. The IOSCO dealt with policy measures on MMFs, hedge funds, other investment funds, and criteria for securitization, jointly with the BCBS. The BCBS dealt with capital requirements for banks' exposures to shadow banking, including securitization. Overall, the international regulation of shadow banking was neither a 'silos-like' model, such as in banking, nor a 'hierarchical model', given that the FSB had only a coordination role, which was sometimes ineffective, as elucidated in the following chapters. It was a regime complex, whose elemental regimes are outlined in the following section.

At the domestic level, shadow banking was regulated and supervised in various jurisdictions through fragmented institutional frameworks. In the US, the prudential banking regulators were the Federal Reserve, the Office of the Comptroller of the Currency, and the Federal Deposit Insurance Corporation, hence these authorities dealt with bank exposures to shadow banking. The SEC regulated securities markets, including securities-related derivatives, MMFs, and investment funds (hedge funds, managed funds, and asset management). The Commodity Futures Trading Commission was the regulator for commodity futures and most derivatives. The Financial Stability Oversight Council (FSOC) was established by the Dodd-Frank Act (2010), with the mandate to prevent the build-up of systemic risk. The Council, which consisted of ten voting members and five non-voting members and chaired by the Secretary of the Treasury, brought together federal financial regulators, state regulators, and an independent insurance expert appointed by the President. The FSOC had the power to designed non-bank financial institutions as systemically important and to be supervised by the Federal Reserve.

In the EU, the ECB, in cooperation with national central banks, was responsible for banking supervision in the euro area within the Single Supervisory Mechanism. The European Banking Authority (EBA) brought together banking supervisors of all the EU member states. The ESMA brought together securities market regulators all the EU member states. The European Systemic Risk Board (ESRB), which was established in 2010, had a macroprudential mandate, it monitored and assessed systemic risks, issuing warnings and recommendations, if necessary. The ESRB, which was hosted by the ECB and chaired by the president of the ECB, brought together as voting members the President and the Vice-President of the ECB, the Governors of the national central banks of the member states, the chairpersons of the European Banking Authority, the ESMA, the European Insurance and Occupational Pension Authority, and one member of the European Commission.

Overview of Post-crisis International Shadow Banking Governance

At their summit in Seoul in November 2010, the Leaders of the G20 (2010) warned that, following the agreement on the new capital and liquidity requirements for banks, the Basel III Accord (see Goldbach 2015a, b; Howarth and Quaglia 2016; Lall 2012; Young 2012), 'regulatory gaps may emerge in the shadow banking system'. Therefore, the G20 (2010) asked the FSB to work in collaboration with other international standard-setting bodies to develop recommendations to strengthen the regulation and oversight of the shadow banking system. To this end, the FSB set up a Task Force on Shadow Banking, co-chaired by two authoritative figures, Adair Turner of the British Financial Services Authority and Jaime Caruana of the BIS. The primary goals of the Task Force were to: clarify the definition of the shadow banking system; set out potential approaches for monitoring it; and explore possible regulatory measures to address the systemic risk and the risk of regulatory arbitrage.

The FSB (2011a: 3) began with a broad definition of shadow banking, that is to say, 'the system of *credit intermediation* that involves entities and activities *outside the regular banking system*'. It, then, pointed out two major risks related to shadow banking: systemic risk, which predominately arose from activities that generated maturity transformation, liquidity transformation, credit risk transfer, and leverage; and regulatory arbitrage, whereby shadow banking activities could be used to circumvent banking regulation. In light of these risks, the definition of shadow banking was revised as follows 'a system of credit intermediation that involves entities and activities outside the regular banking system and raises i) *systemic risk* concerns, in particular by maturity/liquidity transformation, leverage, and credit risk transfer, and/or ii) *regulatory arbitrage* concerns' (FSB 2011a: 3, all *emphasis* added). The document included also an important footnote (n. 3) noting that 'some authorities or market participants prefer to use other terms such as "market-based financing" instead of "shadow banking". It is important to note the use of the term "shadow banking" is not intended to cast a pejorative tone on this system of credit intermediation. However, the FSB has chosen to use the term "shadow banking" as this is most commonly employed and, in particular, has been used in the earlier G20 communications.'

The FSB recommended that the authorities should focus first on activities that gave rise to either or both of these dangers. It also made clear that, given the broad definition of shadow banking activities and entities, a single regulatory approach was unfeasible. Thus, the regulatory response should be 'balanced and targeted' to the risks that shadow banking created, taking into account the expected costs and benefits of potential policy interventions. A two-step strategy was put forward. The first step was to cast the net wide by looking at all non-bank credit intermediation to ensure that data gathering and surveillance covered all the activities within which shadow banking-related risks could arise. The second step should narrow the focus by focusing on 'the subset of *non-bank credit intermediationwhere maturity/liquidity transformation and/or* flawed *credit risk transfer* and/or *leverage* created important *risks*'.

Four approaches can be used to regulate shadow banking. The first approach is to regulate the banks' interactions with shadow banking entities (*indirect regulation*), to limit the spillover of risks into the regular banking system and reduce opportunities for regulatory arbitrage, whereby banks conduct transactions through shadow banking entities to reduce capital and liquidity requirements. The second approach is to regulate shadow banking *entities* (direct regulation), to reduce the risks they pose to the system. For instance, Lord Turner, Chair of the British Financial Services Authority, said 'If it looks like a bank and quacks like a bank, it has got to be subject to bank-like safeguards' (cited in *Financial Times*, 18 November 2012).[6] The third approach is to regulate shadow banking *activities*, in particular, the instruments that facilitate credit intermediation. The fourth approach consists of *macroprudential measures* designed to address systemic risk in the shadow banking system more

[6] *Financial Times*, 'FSB seeks to tame shadow banking' by Masters, B., 18 November 2012.

broadly (e.g. measures to mitigate procyclicality). The FSB defined shadow banking and framed it in such a way that encompassed all four regulatory approaches (Center for the Study of Financial Market Evolution 2011).

In October 2011, the FSB (2011b) released a report *Shadow Banking: Strengthening Oversight and Regulation*, which dealt with the definition of principles for the monitoring and regulation of shadow banking; the mapping process to identify and assess systemic risks involved in shadow banking; and the scope of possible regulatory measures. The document proposed seven high-level principles for monitoring the shadow banking system and three phases for the monitoring process: phase 1—scanning and mapping the shadow banking system; phase 2—identifying the aspects of the shadow banking system posing systemic risks or regulatory arbitrage concerns; phase 3—assessing systemic risks and/or regulatory arbitrage. The FSB (2011b) also developed 11 recommendations for strengthening the regulation of the shadow banking system, arguing that while regulatory measures should take jurisdiction-specific features into account, international regulatory consistency was also necessary to address common risks and reduce opportunities for regulatory arbitrage across jurisdictions (FSB 2011b: 4). The Deputy Governor of the Bank of England, Paul Tucker (2010), argued that 'in each case, we need to decide whether or not we want to set constraints around the operation of those forms of shadow banking. And we need some principles to guide us when, inevitably, we confront new variants of shadow banking in the future.' Thus, regulators faced considerable uncertainty and were themselves 'puzzled' about shadow banking.

Following its report, the FSB established five work-streams on shadow banking, three focused on entities, and two on activities (see Figure 3.1). The five work-streams were: (i) the IOSCO's work on regulating MMFs; (ii) the work of an FSB subgroup concerning the regulation of shadow banking entities other than MMFs; (iii) the work of another FSB subgroup dealing with securities lending and repos; (iv) the IOSCO's and the BCBS's work on securitization; (vi) the BCBS's work to regulate the interaction between banks and shadow banking entities (indirect regulation). The FSB, through its Standing Committee on Supervisory and Regulatory Cooperation, was to review all the work-streams to provide consistency to the overall project (FSB 2011b: 15).

At the summit in Cannes in November 2011, the G20 (2011) endorsed the FSB's report and noted that

> the shadow banking system can create opportunities for regulatory arbitrage and cause the build-up of systemic risk outside the scope of the regulated

> banking sector. To this end, we agree to strengthen the regulation and oversight of the shadow banking system and endorse the FSB initial eleven recommendations with a work-plan to further develop them in the course of 2012, building on a balanced approach between indirect regulation of shadow banking through banks and direct regulation of shadow banking activities, including money markets funds, securitization, securities lending, and repo activities, and other shadow banking entities.

In August 2013, the FSB published several documents, which are discussed in the following chapters: *Strengthening Oversight and Regulation of Shadow Banking: An Overview of Policy Recommendations* (FSB 2013a); *Policy Framework for Strengthening Oversight and Regulation of Shadow Banking Entities* (FSB 2013b), prepared by the Workstream on Other Shadow Banking Entities; and *Policy Framework for Addressing Shadow Banking Risks in Securities Lending and Repos* (FSB 2013c), prepared by the Workstream on Securities Lending and Repos. On the one hand, the FSB policy frameworks did not create major legal obligations to tighten the regulation of non-bank financial intermediaries or securities lending and repos, partly because the FSB recommendations were soft law and partly because they were deliberately very general, to be applicable across jurisdictions that had different financial systems and regulatory frameworks. On the other hand, all the member jurisdictions of the FSB declared their willingness to participate in an annual system-wide shadow bank monitoring exercise and peer reviews. Although participation in monitoring

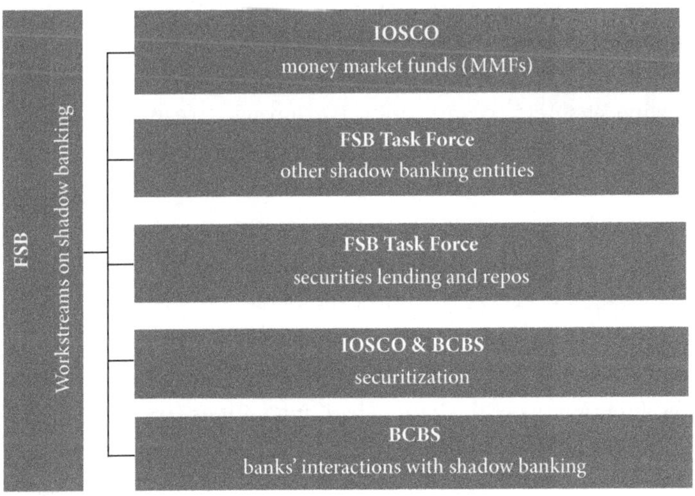

Fig. 3.1 FSB's workstreams on shadow banking (adapted from FSB 2011b)

exercises and peer reviews did not reduce *de jure* regulatory sovereignty, *de facto* it constrained regulatory agencies dealing with large portions of the shadow banking sector (Gruin and Knaack 2020). It should, however, be noted that searching for a compromise, the FSB softened the requirements of the policy framework implementation. Thus, jurisdictions were able to agree to it without much concern for subsequent compliance failures (Woyames Dreher 2019).

In September 2013, the G20 at the summit in St Petersburg welcomed

> the progress achieved in developing policy recommendations for the oversight and regulation of the shadow banking system, as an important step in mitigating the potential systemic risks associated with this market while recognizing that nonbank financial intermediation can provide an alternative to banks in extending credit to support the economy. We will work towards the timely implementation of the recommendations while taking into account country-specific circumstances (G20 2013a).

The G20 (2013b) agreed on a *Road Map* on shadow banking, which was updated over time and which envisaged: an annual shadow banking monitoring exercise; an information-sharing exercise on implementation of the Policy Framework; and a peer review to evaluate progress in implementing the Policy Framework. The monitoring exercise was conducted annually from 2011 onwards. The information-sharing exercise on implementation of the Policy Framework was for the first time undertaken across all FSB jurisdictions in 2015. Finally, the peer review that evaluated progress in implementing the Policy Framework (FSB 2013b) took place in 2016 (FSB 2016a), drawing on the previous exercises (monitoring and information sharing), as discussed in the following chapter. To sum up, a two-pronged regulatory and oversight framework was set in place internationally for shadow banking. The first part was a system-wide monitoring framework to identify potential systemic risks. To this end, the FSB collected data through macro and microchannels. The second part was a policy framework that identified five areas where regulation and oversight needed to be improved to reduce systemic risks: (i) MMFs; (ii) shadow banking entities (other than MMFs); (iii) securities financing transactions, such as repos and securities lending; and (iv) securitization; (v) banks' interactions with shadow banking entities (FSB 2014b: 1). This resulted in a multiplicity of partly parallel, partly nested, and partly interlinked elemental regimes, which generated a regime complex on shadow banking (see Figure 3.2).

To begin with, two elemental regimes on shadow banking entities—the *elemental regime* on *MMFs* and the *elemental regime* on *investment funds* (a.k.a. shadow banking entities other than MMFs)—were parallel and were only marginally tightened up after the crisis—they were neither very precise, nor very stringent, as elaborated in Chapter 5. International rules on hedge funds were very general, whereas rules on MMFs included a range of proposals, but jurisdictions were left free to choose which approach to adopt and several policy options initially considered by the IOSCO were eventually discarded. As for investment funds, the international standards issued by the IOSCO did not set a globally harmonized measure of leverage, so jurisdictions were left free to measure leverage in different ways. The standards on the liquidity of investment funds lacked precision and stringency. Indeed, the Governor of the Bank of England, Mark Carney (2019), lamented that these standards did not prescribe how to regulate the liquidity of investment funds and left implementation to national authorities and funds themselves.

Two elemental regimes on shadow banking activities—the *elemental regime on securities lending and repos*, and the *elemental regime on securitization*—were parallel and had a medium level of precision and stringency, as elaborated in Chapters 6 and 7. In the case of securities financing transactions (which included securities lending and repos), the international harmonization of rules on the re-hypothecation and re-use of collateral was set aside as not feasible. The controversial introduction of haircuts for securities financing transactions was significantly watered down by reducing the level of haircuts, narrowing their scope of application only to a small share of the market, and delaying implementation. International rules for securitized products, including bank capital requirements, were tightened up in the wake of the 2008 crisis. Afterward, international standards for simple, transparent, and comparable securitization were issued and bank capital requirements for this type of securitization were lowered.

All the regimes mentioned above partially intersected with the elemental regime on banking regulation, given that banks engaged with shadow banking entities and activities. The international standards for bank exposures to shadow banking were nested into the broader *elemental regime of capital and liquidity requirements for banks*—these rules were significantly tightened up by the BCBS after the 2008 crisis, even though capital rules on bank exposures to securitization were then recalibrated downward, creating some inconsistency across capital rules. Other banking rules, for instance on large exposures and equity investment in funds, remained rather general and lacked stringency, as explained in Chapter 8.

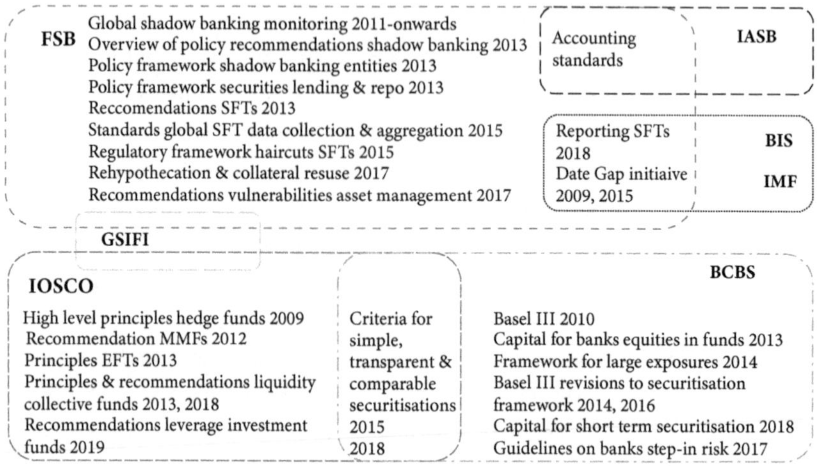

Fig. 3.2 Main international standards in the shadow banking regime complex

International standard-setting bodies sought, to no avail, to establish an *elemental regime for globally systemically important non-bank non-insurer financial institutions* to regulate and supervise these systemic players more stringently and in a way that was consistent with the regulation and supervision of globally systemically important banks and insurers. Yet, in the end, the FSB and the IOSCO were unable to agree on methodologies to identify non-bank, non-insurer G-SIFIs, as explained in Chapter 5. The *elemental regime on the global monitoring of shadow banking*, which was led by the FSB, intersected with all the elemental regimes mentioned above, as well as with *international standards for data reporting, formatting and aggregation*, which also involved the BIS and the IMF, and *international accounting standards* set by a non-financial private standard-setting body, the IASB. To sum it up, the elemental regimes on shadow banking had limited precision, stringency, and consistency, as elaborated in the following chapters.

Conclusion

This chapter has set the context for the rest of the book. First, it has put forward several definitions of shadow banking (the policy implications of these definitions will be elaborated on in the next chapter). It has then outlined the intricate international institutional architecture for the governance of shadow banking, highlighting its fragmentation, the presence of a multitude of international standard-setting bodies, and the lack of a focal institution.

Third, this chapter has provided an overview of the main post-crisis sets of standards in the regime complex on shadow banking, arguing that, despite the prominent role of shadow banking in the run-up to the crisis, post-crisis regulatory reforms were overall rather limited. The next chapter examines the international debate on the definition and monitoring of shadow banking—the first and second steps of the game of shadows identified by this book. The subsequent chapters deal with the third step of the game by examining the international standard-setting in each elemental regime concerning shadow financial entities and activities.

4
Defining, Measuring and Monitoring Global Shadow Banking

The international post-2008 reforms of shadow banking governance began with the definition, measurement, and monitoring of global shadow banking. These steps were interconnected because the definition of shadow banking set the perimeter of what needed to be measured, and the measurement was essential for monitoring. In turn, monitoring preceded regulation. Thus, the definition cum measurement of shadow banking was the first step in the game of shadows singled out by this book. The monitoring of shadow banking was the second step. Regulation, which is discussed in the following chapters, was the third step (see Figure 1.2). The definition of shadow banking and the very use of this term were contested. The term 'shadow' was criticized because it implied something dark, hidden, whereas the term 'banking' was challenged because it was used to describe something very different from 'traditional' banking. Similarly contested were the measurement and monitoring of global shadow banking.

The main jurisdictions influenced the definition, measurement, and monitoring of shadow banking through pace-setting and foot-dragging. Initially, the US and the EU sought to define shadow banking in a way that was most suitable for them, triggering the opposition of emerging economies that had a burgeoning shadow banking system, notably, China. Then, it was the turn of the US and the EU to backtrack on the very use of the term 'shadow banking', which was renamed as 'market-based finance'. Moreover, there was puzzling by regulators, who had to start from scratch by defining what shadow banking was (and what it was not) because this was a new area of regulation at the international and domestic levels and suitable data on various aspects of shadow banking were missing.

At the same time, there was limited mobilization by the financial industry because the definition and measurement of shadow banking were seen as general issues and private actors preferred, instead, to lobby on specific

The Perils of International Regime Complexity in Shadow Banking. Lucia Quaglia, Oxford University Press.
 DOI: 10.1093/oso/9780192866523.003.0004

pieces of regulation that directly affected them. The main exceptions were large transnational associations, notably, the International Capital Market Association and the Institute of International Finance, which mounted a robust defence of shadow banking, while demanding a more nuanced approach to systemic risks, pointing out the need to 'regulate risk, not shadow banking' (cited in *Euromoney*, 22 June 2012;[1] see also Institute of International Finance 2012). Later on, it was the asset management industry—which attracted the attention of regulators, given its massive size—that pointed out the need to distinguish 'market-based finance from shadow banking.... taking market-based finance out of the shadows' (Blackrock 2018: 1). This chapter first examines the definition and measurement of shadow banking and then discusses its global monitoring.

Defining and Measuring Global Shadow Banking

In the wake of the international financial crisis of 2008, it was necessary to define what shadow banking was (or was not) and how it should be measured and monitored. This debate unfolded domestically, but was particularly important internationally, given the cross-border dimension of shadow banking and the need for its global monitoring to reduce systemic risk. The international debate on the definition, measurement, and monitoring of shadow banking mainly took place in the FSB, which, as explained in the previous chapter, was the link between the political level (elected officials of the jurisdictions of the G20) and sectoral international standard-setting bodies (i.e. domestic regulators gathered in the BCBS and the IOSCO). The international debate was led by the US, the EU, and the UK, which were inclined to define shadow banking based on their experience of the 2008 crisis (Knaack and Gruin 2020).

The FSB set up a Task Force, which initially cast the net wide by establishing a workstream to categorize shadow banking entities; assess the scale and risks that they posed; evaluate regulatory frameworks and potential gaps, focussing on prudential measures, rather than investor protection and business conduct. Afterward, the workstream narrowed the scope of its work to certain types of entities: investment funds; exchange-traded funds; hedge funds; private equity funds; securities broker-dealers; securitization entities; credit insurance providers; finance companies; and trust companies. These entities had heterogeneous business models not only across sectors, but also within

[1] Euromoney (2012) 'IIF: Regulate Risk, not Shadow Banking', 22 June.

sectors. Furthermore, they were subject to different regulatory frameworks across jurisdictions.

For these reasons, the FSB's workstream decided to develop an economic function-based (i.e. activities-based) perspective for assessing shadow banking activity in non-bank entities, rather than considering entities' legal forms (FSB 2013b). The framework also contained a set of policy tools from which the national authorities could 'pick and choose' to mitigate the risks related to each economic function. The intention was to provide some consistency across jurisdictions, while allowing the national authorities to adopt tools appropriate for their domestic markets. To maintain consistency across jurisdictions, the FSB set up an information-sharing process and a peer-review process of national implementation. The work of the FSB on these matters was led by the US, the EU, and the UK (Knaack and Gruin 2020).

The term shadow banking and its definition(s) were contested by the financial industry. One of the most powerful transnational financial industry associations, the International Capital Market Association—European Repo Council (2012a) took an issue with the very term shadow banking, arguing that

> It is inherently pejorative. It is also vague, which means that it is arbitrary. This is not a secure foundation for analysis or regulatory prescription. The problem can be seen in the gradual migration of the term. Historically, it described the use of Special Purpose Vehicles. Then, it was applied to funding with uninsured commercial paper. Subsequently, it has gathered in repos. The term may have become too much of a Gladstone Bag.... There are many different objects of (potential) regulation wrapped up in this definition, each manifesting different issues and requiring different regulatory responses... One consequence of the use of the term 'shadow banking' seems to be an acceptance that shadow banking is inherently opaque and an assumption by default that traditional banking is more transparent. Fundamentally, this is wrong.

Similarly, another major transnational financial industry association, the Institute of International Finance (2012), noted that 'starting with the term and then attempting to come up with a definitive list of "shadow banking" activities or entities conducting these activities, or to come up with a single figure for the size of "shadow banking" is unworkable, unnecessary, and risks being a diversion from the real focus of policy, which should be the mitigation of systemic risk'. The decision of the FSB to focus on economic functions related to shadow banking was partly influenced by a paper issued by the Institute of International Finance (*Euromoney*, 22 June 2012),[2] which posited that any attempt to regulate shadow banking by focusing on certain shadow banking entities and activities was 'misguided' and 'unlikely to succeed' (Institute of International Finance 2012).

The FSB's (2013b) *Policy Framework for Strengthening Oversight and Regulation of Shadow Banking Entities* was important for several reasons. To begin with, it laid the groundwork for the measurement and monitoring of shadow banking at the global level through the annual reports prepared by the FSB. In particular, it allowed the FSB to narrow down its definition and measurement of shadow banking, as explained in the following section. Furthermore, jurisdictions agreed to participate in the information-sharing process and undergo the peer review of national implementation, under the aegis of the FSB. Subsequently, the FSB (2016a) noted that there were a variety of institutional arrangements for the regulation and supervision of non-bank financial entities and, in most cases, the regulatory perimeter was ad hoc and informed by concerns about particular activities or entities. There were gaps in the availability of data, particularly for non-regulated entities, given that the authorities' data collection powers often did not extend to such entities. Some jurisdictions provided only partial submissions to the FSB, while others did not provide a joint submission representing a coordinated response from all the relevant authorities in that jurisdiction (FSB 2016a), which highlights the problem posed by the splintered institutional architecture for shadow banking also at the domestic level.

In the meantime, an important internal debate took place within the FSB concerning the definition and measurement of shadow banking, bringing to the fore *pace-setting* and *foot-dragging* by the main jurisdictions. Initially, North American and European regulators framed shadow banking as a potential source of systemic risk that needed to be monitored and, if necessary, regulated (Gruin and Knaack 2020). Subsequently, emerging economies, led by China, contested this definition, arguing that shadow banking, or, to be precise, non-bank financial intermediation, also served important financial development functions. In China, shadow banking assets grew massively from \$500 billion in 2010 to \$2.7 trillion in 2014, and nearly \$8 trillion in 2019. Thus, Chinese regulators and other Asian regulators sought to strike a balance between the promotion of these activities and risk control (Knaack and Gruin 2020; see also Gruin and Knaack 2020; Liansheng 2015). They argued

[2] Euromoney (2012) 'IIF: Regulate Risk, not Shadow Banking', 22 June.

that international cooperation should be based on 'the function of the non-bank credit activities, rather than on the FSB's definition, and that it should take into account differences between countries rather than adopting a single set of integrated standards' (Liansheng 2015: 4). The controversy between the FSB and Asian policy-makers (in particular, Chinese ones) came into the spotlight following the publication of a report prepared by the FSB's Regional Consultative Group for Asia (Knaack and Gruin 2020), which stated that:

> Members [of the Regional Consultative Group for Asia] recognize the beneficial roles played by non-bank financial intermediaries (NBFIs) in filling a credit void and broadening access to finance by individuals and corporations which may not otherwise benefit from access to 'traditional' sources of funding. These positive attributes of NBFIs are of significant socio-economic value to most jurisdictions in the region. NBFIs promote financial inclusion and sustain growth, in particular for emerging and developing markets, where further deepening of financial markets is a priority. In addition, the activities of NBFIs identified in the survey are predominantly domestic and thus, cross-border risks are minimal.... None of the members consider that Asia faces the same shadow banking risks as other jurisdictions such as the US or EU (FSB Regional Consultative Group for Asia 2014: 6).

The report of the FSB's Regional Consultative Group for Asia (2014) disputed the FSB's policy frame on shadow banking as primarily a source of risk, rather than a tool for economic development; it distinguished between domestic and cross-border systemic risk; and it stressed the special needs of emerging economies (Knaack and Gruin 2020). However, the FSB was reluctant to change its policy frame on shadow banking. In response, Chinese regulators acted as foot-draggers and initially limited their cooperation concerning data sharing with the FSB: they did not engage in a detailed classification of shadow banking, and only the China Banking Regulatory Commission, not the Chinese securities regulatory authority, took part in the information-sharing exercise (Knaack and Gruin 2020; Liansheng 2015). In its *Global Shadow Banking Monitoring Report of 2015* the FSB (2015a: 4) explained in a footnote that the 'Chinese authorities did not agree with the classification of certain entity types as shadow banking. Thus, China's entity types are not reflected in this year's economic functions.' In its subsequent report, the FSB (2017a) noted that 'data from China were not received in time to complete an assessment of entities in China for the narrow measure of shadow banking'. However, China provided the necessary data for the *Global Shadow Banking Monitoring Report* of 2017 (FSB 2018c), as detailed below.

On the one hand, the FSB did not respond to the requests made by Asian policy-makers and did not incorporate development issues into its policy work on shadow banking. On the other hand, the FSB's policy discourse gradually changed, morphing shadow banking into market-based finance, and revising (downward) the measurement of shadow banking over time. In fact, initially, the FSB used for measurement a catch-all category of OFIs, but, subsequently, it examined shadow banking by function. Thus, the FSB (2014a) subtracted from the broad measure of shadow banking (the global financial assets of OFIs) non-banks that did not engage in credit intermediation, or maturity and liquidity transformation, and/or leverage. This resulted in a narrower measure of shadow banking, reducing the total value of activities from $75 trillion to $35 trillion.

Over time, the FSB weakened its reformist approach concerning shadow banking (Ban and Gabor 2016), as suggested by the redefinition of the term shadow banking and the narrower, function-based way of measuring its size. In 2014, the FSB (2014b) issued a *Progress Report on Transforming Shadow Banking into Resilient Market-based Financing*, stating that 'transforming shadow banking into resilient market-based financing has been one of the core elements of the FSB's regulatory reform agenda to address the fault lines that contributed to the global financial crisis and to build safer, more sustainable sources of financing for the real economy' (FSB 2014b: 1). Along similar lines, in the same year, the Governor of the Bank of England and Chairman of the FSB remarked that 'now is the time to take shadow banking out of the shadows and to create sustainable market-based finance' (Carney 2014). Thus, shadow banking came to be considered in a rather positive light as an alternative source of funding (Engelen 2018). In 2018, the FSB decided not to use the term shadow banking, but rather 'non-bank financial intermediation', renaming its annual global monitoring report.

The disappearance of the term shadow banking into the shadows was partly due to shifting priorities of the main jurisdictions, first and foremost, the US and the EU (including, at that time, the UK), which were looking for alternative sources of funding for the real economy a few years after the 2008 crisis. This was especially the case of the EU, where banks provided most of the credit to the real economy, but where such a flow was constrained by the need to raise additional capital to comply with the bank capital requirements set by the Basel III accord. Moreover, the sovereign debt crisis in the euro area from 2010 onwards changed the economic agenda of the EU. In 2015, the EU launched the project of Capital Markets Union (Montalbano 2020; Quaglia, Howarth, and Liebe 2016), which partly relied on the expansion of non-bank credit intermediation, including shadow banking (Braun, Gabor, and Hubner 2018; Engelen and Glasmacher 2018; Gabor and Vestergaard 2018).

However, the shift in the FSB's approach to shadow banking was also due to *puzzling* ensuing from the epistemic debate amongst regulators concerning not only the definition, measurement, and monitoring of shadow banking, but also the assessment of the risks it entailed. As the Chairman of the British Financial Services Authority Adair Turner put it, 'shadow banking is like cholesterol. There is good and there is bad. Now we've got the really difficult job of getting the national authorities to dive in and determine which parts really worry us' (*Financial Times*, 19 November 2012).[3] Regulators had to start from almost a clean slate on shadow banking and therefore undertook some 'soul searching'. As Daniel Tarullo acknowledged (2015a), shadow banking was 'not a single, identifiable 'system,' but a constantly changing and largely unrelated set of intermediation activities pursued by very different types of financial market actors. Indeed, the very rigor of post-crisis reforms to prudential regulation may create new opportunities for such activities. The aphoristic warning to avoid too much emphasis on fighting the last war, since wholly new risks may have arisen, seems particularly applicable in this area.' Tarullo (2016b) also noted that a broad definition of shadow banking that embraced all forms of lending outside of prudentially regulated institutions was 'a useful starting point for purposes of consumer protection' but was both

> over- and under-inclusive for purposes of regulation to protect financial stability and the resilience of the economy as a whole. There are certain forms of nonbank lending that do not raise prudential concerns… On the other hand, financial stability concerns can arise where credit extension is only indirectly involved… I think it more productive to focus on the characteristics of shadow banking-related financial activities and institutions that are most likely to pose risks to financial stability and to the economy more generally.

Monitoring Global Shadow Banking

The global shadow banking system grew dramatically in the years before the 2008 crisis. The broad measure of shadow banking, defined as the aggregate

[3] *Financial Times*, 'Lord Turner and Shadow banking' by B. Masters, 19 November 2012.

total assets of OFIs, rose from $26 trillion in 2002 to $62 trillion in 2007. The US had the largest shadow banking system in the world, but non-bank credit intermediation was present in other countries, particularly in the EU (especially, in the UK) and Asia. The US and UK accounted for 46% and 13% of the global shadow banking system, respectively, while Japan and the Netherlands followed (8% each) (Nesvetailova 2015; see also Lysandrou and Nesvetailova 2015). The largest component of shadow banking across all countries was asset-backed commercial paper (Hardie and Howarth 2013), which was a type of short-term security issued by a special purpose company, with additional credit support from the sponsoring bank. The shadow banking system shrunk during the 2008 crisis, but increased afterward.

From 2011 onwards, the FSB conducted annual monitoring exercises to assess global trends and risks of the shadow banking system. Over time, the monitoring exercise was improved by including more jurisdictions and gathering more granular data, some of which were prescribed by the FSB's data reporting and disclosure requirements for shadow banking discussed in the following chapters. The monitoring exercise was conducted by the FSB's Non-bank Monitoring Experts Group, which included representatives from all participant jurisdictions as well as international organizations and standard-setting bodies, specifically: the BIS, the IMF, the OECD, the IOSCO, the IAIS, the European Commission, the ESMA, and the ESRB.

To monitor the global shadow banking system, the FSB established the following measurements. The Monitoring Universe of Non-bank Financial Intermediation (MUNFI) was a measure of all non bank financial intermediation, which comprised OFIs, insurers, and pension funds. OFIs comprised all financial institutions that were not classified as banks, insurers, pension funds, public financial institutions, and central banks. It was a broad measure of shadow banking. The narrow measure of shadow banking included non-bank financial intermediation (NBFI) that was involved in credit intermediation that could pose financial stability risks through liquidity/maturity transformation and/or leverage. The narrow measure was calculated by referring to the economic functions performed by shadow banking, discussed in the previous section.[4]

[4] As explained by the FSB, the economic functions approach was based on the classification of non-bank financial entities into five economic functions through which non-bank credit intermediation could pose bank-like systemic risks to the financial system. Through this process, each jurisdiction removed non-bank entities that in its supervisory judgment did not engage in credit intermediation and also those that were prudentially consolidated into banking groups.

Thus, the FSB's monitoring methodology involved three steps. The first step measured the MUNFI based on the national flow of funds statistics, which provided consistent data on bank and non-bank financial sectors' assets and liabilities. To cast the net wide and cover all areas where shadow banking-related risks could arise, the macro-mapping looked at all non-bank financial intermediation. The second step measured OFIs, which comprised non-bank financial institutions that were not insurers or pension funds and which were used to obtain a conservative estimate of the size of the shadow banking system (the broad measure of shadow banking). The third step focused on NBFI (the narrow measure of shadow banking) by classifying a subset of the MUNFI entities according to five economic functions related to shadow banking, using national financial accounts data and other national sources, such as sectoral data by regulators.

To give an idea of what this 'Russian doll' of measures and data looks like, according to the most recent data of the FSB (2020a), the total financial assets in the financial system amounted to $379 trillion in 2019. The MUNFI was $184 trillion. The OFIs were $114 trillion. The narrow measure of NBFI was $51 trillion, of which collective investment funds were $36.6 trillion (72%), special purpose entities engaged in securitization and asset-backed securities were $4.7 trillion (9.3%) and broker-dealers and securities finance companies were $4.5 trillion (8.8%) (see Figure 4.1).

The remainder of this section discusses the most important data and trends concerning the post-2008 measurement and monitoring of global shadow banking. Three observations stand out. The first observation is that the number of jurisdictions participating in the FSB's global monitoring exercise increased

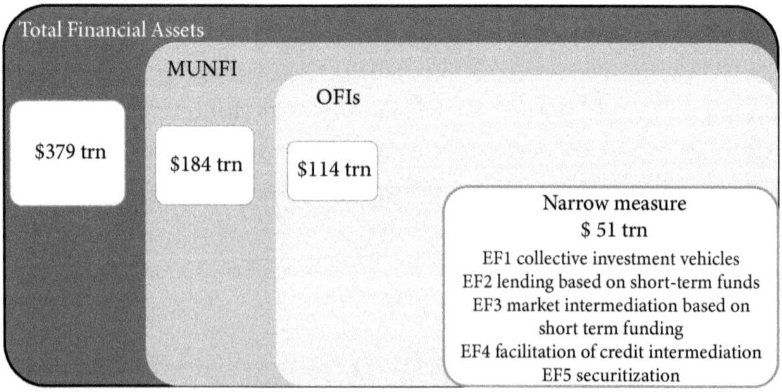

Fig. 4.1 Narrowing down the definition and measurement of global shadow banking (adapted from FSB 2020a)

over time. Small jurisdictions that had a large shadow banking system (notably, Luxembourg and Ireland) were reluctant to submit the relevant data. China was also reluctant to contribute to the FSB's exercise for the reasons explained in the previous section. Thus, the first FSB's (2012e) Global Shadow Banking Monitoring Report covered 25 jurisdictions and the euro area, representing 86% of global gross domestic product and 90% of global financial system assets. In 2015, data from Ireland were included by the FSB for the first time (FSB 2015a). In 2016, data from Belgium and the Cayman Islands were included for the first time, whereas data for the narrow measure of shadow banking were not submitted by China (FSB 2017a). In 2017, data from Luxembourg were included for the first time by the FSB as well as a classification of non-bank financial entities in China into the narrow measure of shadow banking (FSB 2018c).

The second observation is that, initially, some jurisdictions (e.g. China, Russia, Saudi Arabia) lacked a fully developed flow of fund statistics, whereas others (e.g. the UK and the euro area) had low granularity at the sectoral level, resulting in a relatively large share of unidentified non-bank financial institutions (FSB 2011a). The FSB–IMF (2009) *Data Gaps* initiatives were instrumental to improve the flow of funds statistics over time. Moreover, the FSB's *Framework for Haircuts on Non-centrally Cleared Securities Financing Transactions* published in 2015 (FSB 2015e) (see Chapter 7) was instrumental to expand the data collection template to include items from the liability side of the balance sheet, to capture data on wholesale funding and repos of the main financial sectors: deposit-taking corporations, insurance corporations, pension funds, and OFIs (FSB 2017a).

The third and most important observation is that the MUNFI and OFIs continuously increased after the crisis of 2008, with a slight decrease only in 2018 (FSB 2018c). The narrow measure of NBFI continuously increased after the crisis, but, in proportion, less than the MUNFI and OFIs (see Figure 4.2). Hence, the narrow measure of shadow banking increased substantially less than the broad measure, which raises the question of whether the narrow measure was too narrowly defined. Among the components of the narrow measure of NBFI related to five economic functions, the only one that substantially increased over time, superseding by far the pre-crisis period, related to Economic Function 1, that is to say, investment funds (see Figure 4.3), which also explains why regulators began to focus their attention on asset management as time went by, as elaborated in the next chapter.

The most recent report *Global Monitoring Report on Non-Bank Financial Intermediation* was issued by the FSB in 2020 with reference to the previous year.

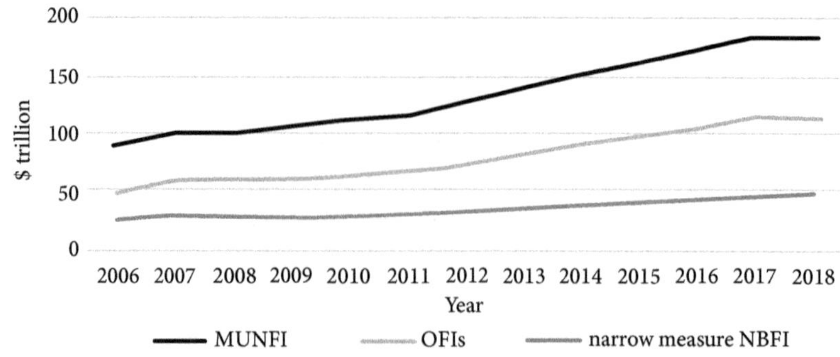

Fig. 4.2 The evolution of the broad and narrow measures of global shadow banking
(data source: FSB 2020a, own elaboration)

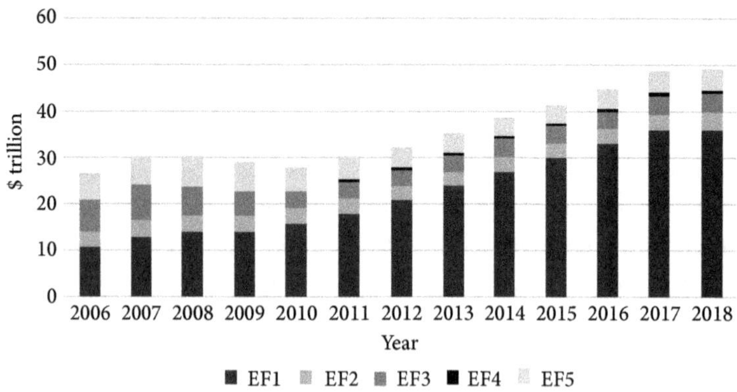

Fig. 4.3 The evolution of the components of the narrow measure of global shadow banking
(data source: FSB 2020a, own elaboration)

In 2019, the global financial assets of all financial entities were $379 trillion. The MUNFI, which comprised 10 subsectors, totalled $183.7 trillion. OFIs, which comprised the biggest share of MUNFI assets, including MMFs, finance companies, structured finance vehicles, hedge funds, other investment funds (OIFs), broker-dealers, and other non-bank financial corporations, were $114 trillion. The euro area had the largest share of OFIs (32% of OFIs), followed by the US (26% of OFIs), China (10% of OFIs), and the UK (9% of OFIs).

Within OFIs, other OIFs—that is to say, investment funds other than MMFs and hedge funds—were the largest share (37% of OFIs, equivalent to $42 trillion), followed by captive financial institutions and money lenders (22% of OFIs, equivalent to $25 trillion), broker-dealers (9% of OFIs, equivalent to $10 trillion), structured finance vehicles (4.4% of OFIs, equivalent to $5 trillion), finance companies (4% of OFIs, equivalent to $4.7 trillion), MMFs (4% of OFIs, equivalent to $6.2 trillion), and hedge funds (4% of OFIs, equivalent to $5 trillion). The US and eight euroarea jurisdictions accounted, respectively, for 43% and 28% of global investment fund assets. Captive financial institutions and money lenders in Canada, Luxembourg, the Netherlands, and the UK accounted for 80% of these assets. Broker-dealers were concentrated in the US (34%), the UK (29%), and Japan (17%) (FSB 2020a).

The narrow measure of shadow banking (i.e. the narrow measure of NBFI) reached $51 trillion, around 75% of all G20 jurisdictions' gross domestic product (including the euro area as a whole) and 13.6% of total global financial assets. The US accounted for 30% of narrow measure shadow banking assets ($15.2 trillion). The eight participating euro-area jurisdictions had a combined amount of $12 trillion (23.6% of the narrow measure, of which, Luxembourg 8%, Ireland 6%, Germany 3%, France 3%, respectively). Then, there were China with $7.8 trillion (15.4% of narrow measure), the Cayman Islands with $5.5 trillion (10.7%), Japan with $3 trillion (5.8%), and the UK (3%). Since the financial crisis, the growth of the narrow measure of shadow banking has been driven primarily by investment funds (Economic Function 1), as opposed to pre-crisis growth, which was driven to a large degree by structured finance vehicles (Economic Function 5) and broker-dealers (Economic Function 3).

Assets related to Economic Function 1—which comprised collective investment funds, such as fixed-income funds, mixed funds, exchange-traded funds, real estate funds, hedge funds, and MMFs—grew to $36.6 trillion or 72% of the narrow measure of NBFI in 2019. The largest share of these assets was held in the US (27%), China (16%), the Cayman Islands (14%), and Luxembourg (9%). The largest Economic Function 1 entity types were fixed-income funds, mixed funds, and MMFs. The majority of fixed income fund assets were held in the US (39%), Luxembourg (15%), and Ireland (6%). The US held the largest share of global mixed fund assets (20%), followed by Luxembourg and Germany (16% each) and the Cayman Islands (9%). The majority of MMF assets were held in the US (53%), China (18%), Ireland (9%), France (6%), and Luxembourg (6%). The assets related to Economic Function 5 (securitization-based credit intermediation) were $4.7 trillion and amounted to 9% of the narrow measure of NBFI. Structured finance vehicles accounted for a significant share of these assets (76%), followed by trust companies (26%). The assets related to Economic Function 3 (market intermediation dependent on short-term funding) were $4.5 trillion, 8.8% of the narrow measure of NBFI. Broker-dealers made up 84% of the total of these assets. The assets related to Economic Function 2 (leading dependent on short-term funding) were $3.6 trillion and represented 7% of the narrow measure. Finance companies held nearly 80% of these assets (FSB 2020a).

Conclusion

This chapter has discussed the first and second steps in the game of shadows, namely, the definition, measurement, and monitoring of shadow banking (for an overview of various explanations, see Table 4.1). At the international level, the most authoritative work was carried out by the FSB, which, together with other international standard-setters, also issued new standards to gather missing data on various aspects of shadow banking. Remarkably, the definition and measurement of shadow banking were narrowed down over time, and ultimately, the term shadow banking disappeared from the official vocabulary, although the problems it posed did not. Indeed, two contrasting trends emerged in the FSB's monitoring of global shadow banking after the 2008 crisis: while the size of non-bank non-insurer financial intermediation (i.e. the broad measure of shadow banking) continued to grow substantially, the narrow measure of shadow banking did not increase to the same extent, and it actually decreased between 2018 and 2019 (see Figure 4.2 and Figure 4.3).

The definition of shadow banking that was initially adopted by the FSB was heavily influenced by the US and the EU (including the UK), which provided the chairs of the FSB and of several of its working groups in the post-crisis period. The initial definition was challenged by China and other emerging economies, which argued that the FSB's approach was not suitable for their

Table 4.1 Defining, measuring, and monitoring global shadow banking: actors, pathways, and outcome

States	Regulators	Industry	Outcome
Initial *pace-setting* by US & EU *Foot-dragging* on measurement and data provision by China before 2016 *Pace-setting* to change definition by US and EU after 2016	*Puzzling* re. definition and measurement, need for data gathering	Limited *lobbying*	Increasingly precise rules, but narrower measure and change of definition by FSB

shadow banking, which had a distinctive configuration, as compared to that in developed countries. Actually, the argument went, what the FSB labelled shadow banking in the Asian context was not shadow banking at all and should not be labelled in this way. Then, it was the turn of the US and the EU to challenge the use of the term shadow banking by the FSB, arguing that the term was misleading and the definition of market-based finance should be used instead. These dynamics concerning the definition, measurement, and monitoring of global shadow banking were also influenced by cognitive uncertainty, hence, puzzling by regulators, as well as lobbying from the financial industry, whereby various private financial actors argued that they were not part of shadow banking and should not be included in the measurement of the global shadow banking system. The following chapters examine the third step of the game of shadows, that is to say, the attempts to set international standards to regulate shadow banking entities and activities.

5

Shadow Banking Entities

The Age of Asset Management?

This chapter discusses the international governance of shadow banking entities, notably, MMFs, hedge funds, and other investment funds undertaking asset management. MMFs played a major role in the unfolding of the international financial crisis of 2008, not only in the (relatively, few) jurisdictions in which they were based (mainly, the US, Luxembourg, Ireland, France, and China). Hedge funds and their managers, which were mostly based in the US and the UK, amplified the effects of the crisis worldwide. By contrast, other investment funds were not major culprits of the crisis, but asset management increased substantially afterward, especially in the US and the EU. Nonetheless, the international governance of all these funds remained relatively weak: post-2008 crisis international standards lacked precision and stringency and were partly inconsistent with other international financial standards.

Three factors account for this outcome, even though some of them were more influential concerning the regulation of certain types of shadow banking entities than others. First, there were disjointed pace-setting efforts by some jurisdictions, and resolute foot-dragging by others. The US was unable to take the lead at the international level because domestic regulators (first and foremost, the Federal Reserve and the SEC) logged horns on these matters. The SEC and the Federal Reserve disagreed on the risk posed by MMFs and investment funds. The US and the UK joined forces and acted as foot-draggers against international rules on hedge funds. The EU was internally divided because the member states with a large hedge fund industry (the UK) and MMF industry (Luxembourg and Ireland) resisted new rules. Eventually, the EU adopted domestic legislation on these financial entities. China, which had a flourishing MMFs industry, was a foot-dragger internationally.

The second explanation for the thin international regulation of shadow banking entities was puzzling (epistemic disagreement) and turf fighting

The Perils of International Regime Complexity in Shadow Banking. Lucia Quaglia, Oxford University Press.
 DOI: 10.1093/oso/9780192866523.003.0005

(bureaucratic disagreement) among sectoral regulatory agencies concerning the risks posed by investment funds, and how to tackle these risks. Securities markets regulators, which were the competent regulators for these funds, were reluctant to act, either domestically or internationally. Most securities markets regulators were not persuaded that there was a problem that needed to be addressed (in other words, that investment funds posed systemic threats to financial stability) and, at any rate, they feared that prudential regulation applied to funds could have negative effects. By contrast, macroprudential regulators (mostly, central banks) and microprudential banking regulators, advocated new prudential 'bank-like' rules on investment funds, even though these financial entities fell outside their regulatory and supervisory purview. Prudential regulators took the lead in the policy debate, especially on G-SIFIs, with very limited success.

The third factor that affected the governance of shadow banking entities was lobbying cum venue shopping by the financial industry, which mobilised at the domestic and international levels and skilfully played domestic sectoral regulators against each other. To begin with, some private financial actors (for instance, MMFs and hedge funds, which were mostly concentrated in few jurisdictions) had preferences that mainly run along national lines and tended to coalesce with those of their national regulators. Investment funds sought either to be excluded from the perimeter of the new rules, or to extend the scope of the new rules to competing types of funds (for instance, sovereign wealth funds). Hence, these private financial actors exerted pressure at multiple levels of governance and in various venues so as to hamper post-crisis regulatory reforms. The result was the watering down of the regulation for MMFs, hedge funds, and other investment funds, while blocking the work on non-bank non-insurer G-SIFIs.

Main Issues in the International Governance of MMFs

MMFs are mutual funds that invest in highly liquid, short-term financial instruments, such as cash, commercial paper, and debt-based securities with short-term maturity (e.g. US treasury bills). MMFs are intended to offer investors high liquidity with a low level of risk, preserving capital and liquidity. They act as intermediaries between shareholders seeking liquid investments and diversification of credit risk exposure and borrowers seeking short-term funding (IOSCO 2012a: 1). In some jurisdictions, such as the US and the EU, MMFs serve as an important source of funding for governments, financial institutions, and businesses. However, they also provide funding to shadow banking. In China, MMFs mainly provide funding to non-financial companies, rather than other financial institutions and savers often invest in MMFs, rather than bank deposits (Sun 2019).

MMFs played an important role in the unfolding of the international financial crisis of 2008. To begin with, in the run-up to the crisis, MMFs provided short-term funding and were often part of the credit intermediation chain that transformed maturity/liquidity and built-up leverage. Thus, MMFs pooled investors' funds to purchase commercial paper[1] or mortgage-backed securities. Once the crisis started, these funds suffered massive losses and experienced the equivalent of a bank run. Indeed, following the bankruptcy of Lehman Brothers in 2008, the Reserve Primary Fund experienced a run due to its holdings of Lehman's commercial paper. The run spread to other funds, triggering investors' redemptions of more than $300 billion in a short period of time. In order to safeguard financial stability, the US authorities provided unlimited deposit insurance to all MMF deposits. This intervention was successful in stopping the run, but it transferred the risk from MMFs to the government (Kacperczyk and Schnabl 2012).

Before the 2008 crisis, investors generally regarded MMFs as a low-risk investment and, indeed, in the past, MMFs had invested in safe assets with steady returns similar to those of US Treasury bonds. However, in the run-up to the financial crisis of 2008, some funds started to generate returns that were significantly higher than those of US Treasury bonds because the underlying assets became riskier. Unlike other mutual funds, MMFs used historical cost accounting, not mark to market accounting, to assess the value of their holdings. By doing so, MMFs were able to maintain a constant net asset value of $1 per share (this paragraph draws on Kacperczyk and Schnabl 2012). This valuation approach exposed MMFs to runs because if the market value of a fund's holdings was expected to drop, investors would all redeem their shares at the same time, forcing liquidation at fire-sale prices. To mitigate the threat of runs, MMFs drew on support from their sponsors, which were large financial institutions that managed funds on behalf of their investors. Even though fund sponsors had no contractual obligation to support their funds, they did so for reputational reasons, also because the default of a fund could generate negative spillovers to the remaining operations of the sponsor (for instance, other mutual funds managed by the same sponsor) (Kacperczyk and Schnabl 2012).

[1] Commercial paper is not usually backed by collateral, so it is a form of unsecured debt.

When international standards on MMFs were discussed in 2012, this industry had approximately $4.7 trillion of assets under management, of which $2.7 trillion in the US and $1.5 trillion in Europe, which together had around 90% of the global MMF industry (IOSCO 2012a). Within Europe, three countries (France, Luxembourg, and Ireland) had a combined market share close to 90% of the EU total. In 2019, MMFs were $6.2 trillion, and accounted for 4% of the share of OFIs. The majority of MMF assets were held in the US (53%), China (18%), Ireland (9%), France (6%), and Luxembourg (6%). Two business models of MMFs co-existed: constant net asset value (NAV) funds, which were offered in the US and other jurisdictions, such as Canada, China, Luxembourg, Ireland, and Japan; and variable net asset value (NAV) funds, which were offered, for instance, in France. Constant NAV funds dominated the MMF markets with an estimated market share close to 80% globally (around 40% in Europe) (IOSCO 2012a).

There were several vulnerabilities of MMFs that could have negative consequences for financial stability. To begin with, the constant NAV gave investors an impression of safety, even though MMFs were subject to credit, interest rate, and liquidity risks. There was also a first-mover advantage because investors had an incentive to redeem their shares from a MMF at the first signs of distress on the basis of the constant NAV, leaving the cost of any loss to be borne by the remaining shareholders. Such advantage was also present, albeit less prominently, in variable NAV funds. Finally, MMFs had implicit support from their sponsors, which stepped in on numerous occasions (IOSCO 2012a). A crucial issue was whether the regulatory approach to MMFs needed to encourage or require a shift to variable NAV, imposing capital and liquidity requirements on MMFs that continued to offer constant NAV to investors.

Main Actors in the International Governance of MMFs

In the wake of the global financial crisis, it was necessary to assess the risks posed by MMFs and regulate them accordingly. The first factor that weakened the international governance of MMFs were timid *pace-setting* by certain *jurisdictions* (the UK and some continental EU countries, notably France) and the resolute *foot-dragging* by other *jurisdictions* (notably, China, Luxembourg, and Ireland) due to domestic political economy considerations. In the US, a pivotal player, there were disagreements among sectoral *regulators* due to *puzzling* and *turf fighting*. Whereas prudential regulators called for more stringent rules on MMFs to protect financial stability, securities markets regulators, notably the SEC, remained unconvinced that MMFs could pose significant systemic threats and, therefore, needed to be subject to more stringent regulation. Securities market regulators generally prioritize investor protection and market integrity through rules on business conduct and transparency. Thus, their approach to regulation and supervision differs significantly from those of banking and insurance regulators (Kempthorne 2013). This discrepancy is due to distinctive regulatory outlooks as well as different mandates and competences. Epistemic disagreements and bureaucratic politics among regulators come to the fore in the post-crisis regulation of MMFs both domestically and internationally. Let us examine these points in more detail.

In the US, given the massive losses suffered by MMFs and the need for government intervention to protect fund depositors, the Federal Reserve supported stringent rules on MMFs because they combined fixed net asset value with a lack of loss absorption capacity (Tarullo 2012a). However, it was the SEC that was responsible for the regulation and supervision of MMFs in the US and, therefore, had the power to address the risks posed by MMFs, in particular, those using a constant NAV. The SEC was internally divided on this matter. Some SEC commissioners, notably, the Chair, Mary Schapiro, supported the attempts by the Federal Reserve to introduce financial stability-oriented regulation (Schapiro 2012). Among the proposals floated by the SEC Chair, there were the requirements for MMFs to abandon the fixed $1 share price and, instead, use mark-to-market valuations and the introduction of a tailored capital buffer of less than 1% of fund assets.

Yet, these reforms were opposed by a majority of the SEC commissioners in 2012 (Schapiro 2012), following intense lobbying by the MMFs industry (*Reuters*, 5 June 2013). For instance, the Investment Company Institute, a fund industry trade body in the US, sent a letter to Mary Schapiro, urging her to set aside her plans to impose capital requirements and redemption gates on MMFs. The letter was also signed by more than 30 elected officials with cross-party affiliations in state and local governments.[2] Eventually, the chairman of the SEC decided to suspend the crucial vote, killing off the reforms. Whereas SEC commissioners and the MMF industry managed to block domestic regulatory reforms, they were unable to prevent the publication of the IOSCO's recommendations on MMFs, which, however, noted that 'a majority of the commissioners of the US Securities and Exchange Commission did not support its publication' (IOSCO 2012b: 1). Although many officials at the SEC

[2] Municipalities relied heavily on MMFs for funding and tighter SEC rules would raise the costs of that funding.

and in other US agencies agreed on the need for more stringent regulation of MMFs, the SEC was slow to act due to an over-crowded agenda and a fierce backlash from the private sector (*Financial Times*, 4 May 2012).[3] This weakened the ability of the US to act as a pace-setter internationally. Eventually, the SEC issued more stringent rules on MMFs in 2014 and 2016.

In the UK, in the wake of the crisis, the Bank of England argued that constant NAV MMFs should not exist—they should become either regulated banks or, alternatively, variable NAV funds (Tucker 2010). Afterward, the Bank of England postulated the choice between either variable NAV funds, or constant NAV funds, subject to some form of capital requirements because MMFs resembled 'narrow banks in mutual fund clothing' (Paul Tucker, cited in *Financial Times*, 14 May 2012).[4] Global standards or, at least, a globally consistent approach to MMFs, were needed because many MMFs were based in the US, but they were internationally active, lending to banks, corporates, and sovereigns around the world. The Bank of England called for the US authorities responsible for MMFs (the SEC and the FSOC) to take action—'making not only their domestic financial system safer, but the global system safer' (cited in *Financial Times*, 14 May 2012).[5] In May 2012, at an event organized by the European Commission, Paul Tucker, suggested that if the US did not implement badly-needed reform to their US MMFs sector, the Europeans could act unilaterally (*Financial Times*, 4 May 2012).[6] At the very least, regulators should limit European banks' reliance on short-term funding from US funds, unless the sector was reformed to make it less susceptible to quasi-bank runs.

The EU was internally divided on this matter, which weakened the ability of the EU to act as a pace-setter internationally. The *Green Paper on Shadow Banking* issued by the European Commission (2012) argued that MMFs could pose huge liquidity risks and that a run on funds could seriously affect financial stability. Indeed, two-thirds of the dollar-denominated funding provided by US MMFs to European banks disappeared in 2011—France was particularly badly hit (*Financial Times*, 14 May 2012).[7] The priority of MMFs reform was also highlighted by the ESRB (2012), whose first 'occasional paper' focused on MMFs. For several years, EU officials expressed concern that the flawed structure of the US MMF industry created the potential for quasi-runs.

[3] *Financial Times*, 'Beware pitfalls of rulemakers pursuing their own agendas' by Tett, G., 4 May 2012.

[4] *Financial Times*, 'The net is closing in on money market funds' by Amery, P., 14 May 2012.

[5] *Financial Times*, 'The net is closing in on money market funds' by Amery, P., 14 May 2012.

[6] *Financial Times*, 'Beware pitfalls of rule-makers pursuing their own agendas' by Tett, G., 4 May 2012.

[7] *Financial Times*, 'The net is closing in on money market funds' by Amery, P., 14 May 2012.

The European Commission was keen on overhauling the rules on MMFs, despite the decision of the SEC to set aside the reform of the US sector. As Emil Paulis, a senior official of the European Commission, put it 'We are very disappointed that, in the US, MMFs have not yet been successfully regulated by the SEC.... We regret what is happening there and we do not intend to follow that route' (cited in *Financial Times*, 29 September 2012).[8] Hence, the Commission supported international standards and, afterward, prosed domestic (EU) legislation based on the IOSCO (2012b) standards for MMFs in 2013. The EU legislation on MMFs was adopted in 2017, after protracted negotiations among the member states.

In fact, France, Luxembourg, Ireland, and the Netherlands had a large MMFs industry. In France, these funds were already regulated according to the variable NAV approach. French regulators, therefore, wanted to include similar rules in EU legislation as well as in the IOSCO's policy recommendations. Edouard Vieillefond, a senior official at the French Autorité des Marchés Financiers, stated that he was in favour of a ban on constant NAV funds, or at least a set of strong prudential rules (cited in *Financial Times*, 1 October 2012), a position similar to that of British regulators. By contrast, Ireland and Luxembourg opposed this reform in the EU as well as internationally. In the international debate taking place at the IOSCO, the EU did not have a clear-cut position because it lacked domestic rules on MMFs at that time (hence, it did not have an EU regulatory template to 'upload' to international standards, see Quaglia 2014a, b) and its member states had different preferences on this matter.

China had a thriving MMFs industry, which was lightly regulated before the crisis and in its aftermath. In China, MMFs employed constant NAV and had been marginally affected by the international financial crisis of 2008. These funds boomed after the crisis and, therefore, Chinese regulators and Chinese MMFs were wary of international standards, which could potentially constrain this flourishing sector (Woyames Dreher 2019). The growth of MMFs in China was driven by investors' quest for high yields relative to bank deposits. Chinese MMFs differed from similar products in other countries: they tended to be more leveraged, and they offered more liquidity and maturity transformation (McLoughlin and Meredith 2017). Internationally, Chinese regulators (the China Securities Regulatory Commission) and the Chinese MMFs industry opposed precise and stringent international standards and took the unusual step of submitting a joint response to the IOSCO's

[8] *Financial Times*, 'Brussels sticks to money market reform', by Ricketts D., 29 September 2012.

consultation (China Securities Regulatory Commission and Chinese Money Market Funds Association 2012). Hence, China acted as a foot-dragger in international standard-setting.

By 2017, the MMFs industry in China was the world's second-largest by assets, though it was small compared to domestic bank deposits. After some domestic policy failures, rules on MMFs were tightened up in China. In 2016, the China Securities Regulatory Commission brought the domestic regulatory framework closer to international standards. However, even under the new rules, MMFs in China were able to obtain leverage of up to 20% (revised down from 40%), compared with 10% in the EU and the US (McLoughlin and Meredith 2017). Chinese MMFs also undertook considerable maturity transformation because they were allowed to hold assets with a maximum weighted average maturity of 120 days, twice the period allowed in the US. Furthermore, post-crisis reforms required funds to adopt a variable NAV in the US, while constant NAV funds were subjected to a capital cushion (a 3% buffer) in the EU, not so in China (McLoughlin and Meredith 2017).

Besides conflicts among jurisdictions and sectoral regulators, the third factor that weakened the international elemental regime concerning MMFs was *lobbying cum venue shopping* by the *financial industry*. MMFs had different preferences that mainly run along national lines, depending on the domestic configuration of the sector and the existing national regulatory framework. Hence, these private financial actors mobilized at multiple levels of governance and in various venues to shape post-crisis regulatory reforms, especially in countries that had a large MMFs industry. The most threatened by proposed reforms were MMFs using constant NAV. Domestically, MMFs preferred to target their direct regulators, that is to say, securities market regulators, which were more likely to give this industry a sympathetic hearing as compared to prudential regulators. Internationally, the FSB, where prudential regulators were the majority, pushed for reform, whereas the IOSCO, which brought together securities markets regulation, delivered rather general international standards.

International Standards for MMFs

Before the international financial crisis that began in 2008, there were no international standards on MMFs. After the crisis, the FSB (2011b) recommended that the regulation of MMFs should be improved, given that these funds could pose systemic risks because they were vulnerable to runs and played an important role in short-term funding markets. The FSB, prompted by US, UK, and EU prudential regulators, asked the IOSCO to work on this matter, which was discussed by the IOSCO Standing Committee on Investment Management. The post-crisis reform of capital markets did not fit well with the IOSCO's practices and policy tools. In particular, whereas the FSB and prudential regulators advocated the introduction of variable NAV,[9] as opposed to the prevalent constant NAV, securities markets regulators remained sceptical (Woyames Dreher 2019).

The IOSCO (2012a) proposed some policy recommendations on MMFs in early 2012, inviting interested parties to respond to the public consultation. Although the respondents to the IOSCO's consultation favoured some international harmonization and the establishment of common principles for the regulation of MMFs, they stressed that the national implementation should take into account the characteristics of the domestic MMFs industry, warning against a 'one size fits all' approach (IOSCO 2012a). Many respondents (first and foremost, MMFs) did not consider MMFs as entities posing systemic risks and challenged the inclusion of MMFs in the shadow banking system. Respondents provided divergent views regarding the differences between constant NAV and variable NAV, reflecting different business models. The possibility of a mandatory move from constant NAV to variable NAV was criticized, stressing that it would likely result in massive outflows from MMFs. Several respondents also highlighted the practical challenges associated with this move because constant NAV funds represented approximately an 80% market share of global MMFs. Other proposals, such as the establishment of a private insurance scheme for MMFs, were considered unfeasible (IOSCO 2012a).

The IOSCO (2012a: 8) was particularly concerned about bank sponsorship of constant NAV funds and argued that this had become an 'unreliable business model' because of the significant amounts potentially involved to support the funds. The IOSCO considered an array of policy options to deal with these risks, ranging from the shift from constant NAV to variable NAV, to the categorization of MMF types by client segments. Crucially, the IOSCO warned against the conversion of all funds to mark-to-market accounting, which was a controversial option for a large part of the industry and some jurisdictions (notably, China). Although converting to variable NAV could lower investor expectations that MMFs were resistant to losses, a transition to variable NAV could be systematically risky (IOSCO 2012a: 14). As an alternative

[9] Consequently, investments in MMFs would vary with market movements.

to a mandatory move from constant to variable NAV, one option was to impose NAV buffers, whereby a fund would create a capital reserve by retaining a portion of its income as a potential backstop against losses.

Eventually, the IOSCO (2012b) issued *Policy Recommendations for Money Market Funds*, putting forward key principles for valuation, liquidity management, use of ratings, and disclosure to investors. The 15 recommendations sought to complement the reforms of MMFs undertaken in the US and the EU. Compared to national reforms, which mainly focused on the asset side of funds, the IOSCO (2012b) recommendations concerned vulnerabilities arising from the liability side, as well as the crucial issue of valuation based on constant NAV (Woyames Dreher 2019). In the IOSCO debate, the SEC was ambivalent about this issue, European regulators had divergent views and Chinese regulators opposed prescriptive international rules on MMFs tout court.

The international standards adopted by the IOSCO (2012b) lacked precision and stringency: they included a range of proposals, such as the possibility of moving to variable NAV, or increase capital and liquidity buffers for funds that did not adopt variable NAV. Yet, jurisdictions were free to choose which approach to adopt. Many policy options that had been mentioned in the IOSCO's consultative paper (2012a) were eventually discarded, notably, the mandatory move to variable NAV, the use of capital buffers for MMFs, especially for those based on constant NAV, and the possibility of subjecting MMFs to bank-like regulation. Other potential requirements were watered down, or made optional, such as the use of redemption gates (Woyames Dreher 2019).

In 2015, the IOSCO (2015a) published a peer review of the regulation of MMFs, which discussed the progress of 31 jurisdictions in adopting regulation concerning MMFs in three areas of reform: (i) valuation practices of MMFs; (ii) liquidity management for MMFs; and (iii) the risks that could affect the stability of MMFs that offered a constant NAV. The peer-review published in 2019 (IOSCO 2019c) revealed that the implementation was most advanced in 12 jurisdictions (approximately 78% of the global market), including two of the largest markets (the US and China). Most jurisdictions implemented the fair value approach for the valuation of MMF portfolios. Progress in liquidity management was less advanced, with only nine out of 24 jurisdictions reporting draft implementation measures. As for the constant NAV, 13 jurisdictions—including four of the five largest jurisdictions for MMFs (the US, China, Ireland, and Luxembourg)—permitted it, subject to safeguards (FSB 2019b). As a consequence of these limited regulatory reforms, when the covid pandemic began in 2020, there was a run on MMFs[10] and central banks had to intervene to provide 'liquidity of last resort' to them (Li, Macchiavelli, and Zhou 2020), as discussed in the concluding chapter.[11]

Main Issues in the International Governance of Investment Funds (Other than MMFs)

Investment funds other than MMFs encompass mutual funds (including, open-end funds and exchange-traded funds) and hedge funds. The asset management industry grew considerably in the run-up to the international financial crisis of 2008, reaching $48.2 trillion in 2007.[12] This trend fell in the wake of the crisis, but was reversed afterward, eventually surpassing the pre-crisis level and reaching approximately three-quarters of the assets of the global banking industry. In 2019, OIFs—that is to say, investment funds other than MMFs and hedge funds—were $42 trillion. MMFs and hedge funds were $6.2 trillion and $5 trillion, respectively, even though the amount of hedge funds assets was somewhat underestimated due to limited data availability (FSB 2020a). The US and the eight euro-area jurisdictions accounted for the bulk of investment fund assets, representing, respectively, about 43% and 28% of global investment fund assets. The vast majority of hedge fund managers worldwide were located in the US and the UK, whereas many hedge funds were domiciled in off-shores jurisdictions (Fioretos 2010; Rixen 2013).

Not only market-based intermediation through asset management entities increased over time, but also the industry became more concentrated, with some very large players. The degree of concentration across the banking industry and the assets management industry was broadly similar. When tighter international regulation of asset managers began to be discussed in 2013, the top ten asset managers accounted for approximately 30% of the sector, the top ten banks for a little more than 20%. Their balance sheets were of similar size. In aggregate, the top ten banks and asset managers totalled $20 trillion and $25 trillion in assets, respectively. The world's largest asset manager (Blackrock) was around a third larger than the biggest bank (the Industrial and Commercial Bank of China) (Haldane 2014). It is however fair

[10] When the covid pandemic began in the spring of 2020, there were massive investor outflows from prime MMFs. The Federal Reserve had to intervene to backstop the market, as it had done when the Reserve Primary Fund 'broke the buck' in 2008 (Ridding 2020).

[11] For instance, the Federal Reserve established the Money Market Mutual Fund Liquidity Facility (Li, Macchiavelli, and Zhou 2020).

[12] https://www.statista.com/statistics/323928/global-assets-under-management/

to say that the asset management industry, as well as securities markets regulators, are generally critical of this kind of data comparison (which is often made by prudential regulators), arguing that banking and asset management are very different (interviews, see James and Quaglia 2022). In 2019, the top ten asset management companies totalled $33 trillion. The five largest players were Blackrock ($6.8 trillion), Vanguard ($6.2 trillion), UBS ($3.2 trillion), State Street Bank ($3.1 trillion), and Fidelity ($3.2 trillion).[13] However, hedge funds were much smaller. For instance, the largest hedge fund managers by assets were Bridgewater Associates ($59 billion), JP Morgan Global Alternatives Hedge Fund Solutions ($54.2 billion), Man Group ($40 billion), Paulson & Co ($35.9 billion), Brevan Howard ($32 billion), BlueCrest ($35 billion), and Och-Ziff Capital Management ($32 billion).[14]

The evolution of the asset management sector reflected the impact of 'extraordinary' monetary policy measures, which resulted in exceptionally low interest rates after the 2008 international financial crisis. Consequently, investors invested in funds that offered exposures to higher-yielding, less actively traded assets, and sought low-cost funds, like exchange-traded funds. The rapid growth of this sector posed potential risks for financial stability (Adrian and Jones 2018; IMF 2014). On the one hand, asset managers, although highly heterogeneous, had some common characteristics: they typically acted in an agency capacity, rather than as principals; they had vehicles that were insolvency remote; and they did not have an official backstop (Adrian and Jones 2018). On the other hand, the asset management industry was a 'greenfield area' compared to banks with reference to financial stability because prior regulation and supervision had focused on consumer protection and market integrity, not system-wide financial stability (Woyames Dreher 2019). Furthermore, since asset management funds are different from banks, the prudential policy framework developed for banks was not suitable to be extended to asset management (Adrian and Jones 2018). Thus, the first step was to understand the potential vulnerabilities of asset management. Three issues were particularly important: liquidity, leverage, and size.

This first issue of concern was liquidity because asset management funds held relatively less liquid assets, but gave investors the right to redeem their investment on short notice. Hence, funds could run out of liquidity in periods of stress, causing the fire sales of assets and contagion effects for holders of similar assets and other asset management funds. The second issue of concern

[13] https://www.thebalance.com/which-firms-have-the-most-assets-under-management-4173923
[14] https://dealbreaker.com/2011/05/the-25-biggest-hedge-funds

was the leverage of investment funds, which made them less resilient to stress, but also increased the interconnectedness between funds and other financial institutions (Tarullo 2016b). Whereas high leverage was particularly problematic for hedge funds (which, indeed, were also referred to as 'highly leveraged institutions'), the entire asset management sector was highly interconnected with other parts of the financial system through cross-ownership, common asset exposures, and the provision of wholesale funding to banks (de Guindos 2018). Thus, any potential problem in the investment fund sector could rapidly spill over to other parts of the financial system, especially, banks, which is why central bankers and banking regulators paid increasing attention to asset management.

The third issue of concern was the size, complexity, and systemic interconnectedness of certain investment funds, whose distress or disorderly failure would cause significant disruption to the wider financial system (FSB 2010). The FSB's framework for reducing systemic risk required assessment methodologies to determine which institutions were to be designated as G-SIFIs. Assessment methodologies were developed first for banks and then for insurers. Afterward, 30 banks and nine insurers were designated as globally systemically important and, therefore, subject to additional regulation and supervision. As time went by, the regulatory focus shifted towards other financial institutions that could pose systemic risks because the sector-by-sector approach could trigger regulatory arbitrage.

Of particular concern was the asset management industry. That prompted the question of whether some of the biggest investment funds should be designated as G-SIFIs, requiring additional regulation and supervision. The methodologies for the assessment of G-SIFIs were controversial because the designation was the starting point for the development of additional regulatory and supervisory measures for non-bank non-insurer G-SIFIs, as it has been done for banks and insurers. Once the methodologies non-bank non-insurer G-SIFIs were set, the question would then be which additional measures to adopt for these institutions. The expectation was that these measures would probably be similar to those for banks, consisting of capital requirements and loss absorption capacity; enhanced prudential supervision; and resolution planning requirements.

In deciding the methodologies for designating non-bank non-insurer G-SIFIs, several issues had to be tackled because the methodologies used for banks and insurers were not suitable for investment funds. These funds had a wide variety of business models, hence sector-specific methodologies were needed for finance companies; market intermediaries (securities broker-dealers); and investment funds (including hedge funds). Another issue was whether asset funds or fund managers or both should be subject to this assessment. A third issue related to the materiality threshold for the assessment. Some argued that the size of a fund was not per se an indicator of risk because there was not a linear relationship between size and risk, unlike for banks. Investment funds were generally smaller than global systemically important banks and unlike banks, they had no leverage. However, for leveraged funds (notably, hedge funds), the problem was to devise a measure of leverage to assess their systemic significance. Finally, there were limitations in data availability: it was difficult to obtain appropriate data, especially on a globally consolidated basis.

Main Actors in the International Governance of Investment Funds

The first factor that weakened the international governance of hedge funds was resolute *foot-dragging* by the key jurisdictions, namely, the US and the UK, despite some *pace-setting* efforts by France and Germany. In fact, the US and the UK opposed international rules on hedge funds (Fioretos 2010; Woll 2013), which were under the purview of one domestic regulatory agency, the SEC, and the British Financial Services Authority (before it is dismantled), respectively. However, as far as the regulation of other investment funds is concerned, there were neither pace-setting jurisdictions nor foot-dragging ones, the main obstacle to regulatory reforms was disagreement among sectoral regulators, notably in the US and at the international level.

The US had the largest asset management industry in the world, but the main domestic regulatory agencies disagreed on this matter, which was consequential for the international standard-setting bodies where these domestic agencies sat. After the 2008 crisis, the Federal Reserve worried about the macroprudential risks posed by asset management. For instance, Daniel Tarullo (2015a), a member of the Board of Governors at the Federal Reserve, underscored the liquidity and leverage risks posed by investment funds, noting that the asset management industry had grown rapidly after the financial crisis, both in terms of the amount of assets under management and the concentration of assets managed by the largest firms. These regulatory discussions intersected with the attempt to develop what Tarullo (2016a) called 'prudential market regulation',

> that is, a policy framework that builds on the traditional investor protection and market functioning aims of securities regulation by incorporating a system-wide perspective. Like the reforms to banking regulation that followed the crisis, this new form of regulation might start by strengthening some of the firm—or fund-specific measures associated with those traditional regulatory aims, but then move forward to take into account such considerations as system-wide demands on liquidity during stress periods and correlated risks among asset managers that could exacerbate liquidity, redemption, and firesale pressures. The specific policies associated with prudential market regulation might be transaction-specific, or apply to certain kinds of business models.

By contrast, the SEC, which was the direct regulator of investment funds in the US, was somewhat less sanguine about the risks they posed and some SEC Commissioners also explicitly opposed the call for 'prudential market regulation' of capital markets actors (Piwowar 2016b). Moreover, the SEC was not particularly concerned by the systemic risks posed by hedge fund and, in fact, in 2011, it only mandated the registration of hedge fund managers—like other investment fund managers—and the reporting of relevant information, but did not adopt prudential requirements (Paredes 2011). In 2016, the Chair of the SEC, Mary Jo White (2016a, b), outlined a roadmap to develop a prudential regulatory approach for the asset management industry, which mainly consisted in issuing new rules on liquidity for mutual funds, whereby mutual funds with assets of more than $1bn were required to classify their portfolio holdings into four liquidity 'buckets'.

The FSOC, which was established post-crisis and brought together the main US financial regulatory agencies, the Federal Reserve and the Treasury, indicated in 2011 that it would consider designating certain non-bank financial institutions as systemically important, and, therefore, subject to higher capital, liquidity and reporting requirements, as prescribed by the Dodd-Frank Act. The FSOC then designed two insurance companies as systemically important financial institutions. In 2014, the FSOC, under the impulse of the Federal Reserve, examined whether asset managers contributed to systemic risk (*Financial Times*, 26 May 2014) and asked the competent regulatory agency, the SEC, to take action concerning the designation of individual investment firms as systemically important (Gelzinis 2019). Once the SEC refused to do so, the Federal Reserve sought to pursue this course of action at the international level. As illustrated below, the domestic policy debate on non-bank non-insurer systemically important financial institutions in the US ran in parallel to and intersected with the international debate on G-SIFIs.

The UK, which together with the US hosted the majority of hedge fund managers worldwide, firmly opposed international rules on hedge funds (James and Quaglia 2020; Fioretos 2010; Woll 2013). However, the UK was not a foot-dragger concerning the regulation of other investment funds. On the contrary, the Bank of England, which was responsible for macro and microprudential regulation, worried about the potential financial stability risks posed by these funds. Specifically, the Bank was concerned about the size and liquidity of investment funds. In a revealing speech entitled 'The Age of Asset Management', Andrew Haldane (2014), Executive Director of the Bank of England, argued that 'the financial crisis alerted us to the perils of banks that are "too-big-to-fail". One natural question, then, is whether the asset management industry has spawned similar such behemoths.... It is often said that banks are special. Compared to banks, asset managers generate a completely different risk and opportunity set. But they, too, are special both for the financial system and the wider economy.... Distress at an asset manager may aggravate frictions in financial markets, in particular frictions in market liquidity.'[15]

The Governor of the Bank of England, Mark Carney, reiterated the point, arguing that banks were safer as a result of more stringent regulation after the crisis. By contrast, the regulation of investment funds had not been substantially tightened up. He also noted that over half of investment funds had a structural mismatch between the frequency with which they offered redemptions and the time it would take them to liquidate their assets (*The Guardian*, 6 June 2019).[16] The problem of holding illiquid assets in open-ended investment funds came to the fore after the Brexit referendum in June 2016, when most open-ended property funds in the UK were forced to suspend dealing due to market turmoil. The Financial Conduct Authority had explored several regulatory options following the Brexit referendum, but the policy conclusions were very slow to emerge (*Citywire*, 27 June 2019). In 2019, a run on a large investment fund managed by Neil Woodford renewed the interest of the Bank of England on this matter (*Financial Times*, 13 July 2019, 16 December 2019).

In the EU, the regulation of hedge funds was very controversial, pitting continental European countries against the UK. France and Germany, which had long been critical of hedge funds (Fioretos 2010; Quaglia 2011; Woll 2013),

[15] Similarly, Sarah Breeden, a senior official at the Bank of England pointed out that the 'run risk' inherent in mutual funds could have systemic implications (*Financial Times*, 26 May 2014).

[16] *The Guardian*, 'Investment funds need closer Bank of England scrutiny, says Carney' by Elliot, L., 6 June 2019.

sponsored new EU legislation on hedge funds, arguing that 'Europe should play an instrumental role in shaping a global regulatory regime for hedge funds through the creation of a "European label"' (European Commission 2009: 8). By contrast, for the UK, which hosted four-fifths of hedge fund managers in the EU, EU legislation would be highly damaging to the competitiveness of the sector and would trigger international regulatory arbitrage (*Financial Times*, 12 September 2009). After a heated intra-EU policy debate, the EU issued the Alternative Investment Fund Managers Directive in 2011, which also applied to hedge funds (the main category of alternative investment funds). This piece of EU legislation introduced a legally binding authorization and supervisory regime for all alternative investment fund managers in the EU, irrespective of the legal domicile of the alternative investment funds managed. Alternative investment fund managers were subject to authorization, reporting requirements, and a minimum level of capital.

As for asset management, investment funds total assets expanded by approximately 170% between 2008 and 2017 in the EU. In 2008, total assets held by investment funds were only 15% of banking sector assets in the euro area. In 2017, euro-area investment fund assets were 42% of total banking sector assets, amounting to €12 trillion (de Guindos 2018). The asset management industry was highly regulated by various reiterations of the Undertakings for Collective Investment in Transferable Securities directives, which, however, dealt with microprudential risk and investor protection, not macroprudential risk. The ESRB, which was responsible for macroprudential regulation in the EU after the 2008 crisis, had no regulatory tools at its disposal. The ESMA, which was the competent authority for investment funds, worried about the potential financial stability risks that the asset management sector posed to the functioning of the broader financial system (Maijoor 2014; Maijoor 2019). Since the asset management sector was highly interconnected with banks, the ECB also paid attention to this sector, especially once the ECB became responsible for prudential banking supervision in 2015. In a revealing speech entitled 'Coming to the forefront: the rising role of the investment fund sector for financial stability in the euro area', Luis de Guindos (2018), Vice-President of the ECB, noted that

> The asset management industry keeps reminding us that vulnerabilities in funds cannot be presumed to resemble those of banks. And it is true that investment funds do not issue deposits and that potential losses in a fund are borne by end-investors. But there is a fundamental difference between the equity in banks and the equity in funds. Investors in an open-end fund can

run by redeeming their units, whereas equity holders in a bank can only run by selling their shares to other market participants. A run by investment fund unitholders can, therefore, resemble a run by bank depositors. In both cases, the institution is, in principle, forced to sell assets in a fire sale in order to meet its short-dated liabilities.

The second factor that explains why investment funds were not subject to substantially more stringent regulation after the crisis was *puzzling* and *turf fighting* among *regulators*. Regulators within jurisdictions and in different international standard-setting bodies disagree on the risks posed by investment funds and asset management and, hence, on how to regulate these entities. Thus, epistemic disagreement unfolded among different regulatory agencies at the domestic level as well as among different standard-setting bodies at the international level. The main line of division was between macro and microprudential regulators—respectively, central bankers and banking regulators—versus securities markets regulators. This clash had to do with different regulatory outlooks (hence, different epistemological views) as well as bureaucratic politics (hence, different mandates and turf fighting for competences).

The most worried about the systemic risks posed by investment funds and asset management were prudential banking regulators, whose mandate concerned the soundness of individual banks and the banking system. They also worried about the interconnections between banks and investment funds, and the risks that these funds could pose for banks. Central bankers and banking regulators favoured, respectively, macroprudential tools as well as bank-like, entity-based, microprudential tools. By contrast, securities market regulators paid less attention to financial stability tout court and the interactions between banks and investment funds, prioritizing their mandate to protect investors and market integrity. Securities market regulators favoured transaction-based tools. Besides different regulatory outlooks, bureaucratic turf fighting was also at play because prudential regulators were eager to regulate entities, notably, large investment funds (such as Blackrock), that were regulated by securities market regulators, and wanted to use a bank-like approach to do this. Securities market regulators disagreed and pushed back (James and Quaglia 2022).

This epistemic disagreement, which also had some bureaucratic connotations, came to the fore at the domestic and international levels. Domestically, two 'heavyweight' regulatory agencies, namely, the SEC and Federal Reserve, locked horns in the US. The Federal Reserve called for 'prudential market regulation', pointing out the need to broaden the 'perimeter of prudential regulation, both to certain non-bank financial institutions and to certain activities' (Tarullo 2016a), and urging the macroprudential regulation of asset management. The SEC opposed prudential market regulation. Commissioner Piwowar (2016b) noted that 'If we were to apply "macroprudential" regulation to capital markets and, in particular to the asset management industry, as many prudential regulators are calling for, the results could be catastrophic.'[17]

The tug of war between sectoral regulators was underplayed in the UK and the EU. In the UK, the number of regulatory authorities was limited and the Bank of England was in the driving seat. Yet, the Bank of England and the Financial Conduct Authority criticized for the lack of precision the work on liquidity for investment funds done by the IOSCO in 2018, eliciting a brisk response from the IOSCO. In the EU, until 2015, the ECB was not responsible for prudential banking supervision, the ESMA was in the process of building up its structure and expanding its competences, and a third body, the ESRB was responsible for macroprudential regulation, but without regulatory tools at its disposal. The ESRB (2019) and the Bank of England (2019a), separately, although in a coordinated manner, took the unusual step of responding to the IOSCO consultation on investment funds leverage to call for further international harmonization.

The ECB also welcomed the too-big-to-fail strand of work of the FSB and the IOSCO because it would help regulators to assess this 'broad and heterogeneous segment of the financial system' in a way that was 'consistent and comparable' with what the BCBS had already done for the global systemically important banks, and the IAIS planned to do for global systemically important insurers (Constâncio 2014). The ECB was keen on moving from designation to stricter regulation. 'Once the methodology for identification of non-bank non-insurers G-SIFIs is agreed, the discussion should move quickly to and focus on the appropriate incremental policy measures that these identified institutions should be subject to… it is key to design measures that ensure that these entities internalize the potential costs they impose on the financial system, and at the same time provide for incentives to reduce their systemic footprint' (Constâncio 2014).

[17] Piwowar (2016b) also argued that the introduction of prudential market regulation was problematic because it could conflict with existing securities markets regulation. 'Prudential market regulation could force, for example, asset managers to face the impossible task of balancing their fiduciary duties to their clients and investors with regulatory obligations to do what is best for the financial system as a whole'.

The third factor that weakened the international governance of investment funds was *lobbying* cum *venue shopping* by the *financial industry* vertically (across levels of governance) and horizontally (across venues). On certain issues, the investment fund industry was internally divided because different typologies of funds (e.g. hedge funds, collective funds) were keen on being excluded from the scope of application of the regulation or, if they could not secure exemptions from certain rules, they wanted to extend those rules to competing typologies of funds. For instance, mutual funds argued that they represented less than a fifth of all assets invested globally, while other large investors, such as pension funds and sovereign wealth funds, were not subject to similar requirements. However, all investment funds challenged the need for precise and stringent rules on leverage and, especially, liquidity. The large funds also challenged the concept of non-bank non-insurer G-SIFIs, as elaborated below.

Not surprisingly, investment funds and their associations sided with securities markets regulators concerning the regulation (or otherwise) of investment funds. The industry repeatedly stressed that securities market regulators, and not central bankers and banking regulators, were responsible for monitoring and regulating this specific segment of the financial sector. For instance, the Investment Company Institute (2016) urged the IOSCO to reflect the exhortations of its former Chairman, Greg Medcraft (2015), who warned against 'jumping to conclusions' about the nature and extent of risks in the asset management sector and the 'need to act'. The IOSCO's Chairman also stressed that regulators should only 'think about solutions' once they were satisfied there was strong concrete evidence that there was a problem. As for the measurement of leverage, investment funds called for securities markets regulators (not prudential regulators) to perform leverage assessments. On liquidity, investment funds opposed a 'one-size-fits-all' approach, called for flexibility in the use of liquidity tools, and supported the 'principles-based approach' taken by the IOSCO.

International Standards for Hedge Funds

Before the international financial crisis of 2008, there were no international standards on hedge funds. To be precise, the IOSCO (1999) and the BCBS (1999a, b) endorsed the indirect regulation of hedge funds—meaning the regulation of financial institutions that interact with hedge funds, notably, banks—and well as private sector governance (Quaglia 2011). In the wake of the crisis, under the pace-setting efforts of France and Germany, the attention focused on hedge funds both internationally and in the EU (*Financial Times,* 23 February 2009). In a joint letter, French President Nicolas Sarkozy, the German Chancellor (Merkel and Sarkozy 2009) argued that 'The European Union must assert a common position and take the lead on this .... The European Union must propose that all hedge funds and other funds presenting a potential systemic risk be subject to appropriate registration, regulation and oversight.' By contrast, US and UK policy-makers were foot-draggers, they supported greater disclosure over more stringent regulation, proposing that funds be required to register with regulators and disclose more information to increase transparency (*Wall Street Journal,* 14 March 2009).

After a heated debate, G20 jurisdictions at the summit in London in April 2009 agreed that:

> ... hedge funds or their managers will be registered and will be required to disclose appropriate information on an ongoing basis to supervisors or regulators, including on their leverage, necessary for assessment of the systemic risks that they pose individually or collectively. Where appropriate, registration should be subject to a minimum size. They will be subject to oversight to ensure that they have adequate risk management....
>
> (G20 2009a)

Following the G20's agreement, the IOSCO's Task Force on Unregulated Financial Entities decided to focus its work on hedge funds. On the one side, regulators in France, Germany, and Italy, where hedge funds (not just hedge fund managers) were already subject to registration and supervision, favoured the regulation of both hedge funds and fund managers. They also called for more prescriptive prudential requirements, somewhat akin to those for banks or regulated funds. On the other side, UK and US regulators, together with the hedge fund industry, which undertook targeted lobbying, wanted to limit the application of the IOSCO's principles to hedge fund managers and opposed prudential requirements.

Only a dozen or so financial associations, first and foremost those representing hedge funds, responded to the IOSCO's consultation. Notably, the UK-based hedge fund association, the Association of Alternative Investment Fund Managers (2009), noted that the international financial crisis of 2008 was not a 'hedge fund crisis' and that hedge funds were 'not bank-like in their activities'. Like its British counterpart, the US-based Managed Fund Association (2009) believed that certain proposed regulatory measures would be inappropriate for hedge funds, in particular: standardized disclosure by hedge funds to their investors, minimum capital requirements, and regulatory restrictions on the types of investments that can be made by hedge funds. None of these measures made it into the final IOSCO report (2009a), which was a rather general and short document: it put forward six high-level principles for hedge fund oversight. The IOSCO could not even agree on whether certain principles should apply to hedge funds and/or their managers (Quaglia 2011).

International Standards for G-SIFIs

G-SIFIs are institutions whose distress or disorderly failure would cause significant disruption to the wider financial system because of their size, complexity, and systemic interconnectedness. At the Seoul Summit in 2010, the G20 (2010) Leaders endorsed the FSB's framework for reducing the systemic and moral hazard risks posed by G-SIFIs. Prudential regulators in the US and the UK, which were heavyweight in the FSB, were particularly worried about G-SIFIs because these countries had large financial sectors and large financial players therein. The implementation of the framework required, as a first step, the assessment of the systemic importance of financial institutions at a global level (or G-SIFIs), bearing in mind that these institutions varied in their structures and activities. Thus, the FSB and the national authorities, in consultation with other international standard-setting bodies, had to devise the assessment methodologies to determine which institutions were to be designated as G-SIFIs.

Initially, assessment methodologies were developed for banks and insurers and 30 banks and nine insurers were designated as globally systemically important and, therefore, subject to additional regulation and supervision. As time went by, the regulatory focus shifted towards other financial institutions that could pose systemic risks. Of particular concern was asset management that gave investors the possibility to withdraw their money on a daily basis, while these funds often invested in illiquid assets (*Financial Times*, 19 June 2015). Two important factors were the relative degree of concentration of the asset management industry and the scale of the largest players (Haldane 2014). Hedge funds were much smaller, but since the use of leverage was widespread by hedge funds, regulators also proposed to measure financial leverage (the 'gross notional exposure' discussed below), as an additional criterion to quantify the significance of hedge funds.

The FSB-IOSCO began joint work on this matter in 2014. The asset management industry mounted ferocious lobbying against the FSB-IOSCO's proposal for assessment methodologies for non-bank non-insurer G-SIFIs (*Financial Times*, 15 July 2015), emphasizing the differences between the asset management sector and the banking sector. Unlike banks, asset managers were not leveraged; they acted as agents; and they did not have access to central bank funding in times of distress. For instance, Fidelity and Pimco argued that the initial approach of the FSB was 'irredeemably flawed' and 'without empirical justification'. Blackrock did not openly criticize the FSB, and instead suggested other ways to deal with risks, considering 'the overall market ecosystem', of which asset managers and funds were only one component (*Financial Times*, 14 July 2015).

The Investment Company Institute (2014), a global association of regulated funds primarily based in the US, issued a very critical response of about 100 pages (single-spaced) to the FSB-IOSCO (2014) proposal for assessment methodologies for G-SIFIs. First, it criticized

> the inclination, on the part of some, to paint the entire canvas of the financial system with a single broad brush and dramatically expand the authority of bank regulators, as well as the applicability of bank regulatory standards that are entirely out of keeping with the way in which other types of financial institutions are structured, operated and currently regulated... The process appears designed to permit the FSB, other international regulatory bodies, and central bank representatives to exercise maximum discretion over matters with very serious potential consequences for regulated funds and other affected entities.

Second, the Investment Company Institute noted that the proposed assessment methodology for investment funds would embrace 14 large US funds simply by virtue of their size. These investment funds were much smaller than global systemically important banks and unlike banks, they had virtually no leverage. The concepts of 'distress', 'disorderly failure', and 'public bailouts' were derived from experience with banks and had little relevance for investment funds. Third, the Investment Company Institute argued that size, as such, was not an indicator of risk because it incorrectly theorized a 'linear relationship between size and risk'. Then, in the rest of its response to the FSB's consultation, the Investment Company Institute complained about the process underway in the US to designate funds as systemically important, noting a parallelism between what the FSOC sought to do in the US and what the FSB sought to do internationally.

The European Fund and Asset Management Association (2014a) pointed out that asset managers were not a source of systemic risks because of their agency business model. Like the Investment Company Institute (2014), and the Institute of International Finance (2014), the European Fund and Asset Management Association did not believe that size alone was an appropriate criterion to assess the systemic relevance of investment funds. PIMCO (2014), a very large asset management company in the US, argued that, according to the proposed methodology for the designation of non-bank non-insurer G-SIFIs, only US funds were eligible for designation. Blackrock (2014) reiterated that asset managers were not a source of systemic risks because they did not fail, like banks. Thus, using size to screen funds would generate 'false positives and false negative'.

In 2015, the FSB-IOSCO (2015) revised their previous proposal, deciding in favour of a more inclusive approach (i.e. a dual approach) that focused on two categories of actors in the asset management industry: investment funds and asset managers. Not surprisingly, the response from the financial industry was even more critical than that in the first round of consultations. The Investment Company Institute (2015) submitted a response letter of more than 200 (single-spaced) pages, noting that the second consultation paper added criteria to include large asset managers into the designation of G-SIFIs appearing to target large US firms.[18] The Investment Company Institute underscored

> The continued propensity of banking-oriented regulators, in various jurisdictions and on the global stage, to view the asset management industry through the lens of banking—in particular, the 'safety and soundness' goals of bank regulation.... From the outset, we have strenuously objected to the characterization of all portions of the financial system other than banks as mere 'shadow banks'—a term that describes this FSB workstream and that betrays the kind of bank regulatory 'group think' that pervades the current consultation. This distorted 'shadow-banking' perspective, when applied to investment funds and asset managers, has predictably led to the view that the largest participants in asset management, in case they are not regulated like banks, may pose unaddressed and unacceptable risks to other market participants and the financial system as a whole. Indeed, many of the FSB's choices as reflected in

[18] Based on the global assets under management threshold, four American asset managers would be considered as systemically important, compared to *zero* non-US asset managers.

> the proposed methodologies for investment funds and asset managers remain stubbornly rooted in the banking mindset.

The European Fund and Asset Management Association (2015) noted that the growing attention around the systemic nature of asset management entities was led by multilateral institutions (such as the IMF or the BIS), prudential regulators, and central bankers, whose mandate was not to supervise directly asset managers, or their funds. This association argued that the 'bank-centric' approach taken was problematic[19] and that the new bodies that were established post-crisis to monitor systemic risk (notably, the FSOC in the US and the ESRB in the EU) drew conclusions sometimes at odds with those of securities markets regulators (e.g. Gallagher 2014). Individual investment funds were also very critical of the revised proposal of the FSB-IOSCO (2015). Fidelity (2015), which submitted a response letter of more than 150 pages, reiterated that 'investment funds and asset managers do not, and cannot, present the type and scale of risk required to justify a G-SIFIs designation'. Blackrock (2015) pointed out that the designation of individual funds or asset managers as G-SIFIs could shift risk around the system, without reducing it. The only supportive statement of the FSB-IOSCO's (2015) work came from Occupy the SEC (2015), which, however, noted, with some dismay, the complete absence of comment letters submitted by 'disinterested parties advocating for the public interest'.

The IOSCO publicly sided with the asset management industry, arguing that it was more important to focus on understanding the risks posed by the sector as a whole than to worry about specific large asset managers. At the annual meeting of the IOSCO, Chairman Greg Medcraft noted that 'We are the frontline regulators; we actually regulate the fund management industry ... it's not the same as bank regulation' (cited in *Financial Times*, 19 June 2015). He described relations with the FSB during the standard-setting process on this issue as 'a journey' adding that 'frankly, the whole designation issue ... we will see if there's a problem before we work out a solution'. Greg Medcraft was adamant that 'We should not use tools developed in the banking and insurance space as our starting point. Those tools were developed to deal with firms that have different risk profiles to asset managers. It is like creating a square peg for a round hole.' The IOSCO and some of its members (e.g. the SEC) also sat on the FSB (although they were a minority there), so their opposition had direct implications for the FSB's work.

[19] See also Collins and Plantier (2015) 'The IMF Is Entitled to Its Opinion, But Not to Its Own Facts', in *ICI Viewpoint*, 10 April.

Furthermore, tensions among domestic regulatory agencies in the US were transmitted to international standard-setting bodies and vice versa. SEC Commission Martin Gallagher (2015) argued that the international work of the FSB concerning asset management and that of the FSOC in the US ran in parallel. In 2014, the FSOC shifted its attention to the activities of asset managers. The following year, the FSB launched a review of asset management activities, while targeting large individual investment funds with its joint work with the IOSCO. Gallagher (2015) concluded that the work of the FSB had been tailored to legitimize

> The FSOC's efforts to import prudential regulation to the US capital markets through the designation of non-banking entities as systemically important financial institutions… The FSB is endeavoring to force a prudential, bank regulatory construct into the capital markets. … Each time the FSB has made an important decision or announced a policy affecting non-bank financial institutions, the FSOC has followed suit…. It is plain to see that the FSOC has entered into an insidiously symbiotic relationship with the FSB, supporting its actions on the international stage while using those actions to justify regulation at home.

Even in the UK, where disagreements among regulators are usually underplayed, the head of the UK's Financial Conduct Authority, Martin Wheatley, questioned the wisdom of designating certain firms as systemically important (*Financial Times*, 18 June 2015). At a press conference, he admitted that regulators at the IOSCO had been influenced by the very critical responses from the financial industry. 'We've been through two rounds of consultation, and the purpose of the consultation is not a rubber-stamping exercise, it's genuinely to listen… What's become clear is that there are actually some questions that we still have to answer before we go through that designation process' (cited in *Financial Planning*, 22 June 2015).[20] Basically, the 'IOSCO had industry on its side and felt on solid ground because industry and securities markets regulators reinforced each other—they formed a "pincer movement"' (interview, see James and Quaglia 2022).

Given the push back from the asset management industry and puzzling and turf fighting among sectoral regulators, the FSB and the IOSCO held a meeting in London in 2015 and decided to postpone the finalization of the assessment methodologies for non-bank non-insurer G-SIFIs until the ongoing

[20] https://www.financial-planning.com/news/big-win-for-fund-managers-fighting-too-big-to-fail-regulation

work of the FSB on financial stability risks from asset management activities was completed. Thus, the FSB and IOSCO decided in favour of a full review of asset management activities and products, identifying potential systemic risks and vulnerabilities. The review, which should take precedence over further work on methodologies for the designation of G-SIFIs, would focus on three areas: leverage; liquidity; and data collection. Regulators in the main jurisdictions—including Mark Carney, the FSB Chair and Governor of the Bank of England, and Dan Tarullo at the Federal Reserve—made clear that they did not intend to single out individual asset managers as systemically important. By deciding not to designate the largest asset managers as G-SIFIs, regulators signalled that they thought that no firm was too big to fail, but that did not mean that the industry posed no risks (*Financial Times*, 14 July 2015). Indeed, regulators questioned whether asset managers could exacerbate market panic due to their interaction with the rest of the financial system. The concern was what would happen if several funds started to sell certain types of assets at the same time, or if many investors withdrew their money from the funds at the same time. The fund industry, in particular, large players, argued that any rules designed to mitigate these risks ought to be imposed across all managers, not just the largest ones.

International Standards for Investment Funds

Since US, UK, and EU prudential regulators worried about the leverage and the liquidity of investment funds, they pushed for further scrutiny of these matters by the FSB, where central bankers carried much weight.[21] By contrast, securities market regulators were less sanguine about the systemic risks posed by investment funds. At the international level, the chairman of IOSCO, Greg Medcraft (2015) argued that there was no evidence that asset managers put financial stability at risk and, in this respect, he found the industry's responses 'compelling'. He held the view that

> we should not look to find new – and possibly inappropriate solutions – before we understand what we are already using and what refinements we may need to make to our current approach. In the asset management space, market regulators and asset managers already have toolkits at their disposal – toolkits

[21] The IMF also pointed out the potential implications of asset management for financial stability (e.g. IMF 2015, Chapter 'The Asset Management Industry and Financial Stability').

> based on conduct supervision and enforcement – which I believe have been effective in managing disruptions in these markets in many jurisdictions.

The IOSCO's views echoed comments made by some domestic securities markets regulators. Commissioner Daniel Gallagher (2015) of the SEC gave a speech with the suggestive title 'Bank Regulators at the Gates: The Misguided Quest for Prudential Regulation of Asset Managers', arguing that after the 2008 financial crisis, the asset management industry became a 'target of both the prudential regulators who performed so poorly' and central bankers 'who kept their foot on the credit bubble gas pedal' in the run-up to the crisis. In his opinion, the goal of these regulators was to subject shadow banking markets, of which the asset management industry was a significant part, to bank-like regulation under the prudential regulators. Gallagher (2015) then went on to argue that

> The worst offenders in this cause are the US Financial Stability Oversight Council, or FSOC, and the Basel-based Financial Stability Board, or FSB. Together, FSOC and the FSB have launched a series of broad-based workstreams aimed at designating asset managers, or the activities of asset managers, as systemically important in order to subject them to oversight by the Federal Reserve and other prudential regulators. The Fed, of course, plays a key role in both institutions, operating as the implementation arm of the FSOC and as the chair of the FSB shadow banking workstreams. The repeated attempts of the FSB and FSOC to characterize asset managers and their activities as systemically risky is nothing more than a ploy to wrest control of a hugely important sector of the capital markets from the SEC. For prudential regulators, this is about regulatory power and jurisdiction.

The FSB's (2016b) work on asset management, which encompassed all investment funds, was motivated by the risks that this part of the financial system could pose to financial stability, given its massive size. Eventually, the FSB issued some policy recommendations to address 'structural vulnerabilities' of asset management (2017b), relating particularly to liquidity and leverage in funds. Some of these recommendations were very general and were to be operationalized by the IOSCO because investment funds fell within the remit of securities markets regulators (IOSCO 2018a, b).

Leverage involves the use of borrowed money and derivatives to amplify a fund's exposure to markets. Leverage can enhance returns, but can magnify losses. It is more problematic for hedge funds, which are also referred to as highly leveraged institutions, than for mutual funds, which tend to be less leveraged. Although the hedge fund industry had tripled in size after the 2008 crisis, reaching $3.2 trillion in 2019, its use of borrowed funding had been reduced after the crisis, even though the use of derivatives for 'synthetic leverage' remained less well understood. For instance, the SEC data showed that hedge fund managers held derivative contracts with a notional value of $14 trillion (353% of their combined net asset value), and almost 30% of the exposure was held by the ten largest hedge funds (*Financial Times*, 14 January 2019).[22]

In 2019, the IOSCO undertook a public consultation to develop consistent measures of leverage to enable comparisons across different jurisdictions over time. The macroprudential regulators in two large jurisdictions, the UK and the EU, took the rather unusual step of responding to the IOSCO's consultation, which was suggestive of puzzling and turf fighting between prudential regulators and securities markets regulators. The Bank of England (2019a) pointed out that investment funds operated globally and were often domiciled and managed in different jurisdictions to the location of their investors, or the markets they operated in. Consequently, a core set of measures of leverage risk for funds across jurisdictions was needed. Similarly, the ESRB (2019) argued that the global nature of the investment fund market required a consistent set of measures of leverage across jurisdictions. In many cases, although funds were domiciled in one jurisdiction, they invested in the markets of another, while their investors could be located in yet another jurisdiction.

By contrast, the financial industry noted that there was no single metric that could appropriately measure leverage. At any rate, investment funds called for securities markets regulators (not prudential regulators) to perform leverage assessments. Hence, the industry engaged in lobbying cum venue shopping, to remain outside the purview of prudential regulators. Eventually, the IOSCO (2019a) issued the *Leverage Framework*, which was not very precise nor stringent—it was designed to strike a balance between precise leverage measures and simple metrics that could be applied to a variety of fund types across jurisdictions. Since there were several varieties of funds and regulatory frameworks worldwide, measures of leverage that were appropriate for one type of fund, or in one jurisdiction, were less appropriate for others. There were also challenges regarding how leverage, both on and off-balance sheets, was captured by different metrics as well as data availability. While some jurisdictions, notably, the US and the EU, required detailed reporting on leverage metrics, others did not.

[22] *Financial Times*, 'Watchdogs drill into the data on leverage risk' by Flood, C,14 January 2019.

As for liquidity, the IOSCO (2018b) issued *Recommendations for Liquidity Risk Management for Collective Investment Schemes*[23] and some good practices (2018c), proposing that asset managers should conduct regular stress tests on their mutual funds. Investment funds challenged the need for liquidity rules, arguing that funds themselves were best positioned to manage liquidity (*Financial Times*, 22 July 2019). The Investment Company Institute (2017) commended the IOSCO for ruling out a 'one-size-fits-all' approach to liquidity risk management, recognizing the need for flexibility in implementation and focusing on investor protection. A similar view was also expressed by the European Fund and Asset Management Association (2017). Likewise, Blackrock (2017) opposed a 'one-size-fits-all' approach, and believed that 'the principles-based approach' taken by the IOSCO stroke 'an effective balance in providing necessary guidance while (in most cases) preserving fund manager flexibility to act'. Amundi (2017) argued that liquidity management was not a field for new prescriptive regulation. It was a matter of good practices adapted to the specific characteristic of a given fund.

Overall, the IOSCO's liquidity standards lacked precision and stringency, as pointed out, for example, by the Governor of the Bank of England, Governor Mark Carney (*Financial Times*, 22 July 2019). Although the Governor had applauded the recommendations on fund liquidity issued by the FSB in 2018, he lamented that subsequent work by the IOSCO did not prescribe how this should be achieved (*Financial Times*, 22 July 2019). In 2019, the Bank of England and the Financial Conduct Authority sought to better align redemption terms and asset liquidity, arguing that the work by the IOSCO in 2018 was not detailed enough. Most funds allowed investors to withdraw cash daily, yet the assets they held were not very liquid. The problem came into relief after £3.7bn of investor money was frozen in the Equity Income fund managed by Neil Woodford in 2019. In the aftermath of the affair, Governor Mark Carney stated that funds investing in illiquid assets that offered daily dealing were 'built on a lie' and that liquidity mismatches resulting from large-scale redemptions could transmit stress to other parts of the financial system (*Financial Times*, 13 July 2019).

The IOSCO's response to the critiques made by British regulators was that its recommendations (IOSCO 2018a) provided 'a comprehensive framework for regulators to deal with liquidity risks in investment funds…it was unequivocal [that] there should be an appropriate alignment between portfolio assets

[23] To be precise, the IOSCO decided to review its *Principles of Liquidity Risk Management for Collective Investment Schemes*, which had been issued in 2013 (IOSCO 2013), rather than start anew.

and redemption terms throughout a fund's lifecycle'. The IOSCO also rejected the suggestion that a global approach was needed to regulate investment fund liquidity: given the diverse nature of the fund industry, it would be 'impractical' to adopt a 'one size fits all prescriptive approach' (cited in *Financial Times*, 18 July 2019). The tension between the IOSCO and the Bank of England was suggestive of a broader pattern of puzzling and turf fight between prudential and securities regulators concerning the regulation of leverage and liquidity of investment funds and the difficulty of bringing together prudential regulation and securities market regulation. As one banking regulator noted:

> Securities market regulators highlight the non-banking nature of investment funds and the fact that risk management policies relating to the proprietary trading of banks cannot be applied to funds as the former operate as principals and the latter as agents. The underlying problem, however, seems to be how to manage systemic risk when the failure of an agent causes spill-over effects similar to those caused by the failure of a principal. Securities market regulators do not pay enough attention to this important aspect… Moreover, there is a gap in the supervisory architecture. Such a gap is particularly visible in the US, but also exists in the EU, even though bureaucratic tensions do not come to the fore in the EU, mainly due to the institutional weakness of ESMA vis-à-vis the ECB-centric Single Supervisory Mechanism. On the one hand, securities regulators have competences concerning, for instance, the rules of conduct, but not capital requirements, of the supervised entities. On the other hand, the opposite is true for prudential regulators. Thus, the entities that do not fall under the remit of the prudential authorities escape prudential supervision (interview).

The asset management fund industry was in tune with the views of securities market regulators. For instance, Paul Schott Stevens, president of the Investment Company Institute, argued the intervention of the Bank of England demonstrated a poor understanding of fund managers, fund investors or fund regulation (cited in *Financial Times*, 22 July 2019). Generally speaking, investment funds and securities regulators concur that prudential regulators miss a good understanding of asset management because they are not the direct regulators and do not have frequent contacts with the industry, which 'clings on' securities regulators as a 'natural home' (interviews, see James and Quaglia 2022). However, this also means that securities regulators tend to be more sympathetic than prudential regulators to the views of the investment funds industry.

A more recent concern for policy-makers worldwide was the potential risk posed by exchange-traded funds, which accounted for $5.2 of assets globally in 2018. The growth in exchange-traded funds, which are also referred to as 'passive funds', was due to the high fees and poor performance of many traditional funds actively managed. In the summer of 2015, a large number of exchange-traded funds stopped trading in the US, following turmoil in the stock markets. This was interpreted as a warning sign of the risk posed by exchange-traded funds (*Financial Times*, 1 April 2019).[24] A first issue that required attention was the liquidity of exchange-traded funds and the possibility of a failure in the market-making activity that underpinned exchange-traded funds (*Financial Times*, 31 May 2019). A second issue to examine was whether exchange-traded funds had the potential to exacerbate broader liquidity problems in securities markets. In fact, if investors were to sell out of exchange-traded funds en masse, this could increase the fire sales of the underlying securities, which, in turn, could affect financial stability (*Financial Times*, 1 April 2019).

In the US, the competent regulator, the SEC, began a review of exchange-traded funds in 2016 (*Financial Times*, 5 December 2016). Ireland, which was Europe's largest exchange-traded funds centre, followed suit. Gerry Cross, a senior official at the Central Bank of Ireland, argued that the review was primarily information-gathering rather than prescriptive. However, these domestic measures laid the groundwork for an international regulatory effort coordinated by the IOSCO.[25] In April 2019, Robert Taylor, Chair of the IOSCO, said the exponential growth of exchange-traded funds was one major reason for securities regulators to review their approach, as well as the liquidity concerns that central bankers had about the fixed income securities market (*Financial Times*, 1 April 2019).

Hence, the IOSCO, together with the FSB, was to examine whether exchange-traded funds posed a broad risk to financial stability. In June 2019, the IOSCO and the FSB held a Joint Workshop on exchange-traded funds and market liquidity at the SEC. In her opening remarks, SEC commissioner Hester Peirce (2019) argued that 'Our experience with exchange-traded funds suggests that most exchange-traded funds are very liquid and their arbitrage mechanisms tend to function well almost all of the time…Even informed by the positive history of exchange-traded funds, nobody would argue that

[24] *Financial Times* 'Watchdogs probe systemic risks of passive fund growth: The growing weight of money committed to exchange-traded funds by asset managers is attracting more scrutiny' by Riding, S., 1 April 2019.

[25] In 2013, the IOSCO had issued the Principles for the Regulation of Exchange Traded Funds, which however focused on transparency for investors and potential conflicts of interest regarding exchange-traded funds, not financial stability.

exchange-traded funds will always function without incident.... It is important for us to consider the channels through which any exchange-traded funds problems would roil the financial markets or affect the rest of the economy.' However, he also added that 'for a risk to implicate financial stability concerns, the bar is quite high'. We discuss in the concluding chapter how exchange-traded funds and asset management more generally coped with the covid-related economic crisis.

Conclusion

This chapter has examined the international governance of shadow banking entities after the international financial crisis of 2008. Although a variety of international soft laws was issued (see Table 5.2), the post-crisis regulatory reforms were limited because the IOSCO's standards on hedge funds, MMFs, and other investment funds were neither precise nor stringent, whereas methodologies to assess G-SIFIs were eventually not adopted by the FSB-IOSCO, creating inconsistency with what was done for banks and insurers (for an overview of the main explanations, see Table 5.1). In the case of MMFs and hedge funds, the main obstacle to more stringent international regulation was disagreement among jurisdictions, which had different preferences, mostly depending on the configuration of the national financial industry, which lobbied intensely on these matters. Particularly consequential was the foot-dragging by major jurisdictions. Thus, China, which had a large domestic MMFs industry, opposed international rules on MMFs. The US and the UK, where most hedge fund managers worldwide are based, opposed international rules on hedge funds. Moreover, the same jurisdiction was at times a footdragger,

Table 5.1 International governance of shadow banking entities: actors, pathways, and outcome

States	Regulators	Industry	Outcome
Limited *pace-setting* by EU (internally divided) on MMFs and hedge funds *Foot-dragging* by China on MMFs and US and UK on hedge funds	*Puzzling and turf fighting* among central bankers, banking and securities regulators about asset management	*Lobbying*: mostly at domestic level by MMFs and hedge funds; *venue-shopping* and 'alliance' with sectoral regulators by investment funds	Very limited precision, stringency and consistency of IOSCO's rules

Table 5.2 International standards for shadow banking entities

International standard-setting body	Date of issuance	Standards (framework, guidance, etc.)
IOSCO	2009	Principles Hedge funds
IOSCO	2011	Principles on the Suspension of Redemptions in Collective Investment Schemes
IOSCO	2012	Policy Recommendations on MMFs
FSB	2013	Policy Framework for Strengthening Oversight and Regulation of Shadow Banking Entities
IOSCO	2013	Principles of Liquidity Risk Management for Collective Investment Schemes
IOSCO	2013	Principles for the Regulation of Exchange Traded Funds
FSB	2017	Policy Recommendations to Address Structural Vulnerabilities from Asset Management Activities.
IOSCO	2018	Open-ended Fund Liquidity and Risk Management—Good Practices and Issues for Consideration
IOSCO	2018	Recommendations for Liquidity Risk Management for Collective Investment Schemes
IOSCO	2019	Recommendations for a Framework Assessing Leverage in Investment Funds

other times a pacesetter or neither. Notably, the UK sponsored new rules on MMFs, but resisted those on hedge funds. France and Germany called for the regulation of hedge funds, but were silent concerning the regulation of asset management.

In the case of asset management, the main hindrance to trading up international regulation was the fact that sectoral regulators had different priorities and disagreed at the domestic and international levels, creating opportunities for venue shopping by the financial industry. Prudential regulators called for new rules concerning the leverage and liquidity of investment funds. By contrast, securities markets regulators opposed these rules at the domestic and international levels, and so did the financial industry. The FSB, where prudential regulators are a majority, sought the spur the IOSCO into action and these international standard-setting bodies jointly worked on the designation of G-SIFIs, to no avail. The domestic policy debate on investment funds in the main jurisdictions intersected with the international policy debate, generating a rather sui generis two-level game, in particular concerning the designation of non-bank non-insurer G-SIFIs. The SEC Commissioner Martin Gallagher (2015, see, also, SEC Commissioner Piwowar 2016a, b) argued that the international work of the FSB and that of the FSOC in the US ran in tandem, concluding that the work of both the FSB and the FSOC were intended to 'force a prudential bank regulatory construct into the capital markets'. Eventually, the regulatory focus, both domestically and internationally, shifted away from examining individual funds or managers for potential designation as systemically important financial institutions (G-SIFIs) and focused, instead, on system-wide measures, which are discussed in the following chapters.

6

Securities Financing

Too Much or Too Little Repos?

The previous chapter has discussed the international governance of shadow banking entities, including MMFs, hedge funds, and investment funds. This chapter examines the international governance of shadow banking activities, specifically, securities financing transactions, which include securities lending and repos. On the one hand, the excessive use of repos can encourage the build-up of leverage and the reliance on short-term funding. On the other hand, these financial instruments facilitate the flow of cash and securities in the financial system, benefitting both financial and non-financial firms. As Andrew Hauser (2013), a senior official at the Bank of England and Chair of the Securities Lending and Repo Committee,[1] noted, there could be 'too little' or 'too much' repo, whereby too little provision of collateral and financing could limit economic growth, but too much could cause the system to overreach.

The international governance of securities financing was weakened by disjointed and half-hearted pace-setting by the main jurisdictions, which worried about the financial stability implications of shadow banking activities, including securities lending and repos. However, the US and the EU were not on the same page on important issues, such as the re-hypothecation/re-use of collateral and haircuts, due to different domestic market structures and regulatory frameworks. It is also noteworthy that while securitization volumes were higher than repo volumes in the US, the opposite was true in Europe (Gabor 2014). Even more consequential was the fact that the regulation of the repo market intersected with the conduct of monetary policy, which was a major concern for central banks, and with fiscal policy (that is to say, the ability of governments to refinance the national public debt on the market), which was of primary interest to finance ministries. In turn, this elicited puzzling and

[1] The Securities Lending and Repo Committee was established in the UK in the early 1990s, bringing together market practitioners, trade associations, infrastructure providers, and regulators.

The Perils of International Regime Complexity in Shadow Banking. Lucia Quaglia, Oxford University Press.
 DOI: 10.1093/oso/9780192866523.003.0006

turf fighting among regulators, which was compounded by the fact that securities financing transactions were activities undertaken by shadow banking entities as well as non-shadow banks (e.g. traditional banks). Whereas it was possible to classify entities as either shadow banks or traditional banks, the same was not true of the markets in which they operated, which were shared. For example, the repo market was used by both shadow banks and traditional banks. Finally, the third factor that weakened the international governance of securities financing and that is strictly interconnected to the previous point was the infrastructural power of the financial industry because the functioning of the repo market impacted upon the conduct of monetary policy and the refinancing of public debts on the market. Thus, private financial actors engaged in lobbying cum venue shopping at the international and domestic levels, targeting central banks and finance ministries, especially in countries that had large public debts.

Overall, post-crisis international standards on securities lending and repos had some precision, but limited stringency. The FSB and its member jurisdictions agreed on the need for data reporting and aggregation to monitor this market and understand the systemic risks it entailed. By contrast, the potential harmonization of domestic regulation concerning the rehypothecation and re-use of collateral was set aside as not feasible and, ultimately, not necessary for financial stability. The most controversial international reform was the introduction of haircuts on securities financing transactions. The level and scope of mandatory haircuts were reduced over time, partially in response to pressure from industry, but also following the impact studies conducted by regulators.

Main Issues in the International Governance of Securities Financing

Securities financing is the lending of securities (stocks, bonds, asset-backed securities) by one party to another against cash. There are different types of securities financing transactions, including, securities lending and repos.[2] They are forms of short-term lending that use securities as collateral. 'Securities lending' is the lending of a security to an investor, whereby the borrower pays a fee to the lender, provides collateral, and becomes the owner of the security. 'Repo' refers to a contract for the sale and repurchase of securities. In a repo

[2] In each of these activities, the ownership of the securities temporarily changes in return for cash. At the end of a security financing transaction, the change of ownership reverts, and both counterparties are left with what they possessed originally, plus or minus a small fee (ESRB 2017).

transaction, one party sells an asset (collateral) to another party, combined with an agreement to buy this asset back in the future. In this way, the seller gets cash without effectively selling the collateral, while the buyer receives interest, creating a securitized loan (International Capital Market Association 2013a). Since the buyer becomes the legal owner of the asset during the transaction, s/he can re-use the same asset, which can lead to long repo-chains, increasing the interconnectedness of the financial system (Gabor 2016a).[3] While repos represent an additional channel of liquidity for banks, they are the main source of refinancing for shadow banks, which use these instruments to increase their leverage (Thiemann, Birk, and Friedrich 2018).

An important difference between repos and securities lending is that the repo market primarily uses bonds and other fixed-income instruments as collateral, whereas an important segment of the securities lending market is in equities. Moreover, whereas most repos are used to borrow cash using securities as collateral, securities lending contracts are mainly used to access securities, using cash as collateral (Baklanova, Copeland, and McCaughrin 2015; International Capital Market Association 2013b). In addition, securities financing via repos entails one important advantage over secured lending against collateral: repos are treated as outright sales and repurchases of collateral, allowing repo lenders to re-use collateral for their own purposes (e.g. short-selling and hedging) (Gabor 2016a). Furthermore, in most jurisdictions, repos are subject to favourable treatment under the insolvency law because they are exempted from the automatic stay under bankruptcy. This means that, in the event of a default by the cash borrower, counterparties have access to the securities and the right to liquidate them. Repos have benefited from a global expansion of the public debt over the last decades because repo transactions typically use high-quality government bonds (International Capital Market Association 2013a).

Securities lenders are generally institutional investors that manage a portfolio of securities. They include mutual funds, pension funds, sovereign wealth funds, insurance companies, and central banks. Securities borrowers are generally securities dealers, who borrow for their market-making activities, or on behalf of their clients. In both repos and securities lending, securities dealers operate as intermediaries between those who lend cash collateralized by securities (e.g. MMFs and central banks) or those who lend securities (institutional investors, such as asset managers and pension, sovereign, and insurance funds)

[3] A reverse repo is the same type of transaction seen from the perspective of the party lending cash and receiving securities as collateral (Committee on the Global Financial System 2017).

and those who seek either funding (leveraged investors and broker-dealers), or to borrow specific securities for short-selling[4] (for instance, hedge funds). Repos and securities lending can be used to borrow cash or securities. Usually, pension funds tend to transact via securities lending, while dealers mainly use repos to obtain funding.

The repo market brings together two types of end-users that interact through intermediaries. The first type includes those that provide collateral in return for cash (e.g. asset managers, pension funds, hedge funds, and insurance companies). The second type of end-users are those investing in cash while receiving collateral (e.g. MMFs) (Committee on the Global Financial System 2017). The repo market has a bilateral segment, which is common in Europe and involves two parties in the transaction, and a tri-party segment, which is common in the US, where a third party acts as an intermediary for collateral management between the borrower and the lender. These two segments of the repo market are subject to different types of instability, as demonstrated by the international financial crisis of 2008. Bear Stearns and Lehman Brothers lost access to tri-party repo funding, whereas the run on bilateral repos resulted in an increased cost of funding against securitized collateral (Copeland, Martin, and Walker 2011). Total repos activity at its peak level before the 2008 financial crisis was estimated as ranging from \$5 to \$10 trillion.[5]

The evolution of the repo markets triggered profound changes in the practices of central banking and the relations between the monetary authorities, the fiscal authorities, and private financiers.[6] As for central banking, Gabor (2020: 50) notes that 'credit creation in market-based finance is structurally different to credit creation in bank-based finance.... In shadow money, repo liabilities collateralized by securities are used to finance credit created via securities markets.' After the failure of Lehman Brothers in 2008, central banks became 'market-makers of last resort' for a set of collateral securities (Gabor and Ban 2016). Besides being important for monetary policy, the repo markets were also important for fiscal policy (Gabor 2020). Over the last two decades or so, the fiscal authorities (i.e. the national governments) that could no longer borrow from their (independent) central banks turned to the repo markets to refinance their sovereign debt. Treasury ministries in Europe, and then the ECB, became active promoters of US-style repo markets (Gabor 2016b).

[4] In short selling, an investor borrows securities or other assets that s/he believes will decrease in value in the future. The investor then sells the borrowed securities to buyers who are willing to pay the market price. The trader bets that the price of the assets will decline, so that they can purchase them later at a lower cost.

[5] https://www.newyorkfed.org/medialibrary/media/research/staff_reports/sr740.pdf.

[6] I wish to thank Daniela Gabor for this point.

The entanglements between private financial actors and the public authorities in the markets where monetary and fiscal (debt management) policies are conducted (Braun 2020; Braun and Gabor 2020) brought to the fore the 'infrastructural power' finance (Braun 2020), which created intricate regulatory dynamics concerning the repo markets.

After the 2008 crisis, there was the need to regulate securities lending and repos, given their role in the playing out of the crisis as well as the sheer size of these markets. Three main sets of issues needed to be addressed to tackle the financial stability risks related to securities financing transactions: the re-hypothecation and re-use of collateral; margin and haircuts on securities financing and repo transactions; data reporting, collection, and aggregation. Let us examine these issues in turn.

'Re-hypothecation' is the use of client assets by a financial intermediary. Thus, securities that serve as collateral for secured borrowing are further used by the dealer or the bank making the loan. In contrast, the 're-use of collateral' is not limited to the use of client assets and broadly includes any use of assets delivered as collateral (FSB 2017c). On the one hand, the re-hypothecation of client assets and the re-use of collateral increased the availability of collateral, reducing their cost. On the other hand, as highlighted by the international financial crisis of 2008, re-hypothecation and collateral re-use could make it difficult for clients to promptly access their securities in case of insolvency of a financial intermediary. Re-hypothecation could also contribute to building-up leverage, increasing interconnectedness among market participants. Furthermore, different domestic regimes on re-hypothecation could generate regulatory arbitrage and disrupt the international level playing field (FSB 2017c).

In finance, a 'haircut' is the difference between the market value of an asset used as loan collateral and the amount of the loan. Thus, the haircut is the discount applied to the value of collateral provided to cover market risks (FSB 2017d). In the context of securities lending and repos, the haircut is supposed to 'provide a buffer against market fluctuations and incentivizes borrowers to adhere to their promise to buy securities back' (Gabor and Vestergaard 2016: 12). If the value of the collateral decreases, the lender can claim additional collateral from the borrower (margin call), translating volatility (pro-cyclicality) in market prices for the underlying collateral into fluctuations in margin and haircuts (Brunnermeier and Pedersen 2009). In securities financing transactions, margin and collateral haircuts were used as risk mitigation techniques. Initially, there were no post-crisis legal provisions for setting margin and haircuts and market participants developed best practices. Whereas there was agreement that haircuts on securities financing transactions could help to restrict leverage, their effects on pro-cyclicality were not entirely clear and depended on their application (ESRB 2015). Procyclical risk management takes the form of low margin and haircuts in good times, followed by large and sudden increases in margin and haircuts in downturns (FSB 2013c; ESRB 2015). At the international level, but also at the domestic level, there was no consensus on how to design a system-wide framework to tackle the build-up of leverage with reference to securities financing transactions.

Finally, there were issues related to the lack of reliable data to assess potential risks of securities financing as well as the impact of the regulatory measures envisaged. The specific contribution of securities financing transactions to the build-up of leverage was difficult to evaluate due to a lack of granular data (for example, on the reinvestment and re-use of collateral) and the different purposes for which securities financing transactions were undertaken. The Federal Reserve (Fischer 2015), the Bank of England (Hauser 2013), the ECB (Constâncio 2016), the ESRB (2016), the ESMA (2016), and the European Commission (2017) repeatedly pointed out the need for better data.

In 2019, the global repo market was approximately €15 trillion, with a turnover of about €3 trillion per day (International Capital Market Association 2019), whereas the amount of securities on loan globally was much smaller, approximately €2.3 trillion (International Securities Lending Association 2019). Repos were crucial components of the funding of the global shadow banking system. OFIs, especially, MMFs, trust companies, investment funds, and special purpose vehicles, were net providers of cash to the financial system through reverse repos, while banks remain net recipients of cash through repos. Among OFIs, broker-dealers, hedge funds, and finance companies were also net recipients of cash. In 2019, OFIs' total repo assets were $4.3 trillion and their total repos liabilities were $3.9 trillion. The total repo assets of banks were $5.9 trillion, while their total repo liabilities were $6 trillion (FSB 2020a).

Main Actors in the International Governance of Securities Financing

In the wake of the international financial crisis of 2008, it was necessary to assess the risks posed by securities financing transactions and repos, which, in turn, required measuring the size of these activities, so as to regulate them accordingly. The first factor that affected the international governance of securities financing was disjointed and half-hearted *pace-setting* by the *main jurisdictions*, namely, the US and the EU, which had large markets for securities financing transactions. In 2018, the US repo market was approximately $4 trillion and the repo market in Europe was approximately €7 trillion, whereas the global repo market was approximately €15 trillion (International Capital Market Association 2019). According to the Committee on the Global Financial System (2017), out of $12 trillion of repo and reverse repo transactions outstanding globally in 2017, nearly $9 trillion were collateralized with government bonds. The largest repo markets collateralized by government bonds in terms of outstanding amounts were the US, the euro area, Japan, and the UK (Committee on the Global Financial System 2017).

Whereas the US and the EU agreed on the need for more stringent regulation and monitoring of securities financing transactions, they had different preferences on important issues. Notably, the US, unlike the EU, opposed the prohibition of the re-hypothecation of collateral because the SEC rules already limited the amount of a client's assets that a prime broker could rehypothecate, whereas there was not such a limit in the EU (Thiemann, Birk, and Friedrich 2018). Moreover, both the US and the EU were internally divided. The crux of the matter was that the functioning of the repo market was of relevance for macroprudential authorities and securities market authorities, but also central banks and finance ministries, which were deeply involved in the '(repo) market-based finance' through the monetary policy frameworks and the government bond markets (Gabor 2016a: 925).

In the US, initially, the Federal Reserve supported market-led action in the repo market at the domestic level. After becoming dissatisfied with the efforts of the industry to address existing problems, the New York Federal Reserve argued that regulatory agencies had to take regulatory and supervisory measures to mitigate potential risks (*Reuters*, 2 May 2012).[7] A major reform of the US tri-party repo market followed. At the international level, the Federal Reserve issued strong warnings about the disruptive potential of the repo market and sought to spur the FSB into action, as elaborated below. By contrast, the US Treasury, which was the largest issuer of public debt in the world, resisted these efforts, in particular the proposal of haircuts on repos (Gabor 2014).

In the EU, the ECB was concerned about the functioning of the repo market, but opposed the introduction of haircuts and so did the Treasury ministries of countries with large public debts (Gabor 2014). There was also a feeble attempt by the European Commission, backed by some member states, to

[7] https://www.reuters.com/article/financial-regulation-fed/more-must-be-done-on-shadow-banking-feds-tarullo-idUSL1E8G200V20120502

introduce a European financial transaction tax, which initially was to apply also to repo transactions. However, finance ministers, prompted by the ECB, eventually removed the repo market from the scope of the financial transaction tax, which anyway was not approved in the end (Gabor 2016b; Braun 2020; Kalaitzake 2017). The European Commission proposed a Regulation on the Transparency of Securities Financing Transactions, which was adopted in 2016. These rules concerned transparency, reporting, and disclosure for securities financing transactions, making it easier to monitor and assess the risks involved in these transactions. The regulation required firms to report their securities financing transactions to a trade repository. However, it did not prescribe mandatory margin or haircut levels applicable to securities financing transactions. Thus, the EU followed the recommendation by the FSB in 2013 to increase transparency in the use of securities lending and repos, but, like the US, did not implement the FSB's recommendations on haircuts, discussed in the following section.

Besides disagreements among jurisdictions on certain issues, there were also *epistemic and bureaucratic* tensions among *regulators*. Whereas there was a consensus on the need for data collection and harmonization, as well as the need to switch the focus of regulation from entities to transactions and markets, technocrats did not agree on important issues concerning the re-hypothecation/re-use of collateral and haircuts. In the case of the re-hypothecation/re-use of collateral, the disagreement among regulators ran along jurisdictional lines, as it was influenced by the distinctive configuration of domestic markets and national regulatory frameworks. However, in the case of haircuts, epistemic discordance among regulators ran across sectoral lines: whereas macroprudential regulators supported the introduction of haircuts, microprudential banking regulators, and securities, market regulators were circumspect about the use of these tools, and so were central banks and finance ministries, albeit for different reasons. In certain cases, the *puzzling* was internal to central banks, if they were also macroprudential authorities, because the macroprudential priorities and the monetary policy priorities of central banks were not fully aligned, if not conflictive.[8]

The crux of the matter was that securities financing transactions appeared to involve 'minimal risks from a microprudential perspective', but created 'sizable macroprudential risks, including vulnerabilities to runs and asset fire sales' (Tarullo 2013). This generated some *turf fighting* among sectoral regulators, which had different mandates and competences. As a senior official at the

[8] I wish to thank Daniela Gabor for this point.

Bank of England, Andrew Hauser (2013) noted, securities financing transactions linked 'lenders and borrowers, lubricating the market-making system, and providing financial intermediaries and investors with liquidity, maturity, and credit transformation. If that all sounds a bit like banking, that's really because it is: indeed, if we were seeking a functional description, we could easily leave out the "shadow" prefix altogether.... Institutionally, however, this is not exclusively banking, because at least part of the business takes place outside the banking system, and therefore outside the regulatory framework designed to contain banking risk.'

Central bankers and macroprudential regulators in the US and the UK took the lead in the post-crisis policy debate on repos. Daniel Tarullo of the Federal Reserve (2013) pointed out the necessity to supplement prudential bank regulation with regulatory tools that could be applied on a market-wide basis. That is, regulation that focused on particular kinds of transactions, rather than entities undertaking certain transactions. Tarullo advocated international rules for haircuts on securities financing transactions to reduce the build-up of excessive leverage and liquidity risk by non-banks during peaks in the credit and economic cycle (cited in *Reuters*, 14 October 2014). Similarly, Paul Tucker (2012), Deputy Governor at the Bank of England, argued that the authorities should be able to set minimum haircuts for the collateralized financing markets (or segments of them).

The ECB paid close attention to the repo market, not only because it was crucial for the transmission mechanism of monetary policy, but also because the powerful shock amplification of this market became evident during the sovereign debt crisis in the euro area (Constâncio 2012b). Government bonds accounted for two thirds of the EU-originated collateral used in repo transactions. Yet, EU regulatory agencies were not on the same page on the issue of haircuts. Whereas the European Banking Authority (EBA 2016) and the ESMA advised against the introduction of haircut floors (to be precise, they recommended a delayed implementation of international standards to better evaluate expected effects), the ESRB (2016), which had macroprudential competences (but no tools) and where central bankers carried much weight, supported the rules on haircuts and, eventually, envisaged their use in a countercyclical way. However, even the ESRB was internally divided on this matter. Some of its members disagree on the extension of the scope of the framework for haircuts on non-centrally cleared securities financing transactions. A couple of members favoured a delayed implementation of the FSB's numerical haircut floors, discussed below, citing the lack of empirical evidence (Thiemann, Birk, and Friedrich 2018).

The third factor that weakened the international standard-setting on securities financing was the infrastructural power of the *financial industry*, which lobbied against the proposal to limit re-hypothecation, establish voluntary haircut methodologies as well as minimal mandatory haircuts. Two principal trade groups participated in the repo market. In the US, the main trade group was the Securities Industry and Financial Markets Association. In Europe, the main trade group was the International Capital Markets Association, especially its European Repo Council, which represented the cross-border repo market in Europe. These trade groups develop standardized documentation, lobbied on regulation, provided training, and conducted studies. As for securities financing, the main trade associations were the Committee on Securities Lending of the Risk Management Association, the International Securities Lending Association, and the Pan Asian Securities Lending Association.

The main industry association in Europe, the International Capital Markets Association—European Repo Council, moved in earnest to influence the international policy debate. Specifically, it prepared two studies: *Haircuts and Initial Margins in the Repo Market* (2012b), which questioned the popular view of the role played by collateral haircuts during the crisis; and *Shadow Banking and Repo* (2012a), which discussed repo markets in the context of the shadow banking debate. The first document argued that the regulatory debate was based on a 'poor understanding' of initial margin and haircuts, as well as 'insufficient empirical data' to assess their impacts. It also noted that the academic literature had focused on the use of structured securities, which was not the predominant form of collateral in the repo market in the US and, especially, in Europe. It is worth quoting one of the key passages of the International Capital Market Association—Repo Council's (2012a) document at length as it is indicative of the positions of the most relevant players in securities financing and repo markets:

> The empirical evidence therefore strongly argues against the hypothesis that initial margins/haircuts were the principal driver of deleveraging in the crisis. And, if initial margins/haircuts were not the principal driver of deleveraging in the crisis, the idea of mandatory through-the-cycle initial margins/haircuts to obviate the need for dealers to raise initial margins/haircuts in a crisis is clearly redundant. In addition, this proposal has serious flaws as a regulatory tool. As a matter of principle, one-size-fits-all mandatory haircuts risk distorting the market… Official concern about excessive leverage has led to calls for mandatory haircuts…There are several objections to trying to control leverage in such an instrument-specific way. Mandatory haircut would

> be a very blunt tool, which would reduce liquidity across the entire market to deal with what should be seen as a problem of risk management specific to individual institutions. In addition, general instrument-based approaches are more likely to have unexpected consequences. Concerns about institutions taking excessive leverage (both levels of borrowing and asset-liability mismatches) should therefore be addressed directly using institution-specific tools such as leverage limits and capital ratio.

More generally, there was the mobilization of an ad-hoc coalition between private financiers, central banks, and ministries of finance, which stemmed from entanglements between the repo market and the public authorities that govern by transacting in that market (Braun 2020). Thus, central banks and finance ministries were also participants in repo markets, and the convergence of public and private interests created new trade-offs that allowed private financial actors to successfully mobilize opposition to major reforms (Gabor 2016a). In this respect, the infrastructural power that the financial industry has in the repo and securitization (see Chapter 7) markets is different from other areas of shadow banking (for an overview of the main explanations, see Table 6.1).

International Standards for Securities Lending and Repos

The repo market was global and whereas securities lending had distinctive nuances in different markets worldwide, many participants acted on a global basis. The FSB set up the Workstream on Securities Lending and Repos to assess financial stability risks and develop policy recommendations to strengthen the regulation of securities lending and repos. The FSB Workstream

Table 6.1 International governance of securities financing: actors, pathways, and outcome

States	Regulators	Industry	Outcome
Limited *pace-setting* by US (internally divided) Limited *foot-dragging* by EU on repos (internally divided)	*Puzzling and turf fighting* among public authorities	Infrastructural power and venue shopping by financial industry, lobbying central banks and treasuries	Precise but not stringent rules by FSB: narrow scope, limited consistency

on Securities Lending and Repos, in cooperation with the IOSCO Standing Committee on Risk and Research, conducted a survey to map the relevant regulatory frameworks in member jurisdictions. The FSB produced a report on securities lending and repos (2012a), which did not put forward specific recommendations (i.e. proposals for regulation). Hence, the respondents to the consultation (a limited number of transnational financial industry associations) took the opportunity to undertake pre-emptive lobbying about forthcoming regulation of securities lending and repos.

The International Capital Markets Association—European Repo Council (2012c) maintained that the repo market provided an efficient source of money market funding and was an essential tool for central banks. One potential measure that was heavily criticized was the imposition of mandatory minimum haircuts. The International Banking Federation (2012) explicitly endorsed the response of the International Capital Market Association—European Repo Council (2012c) and stressed that securities lending, as well as repos, were essential for funding and liquidity. Consequently, regulatory requirements should be balanced to avoid unintended consequences. The Securities Industry and Financial Markets Association (2012) in the US believed that many of the issues raised by the FSB could be addressed by the industry, as it was done, for example, in the tri-party repo market reform in the US.

The Committee on Securities Lending of the Risk Management Association, the International Securities Lending Association, and the Pan Asian Securities Lending Association (2012) focused their joint comment on securities lending. They agreed that it was helpful to consider securities lending and repos as two distinct segments, identifying the specific elements that were relevant to shadow banking. The Bank of New York Mellon Corporation, the Northern Trust Corporation, and the State Street Corporation (2012) submitted a joint response that supported the joint comment letter sent by the Committee on Securities Lending of the Risk Management Association, the International Securities Lending Association, and the Pan Asian Securities Lending Association (2012). They also urged the FSB to focus its proposals on specific regulatory gaps, and avoid duplicative requirements. Basically, the joint responses from a limited pool of private actors extensively cross-referenced each other (on the cross-referencing of responses to public consultation and the re-use of text by private actors see James, Pagliari and Young 2021).

In 2013, the FSB (2013c) issued a *Policy Framework for Addressing Shadow Banking Risks in Securities Lending and Repos*, which set out 11 policy recommendations that were based on the issues discussed in its previous report (FSB 2012a), but were refined by focusing on shadow banking. The recommendations concerned the regulation of securities financing transactions (in particular, the re-hypothecation of collateral and haircuts on non-centrally cleared securities) and data reporting, collection, and aggregation, which are all discussed in the following subsections.

Re-hypothecation of Collateral

The FSB established a Working Group on Re-hypothecation, which undertook a stock-taking exercise of existing regulation on the re-use and re-hypothecation of collateral, before considering potential international harmonization (FSB 2017c). However, regulators in various jurisdictions had different views on this matter (*Euromoney*, 1 October 2013)[9]—whereas the UK and the EU engaged in pace-setting, advocating more stringent rules, the US did not. The Deputy Governor of the Bank of England Paul Tucker (2012) noted that 'anyone with a securities portfolio can build their own shadow bank by borrowing at a call against the securities and then employing the cash in credit assets; that is, borrow short to lend … The hypothecation of client assets gives non-banks the wherewithal to fund their business in this way, effectively becoming a non-bank bank. It can make the financial system fragile. Bank-type risks need to come with bank-type regulation, which itself has needed a massive overhaul.' For the ECB, the re-hypothecation and re-use of securities amplified the creation of liquidity and caused higher leverage, which had negative consequences when the crisis led to an increase in haircuts, causing illiquidity in the repo market (Constâncio 2014). Therefore, the ECB supported the harmonization of regulatory approaches to the re-hypothecation of client assets. By contrast, US regulators were reluctant to endorse international regulatory measures on this matter because there was already a balance sheet constraint for primary brokerage in the US (Thiemann, Birk, and Friedrich 2018). Other jurisdictions had regulatory approaches that were by and large comparable to either the US, or the EU (FSB 2017c).

A general concern of policy-makers was the widespread practice of using the same securities over and over again, creating sources of credit outside the regular banking system (*Financial Times*, 6 September 2013).[10] Broker-dealers and

[9] https://www.euromoney.com/article/b12kjv8mclbh9s/hangover-from-banks-use-of-short-term-funding-refuses-to-go-away

[10] *Financial Times*, 'Regulators take aim at recycling of assets' by Masters, B. and Stafford, P., 6 September 2013.

banks routinely recycled the cash and securities handed to them as collateral by large institutional investors by pledging these securities out in other transactions, usually in the short-term repo market. This serial lending (a.k.a. re-hypothecation, when it involved client assets) lubricated the markets by making more securities available for trading. The FSB sought to constrain securities lending and repos, as part of its crackdown on shadow banking, while the BCBS-IOSCO sought to restrain the re-use of collateral posted as part of derivatives transactions (Quaglia 2020; Spagna 2019). In general, regulators wanted to limit the number of times a security could be passed on to a new counterparty (*Financial Times*, 6 September 2013).

The FSB's Working Group on Re-hypothecation held informal meetings with market participants, who suggested that different national regulatory approaches to re-hypothecation did not trigger cross-border arbitrage and that prudential requirements (e.g. the Basel III framework, discussed in Chapter 8) levelled the playing field across jurisdictions, including how financial intermediaries re-hypothecated client assets (FSB 2017c). Hence, the industry did not lobby in favour of cross-border harmonization. It also became clear that it would be challenging to harmonize regulation concerning re-hypothecation because it was interconnected with national securities and insolvency laws, as well as distinctive market structures (cash versus securities-collateral in the US and EU, respectively; and tri-party versus bilateral repos in the US and the EU, respectively). Finally, individual jurisdictions pursued different rationales, such as financial stability or client asset protection, in the design of re-hypothecation regulation (FSB 2017c).

Overall, international harmonization on this matter was challenging because jurisdictions had different approaches, embedded in their domestic regulatory context, including differences in the bankruptcy treatment of re-hypothecated client assets and customer protection regimes (FSB 2017c). Furthermore, the financial industry was comfortable with existing domestic rules, and regulators in various jurisdictions did not agree on how to address the risks posed by re-hypothecation. The FSB published two reports in 2017. The first report (FSB 2017c), outlined potential financial stability issues associated with the re-hypothecation of client assets and collateral re-use. It described the different national regulatory approaches to the re-hypothecation of client assets and examined the arguments for and against the harmonization of these approaches. In light of the hindrances discussed above, the FSB decided not to pursue international harmonization, but, rather, to monitor collateral re-use at the global level. The ECB, for one, criticized the FSB's report as not being sufficiently far-reaching (Constâncio 2017). The second report of the FSB (2017d) defined non-cash collateral re-use measures and metrics. The FSB was to collect nationally aggregated data related to the measures and metrics from 2020 onwards, as part of its global securities financing data standards.

Haircuts on Securities Financing Transactions

The UK and the US were the pace-setters concerning haircuts on non-centrally cleared securities financing transactions. At the Bank of England, Paul Tucker (2012) noted that the amount of leverage in the system depended to a large extent on the haircuts applied in chains of securities financing transactions—leverage was the reciprocal of the haircuts. Another senior official at the Bank of England, David Rule (2014), reiterated the goal of making securities financing markets resilient through haircuts to stabilize rather than destabilize the financial system in the face of shocks. The Federal Reserve supported a system of numerical haircut floors for securities financing transactions that would require any entity that wanted to borrow against a security to post a minimum amount of margin to its lender, depending on the asset class of the collateral. Numerical floors for securities financing transaction haircuts would serve as a mechanism for limiting the build-up of leverage in the financial system (Tarullo 2015a). They could also mitigate the risk posed by pro-cyclical margin calls during times of financial stress because putting a regulatory floor under securities financing transaction haircuts during good times would reduce the amount by which they would increase during periods of stress (Tarullo 2015a). Given the potential for cross-border regulatory arbitrage, both the US and the UK argued that it was important that the FSB adopted framework applicable in all major financial markets (Tucker 2012; Tarullo 2013).

In 2012, the FSB (2012b) Workstream on Securities Lending and Repos released for consultation a proposal for margin requirements (haircuts) in the repo market that would apply across all types of collateral, including government bonds (Gabor 2016a). A revised proposal on *Regulatory Framework for Haircuts on Non-centrally Cleared Securities Financing Transactions* was included as Annex 2 in the FSB (2013c) *Policy Framework for Addressing Shadow Banking Risks in Securities Lending and Repos*. The proposal comprised qualitative standards for methodologies used by market participants to calculate haircuts; and numerical (quantitative) haircut floors that applied to non-centrally cleared securities financing transactions in which entities not subject to the regulation of capital and liquidity (i.e. non-banks) received financing from regulated financial intermediaries (i.e. banks) against collateral, other than government securities.

In comparison to the previous proposal (FSB 2012b), the revised proposal was less stringent because the level of haircut was lower, but also because government bonds and repos between banks were *excluded* from the scope of haircuts. Securities financing received by banks or between banks was excluded from the scope of application of the proposed numerical haircut floors because banks were already subject to capital and liquidity regulation (FSB 2013c). Transactions backed by government bonds were excluded from the proposed framework because the calibration exercise suggested that numerical haircut floors could harm the functioning of these markets (FSB 2013c). Two interconnected factors account for the backtracking by the FSB. First, finance ministry officials in the FSB worried about the ability to refinance large national public debts in the market (Gabor 2016a). Second, the financial industry strongly opposed minimum haircuts: repos were presented as risk-reducing instruments and therefore harsh regulation could increase systemic risk. Whereas this argument, on its own, would have not been enough to persuade the FSB to change its proposal, repo lobbies forged a strategic alliance with central banks and treasury ministries (Gabor 2014).

Lobbying by the financial industry was intense. The International Capital Market Association—European Repo Council and the International Securities Lending Association (2013), which submitted a joint response to the FSB's (2013c) consultation, believed that overly stringent regulation in this area would deter market participants from using these transactions. A mandatory haircut would do little to prevent pro-cyclicality. The International Banking Federation (2013a) endorsed the response jointly prepared by the ICMA and the International Securities Lending Association, noting that the recommendations could have 'unintended consequences', whereby the focus on the financing of non-banks by banks risked driving financing activity away from banks. The Investment Company Institute (2013) argued that the proposal assumed a direct relationship between the size of haircuts and the amount of leverage in the financial system, but this was a 'flawed assumption'. Furthermore, the initial FSB's (2012b) proposal had envisaged haircuts that were much higher than were those prevailing in the market. Haircuts at those levels threatened to make repos 'economically unviable'. The new proposal went in the opposite direction, setting out a schedule of haircuts at much lower levels, lower than existing market levels.

Hedge funds were keen on avoiding the new rules and, if that was not possible, extending these rules to banks. The Alternative Investment Management

Association (2013) criticized the establishment of numerical haircut floors. If, however, the FSB decided to recommend a framework of numerical floors, the framework should apply to 'regulated intermediaries' (banks) to prevent potential regulatory arbitrage. The Managed Funds Association (2013) criticized the use of numerical floors as a 'blunt instrument'. It also criticized the fact that the proposed framework of numerical haircut floors applied only to transactions in which non-banks received financing from banks, and not the other way around. If such requirements were to be imposed, they should apply to any transactions, regardless of the counterparty and the type of transaction. Hence, the exclusion of transactions backed by government securities was inappropriate. In this respect, it is worth quoting the Managed Funds Association's (2013) response at length:

> Whilst it is true that imposing numerical haircut floors on these transactions could have an impact on the liquidity and functioning of funding markets, this is equally true of imposing such floors on other transactions that are currently within the proposed scope. Sovereign bonds are subject to default risk... Furthermore, as the price of some countries' government debt is more volatile than others, and as price volatility varies between different debt instruments (based on differences in maturity for example), a blanket exclusion of all transactions linked to any government debt is unlikely to adequately encompass the systemic risks that the proposed reforms aim to address. Moreover, excluding transactions backed by government securities from the scope of the proposed requirements may have the unintended consequence of shifting the relevant risks into markets for sovereign debt and connected instruments.

The Global Financial Markets Association—which brings together the Association for Financial Markets in Europe, the Securities Industry and Financial Markets Association in the US and the Asia Securities Industry & Financial Markets Association—submitted a joint response together with the Institute of International Finance (2013). They disagree that 'regulated entities [banks] should be subject to even further regulation in order to indirectly regulate the unregulated sector. Indirect regulation could result in overburdening the regulated sector and lead to unintended consequences (e.g. transactions could move away from the regulated market)'. However, if the FSB recommended indirect regulation, the use of margin requirements was better than the introduction of further capital requirements for banks, stressing the interlinkages between these two sets of international standards.

The FSB's (2013c) proposal had important limitations, as recognized by regulators themselves (see, for instance, Tarullo 2013). First, the new framework would apply only to securities financing transactions in which banks provided financing to non-banks. The proposal would not cover securities financing transactions between banks, or between a non-bank and a bank, or between two non-banks. Second, the proposal would apply only to lending against collateral other than sovereign bonds. Third, the proposed numerical floors were set at relatively low levels, significantly below the haircuts that prevailed in the tri-party repo market. Tarullo (2013), who chaired one of the FSB's standing committees, noted that an alternative approach would be to apply a system of numerical floors to securities financing transactions regardless of the parties to the transactions. Such an approach would partially offset the incentive to move securities financing activity completely into the shadows. As far as the calibration of haircuts was concerned, the level of the numerical floors in the FSB's proposal should be increased.

In October 2014, the FSB published for consultation the semi-final version of the *Regulatory Framework for Haircuts on Non-Centrally Cleared Securities Financing Transactions*. There were only ten responses, partly because the timeframe for consultation was tight, partly because several issues had been discussed in the previous rounds of consultations. The European Fund and Asset Management Association (2014b), like in its previous response, opposed the introduction of a numerical haircut floor framework whose scope would cover an 'extremely large range of very different market players, each subject to diverging regulatory requirements, even within the sole investment management industry'. The International Securities Lending Association (2014) agreed that the application of the framework of numerical floors should be extended to cover non-bank to non-bank transactions to ensure a level playing field between all market participants and limit the build-up of leverage outside of the banking system. However, the level of transactions between non-bank entities was limited and regulators should consider the costs of implementing the regime (which were likely to be higher than for transactions involving banks) versus the benefits of doing so.

In December 2014, the FSB (2014c) published the final version of the Framework, which included recommendations on qualitative standards for methodologies used by market participants that provide securities financing to calculate haircuts on the collateral received; and numerical haircut floors that would apply to non-centrally cleared securities financing transactions in which financing against collateral other than government securities was provided to entities other than banks. Centrally-cleared securities financing transactions and financing provided to banks were excluded. Transactions that used government bonds as collateral were also excluded, amid anxiety from some governments about the potential impact on sovereign debt markets (*Financial Times*, 14 October 2014).

The numerical haircut floors were calibrated at levels above those proposed in the August 2013 Report, taking into account the results of a two-stage quantitative impact study conducted by the FSB, which suggested that the proposed level would have 'minimal' impact on market volume (*Financial Times*, 14 Oct 2014).[11] In developing the numerical haircut floors, the FSB discussed the relative merits of setting a single numerical floor for haircuts as well as a more granular approach, concluding that the numerical haircut floors should be risk-based, but not too granular. The FSB stressed that the haircut floors were intended to serve as 'backstops' to limit the build-up of excessive leverage, thus market participants should continue to set higher haircut levels than the official requirements where prudent.

Afterward, in order to reduce the risk of regulatory arbitrage and maintain a level playing field between bank and non-banks, the FSB decided to expand the scope of application of the numerical haircut floors to include non-bank-to-non-bank transactions. This would discourage a shift of securities financing transactions to non-bank-to-non-bank transactions in order to circumvent regulatory requirements. The FSB issued a consultative proposal on the application of numerical haircut floors to cover non-bank-to-non-bank transactions backed by collateral other than government securities. For bank-to-non-bank transactions, the FSB recommended that the BCBS incorporated the numerical haircut floors into its capital requirements framework (i.e. the Basel III accord). The BCBS was to set significantly higher capital requirements for transactions with haircuts below the numerical haircut floors, to create incentives for banks to set their collateral haircuts higher than the floors, rather than to hold more capital.

In 2015, the FSB extended the scope of numerical haircut floors to non-bank-to-non-bank transactions, albeit recognizing that the potential for non-bank-to-non-bank transactions to pose financial stability risks varied across jurisdictions. Thus, the implementation would depend on the national/regional authorities' assessment of the scale of securities financing activities and the materiality of non-bank-to-non-bank transactions in their jurisdictions. The FSB extended the implementation deadline for bank-to-non-bank transactions to January 2022 (instead of 2018), in line with the

[11] *Financial Times*, 'Rulemakers lay down terms for taming shadow banking risk: FSB imposes minimum requirements on collateral for short-term lending' by Alloway, T. and Fleming, S., 14 October 2014.

implementation of Basel III. It also extended the implementation deadline for non-bank-to-non-bank transactions to January 2024 (instead of 2019).

The fact that the international regulatory debate on securities financing haircut floors, which had been led by the FSB, was interlinked with the discussion of international capital and liquidity rules for banks (see Chapter 8), which was the competence of the BCBS, encouraged lobbying cum venue shopping by the financial industry that resisted the haircuts. For instance, the International Banking Federation (2019) wrote to the BCBS calling for a revision of the FSB's minimum haircut floors for securities financing transactions because the capital impact of the haircut floors was 'greater than necessary to achieve the stated policy objectives'. The International Banking Federation also noted that even though the FSB's study had concluded that there would be a small impact ensuing from the introduction of haircut floors (see FSB 2014c), this impact needed to be assessed by the BCBS in conjunction with other revisions of Basel III framework. Thus, private financial actors, first, lobbied the FSB against precise and stringent rules on haircuts, given that this body was the first international standard setter to examine this matter. Having only partly succeeded in making their case to the FSB, private financial actors subsequently lobbied the BCBS, to which the dossier had been passed by the FSB to incorporate the haircut provisions into the revisions of Basel III (the so-called Basel IV).

Overall, whereas the new rules were relatively precise, their stringency (that is to say, the level of minimum haircuts and the scope of application) was limited (Thiemannn, Birk, Friedrich 2018; Gabor 2016a). The regulation did not apply to government bonds as well as to transactions cleared through central counterparties. Hence, about 80% of repo transactions in Europe, which were backed by sovereign debt, and all bilateral repo trades cleared via central counterparties, were excluded. Furthermore, the minimum haircuts were below average market haircuts at that time. This was partly due to puzzling and turf fighting by regulators, who worried about the impact of the new measures, while the limited data on the repo market constrained evidence-based regulation (Thiemannn, Birk, and Friedrich 2018). One disagreement concerned the risks posed by repo markets and how to tackle them. Andrew Hauser (2013) explained that:

> The very features that make repo so effective in reducing counterparty risk at a microprudential level – collateralization, marking to market, regular remargining, and short maturities – also pose potential new macroprudential risks... Until recently, analyses of these two sets of issues, both in academia and in official circles, have tended to be carried out independently... It is

> easy to characterise these objectives as contradictory. But they are really two sides of the same policy challenge: we need repo markets that are both prudentially sound and sufficiently deep and liquid to perform their crucial functions.... Central banks such as the Bank of England have a big stake in the answer to these questions. We rely on healthy, well-functioning repo markets to implement monetary policy, and to transmit that policy to the wider economy... But we are also charged with maintaining the stability of the financial system as a whole.

Disagreements among sectoral regulators also involved the use of haircuts as a policy tool and came to the fore in the debate that unfolded in the EU. The ESMA (2016), whose work was informed by the transaction-based approach of securities markets regulators, recommended the introduction of the FSB's qualitative standards in the methodology used to calculate haircuts in the EU, but called for a postponement of the introduction of numerical haircut floors. Subsequently, the European Banking Authority (2016), whose work was informed by the microprudential outlook of banking regulators, advised against the introduction of minimum haircut floors for securities financing transactions in EU bank legislation, setting aside the recommendations issued by the FSB and the provisions of the so-called Basel IV accord issued by the BCBS.[12]

By contrast, the ESRB (2016), which had a macroprudential outlook, recommended the immediate implementation of the FSB's framework on numerical haircut floors. In a subsequent paper, the ESRB (2017), which lacked tools to pursue its macroprudential mandate, considered the implementation of the FSB's haircut floors as the 'first step in incorporating macroprudential considerations into the regulatory framework', which could 'lay the foundations for other macroprudential tools', such as the development of minimum levels of initial margins or the extension of the framework to government bonds. There was also scope to develop a framework for the 'use of discretionary add-ons' and 'efforts could be made at microprudential level to better mitigate any procyclical effects of margins and haircuts on these transactions' (ESRB 2017).

In the US, the Federal Reserve shared some of the macroprudential concerns of the ESRB. In a speech entitled 'Advancing Macroprudential Policy Objectives', Daniel Tarullo (2015b) argued that 'One policy response that the Federal Reserve has advocated and that has now been proposed by the FSB, is for minimum margins to be required for certain forms of securities

[12] In addition, if numerical haircut floors for securities financing transactions were to be introduced in the EU, the EBA (2016) took the view that this should occur via *market regulation*, not *banking regulation*.

financing transactions that involve extensions of credit to parties that are not prudentially regulated financial institutions. This system of margin is intended to serve the macroprudential aim of moderating the build-up of leverage in the use of these securities in less regulated parts of the financial system and mitigate the risk of procyclical margin calls by preventing their decline to unsustainable levels during credit booms' (Tarullo 2015b). To this end, the US supported the FSB's effort to develop regulation to establish minimum haircuts for securities financing transactions on a market-wide basis, rather than just for specific classes of market participants.

Not only the setting of international standards was controversial, but also their domestic implementation was contested. To date, no jurisdiction has introduced mandatory haircuts for several reasons. First, the effects of the FSB recommendations on market practices were unclear because the haircuts applied by market participants tended to be higher or at the level of the haircut floors recommended by the FSB (European Commission 2017). Moreover, the framework specifically targeted non-banks, which were less regulated than banks and had less capacity to calculate, validate, and value margin and haircuts. Second, the incorporation of numerical haircut floors for bank to non-bank securities financing transactions into the Basel III framework, which was originally recommended by the FSB for the end of 2015 as a prerequisite for national authorities introducing the haircut floors, was delayed. Finally, the US, the EU, and Japan called for the introduction of numerical haircut floors in a globally coordinated manner to maintain a global level playing field and avoid competitive disadvantages for market participants in the 'first-moving' jurisdiction (see, for example, European Commission 2017).

Reporting and Collecting Data on Securities Financing

In the wake of the crisis, the FSB and the IMF (2009) prepared a report titled *The Financial Crisis and Information Gaps*, and launched the Data Gaps Initiative. With reference to shadow banking, the FSB and the IMF (2009) noted the data challenge presented by entities that fell outside the regulatory perimeter and that disclosed information in a way that was insufficiently granular to allow the assessments of their systemic risk. Moreover, the limitation of the relevant data made it difficult for experts to adopt an evidence-based, data-driven approach. As the Vice-Chair of the Federal Reserve put it 'when it comes to financial stability, what you do not know really can hurt you – and there remains a good bit we do not know' (Fischer 2015). Thus, the FSB and the IMF called for an expansion and refinement in the flow of funds data to cover financial entities and activities in the shadow banking system.

The Inter-Agency Group on Economic and Financial Statistics, which included the BIS, the IMF (chair), the OECD, the UN Statistics Division, the World Bank, the ECB, and Eurostat, was established to coordinate work on economic and financial statistics. The FSB was invited to participate when discussions involved topics of direct relevance to this body. In 2015, the second phase of the data gap initiative was launched, focusing on specific tasks to compile consistent datasets across jurisdictions. As part of these initiatives, the FSB (2015e) issued *Standards and Processes for Global Securities Financing Data Collection and Aggregation*, which was a stream of work on securities lending and repos concerning the harmonization of data gathering. This FSB's document set out, along with the recommendations to national authorities related to the collection of data, the standards and processes for global securities financing data collection, and the reporting of data by national authorities to the FSB.

In 2018, the FSB (2018b) issued *Securities Financing Transactions: Reporting Guidelines*, which spelled out the main information to be collected and their characteristics (i.e. the classification of measures). The standards provided a table for each data element with a code-list that should be used in reporting, and also set out the rules that should be met for the validation of the reported data (FSB 2018b). In 2019, the BIS provided a formal *Data Structure Definition* for reporting the securities financing transactions national aggregates to the BIS. The BIS template was fully based on the data requirements and definitions provided by the FSB in *Standards and Processes for Global Securities Financing Data Collection and Aggregation* (2015d) and the data structures and code lists provided by the FSB (2018b) *Securities Financing Transactions Reporting Guidelines*. Overall, these sets of international standards were relatively precise and consistent.

The work on international data harmonization and collection was moved forward by regulators, in particular the central banks of the main jurisdictions, namely, the Federal Reserve, the ECB, and the Bank of England. A senior official at the Bank of England, Andrew Hauser (2012), in his speech entitled 'Shining a light in the shadows' called for improving the transparency and data collection in the securities lending and repo markets (see also Constâncio 2012b). The Vice-Chair of the Federal Reserve, Fischer (2015) noted that whereas there was consolidated data collection concerning banks (and these data contributed to a quantitative approach to regulation of banks), data securities lending, repos, and derivatives remained inadequate. Regulators were able to gain some insight into these markets via banking supervision, but the activities of important nonbanks, such as asset managers, and the interconnections across institutions remained opaque. Hence, the Federal Reserve endorsed the FSB's finalization of standards for collecting data on securities financing transactions.

The ECB, which also worried about the absence of suitable data, worked jointly with the Committee on the Global Financial System to launch a qualitative quarterly survey on euro-denominated securities financing and over-the-counter derivatives markets. The Vice President of the ECB, Vitor Constâncio (2012a), proposed the establishment of a central database for euro repo markets. He also noted that 'because market interconnectedness knows no borders, a global alignment in terms of repo market transparency is desirable (in results, not necessarily in solutions). On this side of the Atlantic, undoubtedly, I think we should aim for an EU and not only a euro-area central view on the euro repo market and securities lending data' (Constâncio 2012b). Yet, whereas regulators agreed on the need for data collection on securities financing transactions, there was a 'particular contrast' between' market conduct regulators', who wished to have 'trade-by-trade information', and 'macroprudential regulators interested in market-wide stability, where aggregate data on positions and collateral at a counterparty level would be sufficient' (Hauser 2012).

Conclusion

After the 2008-crisis, the building up of the elemental regime for securities lending and repos was a mixed success. On the positive side, international data standardization and collection were undertaken and international rules on haircuts were set. Qualitative standards for methodologies used by market participants and numerical haircut floors were issued by the FSB and their scope was extended over time (for an overview of the main standards issued, see Table 6.2). On the negative side, margin requirements for securities lending and repos were not as stringent as initially proposed. Furthermore, whereas the initial proposal envisaged the inclusion of sovereign bonds in the scope of the regulation, they were excluded in subsequent proposals. That was a major exclusion, given the vast size of sovereign bond markets. Last but not least, the domestic implementation of minimum haircut floors was delayed. It is also

Table 6.2 International standards for securities lending and repos

International standard-setting body	Date of issuance	Standards (framework, guidance, etc)
FSB	2013	Policy framework for addressing shadow banking risks in securities lending and repos
FSB	2013	Recommendations on securities financing transactions
FSB	2015	Regulatory framework for haircuts on non-centrally cleared securities financing transactions
FSB	2015	Standards and processes for global securities financing data collection and aggregation
FSB	2017	Re-hypothecation and collateral re-use: Potential financial stability issues, market evolution and regulatory approaches
FSB	2017	Non-cash collateral re-use: measure and metrics
FSB and BIS	2018	Securities financing transactions: reporting guidelines

noteworthy that haircuts were not the only tool available to the FSB, which could have imposed restrictions on the type of assets used as repo collateral, for instance, excluding government bonds. But this would have been a much stronger regulatory intervention, since minimum haircut requirements do not restrict repos directly but make them more expensive (Gabor 2014).

In regulating securities financing and, especially, the repo market, the main jurisdictions had heterogeneous preferences on important issues concerning re-hypothecation and haircutting. These differences had to do with different domestic regulatory frameworks and market structures. However, on certain issues, notably haircuts, the main hindrance was the fact that sectoral regulators had different views that came to the fore at the domestic and international levels. Thus, macroprudential regulators, first and foremost, the Federal Reserve, the Bank of England, the ESRB, and those at the ECB who dealt with macroprudential issues, supported the use of haircuts and considered them as a macroprudential tool that could be further developed. Microprudential banking regulators and securities market regulators were much more cautious, and so were some central banks (Thiemannn, Birk, Friedrich 2018), notably the ECB, which worried about the implications of the functioning of the repo market for its monetary policy (Braun 2020).

Taking advantage of these divisions, the financial industry engaged in venue shopping, lobbying the FSB first, and the BCBS later. Industry associations also reached out to finance ministry officials, stressing the need to exempt government bonds from the new rules, to facilitate the refinancing of the public debt on the market (Gabor 2016a). Private financial actors (see, for example, the International Capital Market Association—European Repo Council 2012a) also overplayed the concerns about the potential scarcity of collateral and unintended effects of haircut rules, strategically arguing that the demands for collateral increased significantly following post-crisis regulatory reforms, including those concerning derivatives markets. Furthermore, different parts of the financial industry were keen on either remaining outside the scope of the new rules, or making sure that those rules also extended to business competitors.

7

Securitization

A Problem or a Solution?

Besides securities lending and repos, which have been discussed in the previous chapter, another set of international discussions concerning shadow banking activities focused on securitization. Securitized products were major culprits of the 2008 international financial crisis in the US and, to a lesser extent, in the EU, which were the main markets for securitization. In the wake of the crisis, international bank capital requirements for securitized products were increased. These regulatory measures, together with market reactions, led to a steep decline in securitization. From 2015 onwards, however, there were attempts to re-launch 'simple, transparent and standardized securitization' in Europe, as an alternative source of funding for the real economy, in addition to bank lending. This effort was reflected internationally, whereby international criteria for 'simple, transparent and comparable securitization' were jointly issued by the BCBS-IOSCO, while bank capital requirements for this type of securitization were lowered by the BCBS.

The first factor that affected the international governance of securitization was pace-setting by the main jurisdictions, which, however, inverted roles over time. In the aftermath of the 2008 crisis, the US, which worried about the financial stability implications of securitization, sought to curb this financial activity, sponsoring higher capital requirements for banks that engaged in securitization. As time went by, jurisdictions in Europe worried about the opposite problem, that is to say, the relatively low level of securitization, which came to be considered as an alternative source of funding. Hence, the EU and the UK sponsored international criteria for safe[1] securitization and lower capital requirements for banks that engaged in securitization.

[1] Initially, regulators used the term 'safe' or 'high quality' securitization. Afterward, they preferred to use the term 'qualifying' (i.e. 'simple', 'standard', and so on) securitization in order not to attach a 'quality' label to securitized products.

The Perils of International Regime Complexity in Shadow Banking. Lucia Quaglia, Oxford University Press.
 DOI: 10.1093/oso/9780192866523.003.0007

Puzzling among financial regulators contributed to the swings of the regulatory pendulum. Initially, regulatory agencies, especially in the US, considered securitization as a problem to be addressed. Hence, they favoured the trading up of rules. Later on, regulators, especially in the EU and the UK, came to regard securitization as a solution to the problem of providing credit to the real economy and reinvigorating capital markets. Furthermore, there was some turf fighting among sectoral regulators because banking and securities market regulators paid attention to different aspects of securitization, which also has implications for the monetary policy of central banks. Yet, compared to other shadow banking elemental regimes (notably, those on investment funds and securities financing), disagreement among domestic regulatory agencies and the international standard-setting bodies they were members of, was limited.

The third factor that affected the international governance of securitization was lobbying by the financial industry, which strategically articulated the self-serving narrative about the (potential) benefits of securitization and sought to forge an alliance with private actors in the real economy, unlike in the case of the elemental regime on shadow banking entities (see Chapter 5). Moreover, financial associations and companies mobilized in several regulatory venues, vertically and horizontally, to pursue their goals. In particular, they reached out to European regulators and elected officials, which were rather sympathetic to the views of the securitization industry because they were eager to develop this market in Europe. The financial industry also used the international debate on securitization as a way to influence international standard-setting on bank capital to make these rules less stringent—it was a notable instance of venue shopping.

Main Issues in the International Governance of Securitization

Securitization is a process in which certain types of assets are pooled so that they can be repackaged into interest-bearing securities (IOSCO 2012c). The buyers of these securities receive the cash flows from the underlying assets, and can use the securities as collateral in wholesale funding markets (Gabor 2016a). Through securitization, a bank transforms its (usually) illiquid assets, traditionally held until maturity, into marketable securities by pooling these assets and transferring them into a special purpose vehicle, a bankruptcy-remote entity that, in turn, finances the purchase through the issuance of securities backed by the pool (generally referred to as asset-backed securities) (IOSCO 2012c).

In the run-up to the international financial crisis, the size of securitization markets increased considerably, driven both by supply and demand. On the supply side, securitization allowed banks to convert illiquid loans into marketable securities, freeing capital for other investments (Casu, Clare, Sarkysian, and Thomas 2011). On the demand side, the growth of securitization was fuelled by the growth of asset management funds and institutional investors, which were keen on investing in highly rated debt instruments. In the US, the outstanding volume of securitization more than tripled from approximately \$3 trillion in 1996 to approximately \$10 trillion in 2007. In Europe, the annual securitization issuance soared from less than \$100 billion in 1999 to \$1.2 trillion in 2007, most of which comprised residential mortgage-backed securities (Buchanan 2017).

Securitization changed the role of banks as financial intermediaries. The traditional 'originate-to-hold' model, whereby banks originated loans and then held them on their balance sheet until maturity, became the 'originate-to-distribute' model, where loans were pooled and sold to outside investors. Thus, securitization blurred the boundaries between loans and bonds and fragmented banks' traditional role as intermediaries into several specific functions, increasingly outsourced to specialized non-bank financial entities (Cetorelli, Mandel, and Mollineaux 2012). In addition, securitization increased the reliance of banks on capital markets as a source of finance. Banks expanded their funding sources, moving away from retail deposits to include bonds, commercial paper, and repo. Other securitized products that boomed in the pre-crisis period were asset-backed securities and structured investment vehicles.

From the early 2000s onward, the creation of collateralized debt obligations departed from the traditional securitization model because these instruments were backed by heterogeneous assets, including high yield bonds, leveraged loans, and tranches of other securitizations. Before the crisis, policy-makers endorsed securitization as a way of parcelling out risk in the financial system. For instance, the BCBS (2004a: 8) noted that 'securitization is important in helping to provide better risk diversification and to enhance financial stability'. With specific reference to the securitization of mortgage finance, the IMF (2006, Chapter 2) argued that it provided a steady source of funding, reducing the volatility of the provision of housing credit, and contributed to moderating credit cycle dynamics. Nonetheless, the originate-to-distribute model created misaligned incentives between banks and investors because low-quality loans were securitized and since loans could be sold, lenders lacked incentives to screen and monitor borrowers. Securitization weakened lending standards and fuelled the subprime mortgage crisis (Dell'Ariccia, Igan, and Laeven 2012).

In the run-up to the 2008 crisis, securitization became increasingly complex and opaque, with poor quality of underwriting standards, over-reliance on credit ratings, and absence of retention requirements. Bank capital requirements were low and there was a lack of disclosure requirements on banks' exposures to securitization, coupled with accounting rules that allowed many exposures to be held off-balance sheet (Bank of England and ECB 2014b). During the crisis, financial institutions were unable to assess the value of securitized instruments, and stopped accepting them as collateral. This led Malcom Knight (2008), general manager at the BIS, to ask whether securitization was the proverbial 'dog that was wagged by its own tail',[2] that is to say, whether the realization of 'tail risks' wagged the 'dog' of securitization to the point where it was no longer a useful element of the financial system. Or, whether the weaknesses that emerged during the crisis were due to how securitization was implemented.

After the 2008 crisis, several issues concerning the regulation of securitization needed to be addressed. First, there was the need to reduce complexity, given the riskiness posed by re-securitization. Fewer re-securitizations and shorter securitization chains would reduce complexity and better align incentives. Second, better information and more disclosure were needed, for instance, on the nature and performance of the assets underlying securitized products. The relevant information should be standardized to be easily comparable across assets and jurisdictions, to rely less on credit ratings.[3] The specific questions to decide upon were what needed to be reported, to whom, and how it should be disclosed.

Third, loan underwriting standards needed to be strengthened. The originate-to-distribute model—whereby assets were originated to be securitized—posed significant risks that were not adequately controlled by the market. There was a wrong incentive structure, whereby financial rewards encouraged participants to lower their underwriting standards on the securitized assets. In fact, if originators did not retain an interest in the asset pool (the originate-to-distribute model), they did not have sufficient incentives to ensure that lending standards, and by extension, the asset pool, were of appropriate quality (IOSCO 2012c; Joint Forum 2011). One way to correct the flaws in the originate-to-distribute model was to revise the incentive structure

[2] This expression is used to describe a situation in which a small or unimportant part of something becomes too important and controls the whole thing.

[3] Alternatively, there could be to have a distinctive rating system for structured finance instruments.

in the securitization value chain. Credit retention requirements—also known as 'skin in the game'—would better align the incentives of originators and investors (Adrian, Ashcraft, Breuer, and Cetorelli 2019). The specific questions to decide upon were the party on which obligations were to be imposed (i.e. direct and/or indirect regime), the forms of risk retention (e.g. vertical, horizontal, etc.), and the exceptions or exemptions from risk retention requirements.

Finally, given the fact that banks were often both arrangers of and investors in securitized instruments, there was the need for adequate capital requirements for securitized products and off-balance-sheet vehicles as well as the revision of the regulation of the banks' trading books. Hence, the regulations of securitization and banking were interlinked. In the wake of the crisis, bank capital requirements on securitized products were increased, given the concern about the potential risks involved in securitization. Once securitization was relaunched five years or so after the 2008 crisis, bank capital requirements on safe securitization were lowered. Here, the issues to decide upon were the calibration of bank capital requirements for safe securitization and the criteria for securitization to qualify as safe for regulatory capital purposes.

Main Actors in the International Governance of Securitization

Pace-setting by the main *jurisdictions*, first and foremost, the US, whose securitization market had been badly hit by the 2008 crisis, accounts for the initial tightening of international standards for bank capital rules on securitization. However, in the wake of the crisis, neither the US nor the EU sponsored international standards for securitization as such, for instance, rules on retention, disclosure, and transparency. Rather, these jurisdictions preferred to issue domestic rules, not least because the main originators of securitization were based in the US and the EU, hence, it was felt that domestic rules in these jurisdictions would suffice to tackle the problem. Moreover, the timing was of the essence and domestic regulatory reforms are generally quicker than setting international standards. In the aftermath of the 2008 crisis, loan underwriting standards were strengthened in both the US and the EU; information disclosure requirements were increased; and the scope of prudential consolidation was expanded, requiring banks that sponsored securitization vehicles to hold regulatory capital against these exposures. Credit retention requirements—also known as skin in the game—were introduced to better align the incentives of originators and investors (Adrian and Ashcraft 2012). However, a few years after the crisis, the EU and the UK were pace-setters in sponsoring international standards for 'safe' securitization as well as less stringent bank capital rules for securitization. Let us elaborate on these points in detail.

In the US, the Dodd–Frank Act (2010) imposed new requirements on asset-backed securities. Specifically, it prohibited conflicts of interests and prescribed rules on risk retention, disclosure, and reporting. In 2011, the SEC adopted rules requiring issuers to provide additional information, conduct reviews of assets underlying securitized products, and disclose those reviews. In 2014, the SEC revised the rules governing the offering process, disclosure, and reporting for asset-backed securities, setting data format standards for issuers to facilitate comparison among asset classes and to disclose asset and loan-level information.[4] In 2014, the SEC, the Office of the Comptroller of the Currency, the Federal Reserve Board of Governors, the Federal Deposit Insurance Corporation, the Department of Housing and Urban Development, and the Federal Housing Finance Agency issued joint rules requiring mandatory risk retention. These rules required a flat 5% risk retention for all asset classes, except for securitization involving so-called 'qualified residential mortgages' for which the risk retention level was zero (Morgan Lewis 2018). US banking regulators also increased the risk weight on capital requirements for securitization held in the bank's trading book.

The securitization industry in the US sought to push back against these domestic reforms. For instance, in a public hearing before Congress, the American Securitisation Forum argued that tighter rules for safer securitization in the US threatened to make this business 'unviable' and 'suffer death by 1000 cuts' (*Financial Times,* 19 May 2011).[5] Later on, when US banking regulators increased risk weight on bank capital for securitization, Tim Ryan, Chief Executive of the Securities Industry and Financial Markets Association, noted that the main issue was not the risk weight per se, but rather the difference between countries (*Financial Times*, 30 January 2012).[6] Thus, the US, initially, had an incentive to act as a pace-setter concerning international bank capital rules for securitization, to preserve a levelled playing field for the US financial industry and reduce negative externalities ensuing from less stringent rules in other jurisdictions.

[4] https://www.sec.gov/news/press-release/2014-177

[5] Tom Deutsch, Executive Director of the American Securitization Forum, cited in *Financial Times,* 'Bankers warn US securitization reform is "death by 1,000 cuts"', by van Duyn, A., 19 May 2011.

[6] *Financial Times*, 'New capital framework "biased against US"', by Braithwaite, T. and Masters, B., 30 January 2012.

The US market was larger and more sophisticated (meaning, with more complex and opaque products) than the market of other jurisdictions, including that of its main counterpart, the EU. After the 2008 crisis, the US securitization market bounced back more quickly than that in the EU for several reasons. The US securitization market was underpinned by Fannie Mae and Freddie Mac, two government-backed mortgage companies, and the Federal Reserve had $1.7 trillion in mortgage-backed securities on its balance sheet as a result of its bond-buying programme. Furthermore, large investors, such as insurers and pension funds, were buyers of asset-backed securities in the US. While the kind of subprime mortgage-backed securities that played a prominent role in the build-up to the 2008 financial crisis remained dormant, other types of securitization rebounded thanks to investors' quest for yield (Nassr and Wehinger 2015).

In the EU, there was a backlash against securitization in the wake of the international financial crisis of 2008, even though, during the crisis, securitized products in Europe performed much better than those in the US. Of more than 9000 European asset-backed securities issued before 2008, only 2% defaulted, compared with about a fifth of US asset-backed securities (*Financial Times*, 5 June 2014).[7] In 2009, the EU Capital Requirements Directive III was amended to forbid banks from taking on exposure to a securitized product, unless the original lenders had committed to retaining a material net economic interest (i.e. skin in the game) not less than 5%. In 2013, the Capital Requirements Directive IV included higher capital provisions for securitized products as well as requirements for risk retention and due diligence.

Following market reactions and more stringent public regulation, the level of securitization dropped significantly in the EU, also because banks preferred to tap central bank facilities for funding. At the same time, the collateralized debt obligations that caused considerable damage during the 2008 crisis largely disappeared and synthetic securitization, which used derivatives to replicate credit, remained limited (*Financial Times*, 9 May 2013).[8] As time went by, the problem in Europe, which suffered very low economic growth and had to deal with the sovereign debt crisis, became how to revive securitization in an attempt to boost economic recovery, while safeguarding financial stability (Montalbano 2020).

Thus, the EU and the UK engaged in concerted *pace-setting* to reform the regulation of securitization by increasing the transparency and

[7] *Financial Times*, by Alloway, T. and Thompson, C., 5 June 2014.

[8] *Financial Times*, 'ECB's Draghi in drive to revive slicing and dicing: News analysis', by Atkins, R., 9 May 2013.

standardization of securitized products, while reducing bank capital requirements for less risky securitization (Quaglia 2021). In May 2014, the Bank of England and the ECB jointly published a joint paper regarding the impaired securitization market in the EU. At the same time, the EBA (2014) issued a discussion paper on simple and transparent securitization. The ECB, the European Banking Authority, the Bank of England, and the European Commission were keen on assuaging public concerns about securitization, which had a bad reputation as a consequence of the crisis (Braun 2020; Braun, Gabor, and Hubner 2018).

Subsequently, securitization became a key component of the project for Capital Markets Union in Europe, proposed by the European Commission (2015) with the support of the member states, first and foremost, the UK, France, and Germany (Quaglia et al. 2016). The Commission was eager to 'harness financial markets as macro-economic stabilization tools', while ensuring fiscal discipline at the EU level (Braun and Hübner 2018). Hence, the Commission openly endorsed existing market-based initiatives to develop safe securitization. In 2015, two legislative proposals concerning securitization were put forward by the Commission as part of a broader set of initiatives concerning Capital Markets Union. First, a regulation on securitization set criteria to identify 'simple, transparent and standardized' securitization—this was the expression used in the EU. At the same time, the regulation on capital requirements for banks was amended to make the capital treatment of safe securitization more risk-sensitive (i.e. less stringent) for banks and investment firms. These pieces of EU legislation were eventually adopted in 2017.

The emphasis on securitization was due to the fact that Europe had a bank-based financial system, whereby securitization could be used by banks to increase lending to the real economy without increasing their capital requirements. However, the relaunch of securitization was also to encourage small and medium enterprises to bypass banks by securitizing their own assets and selling them on corporate debt markets (Quaglia et al. 2016). Jonathan Hill, European Commissioner for Financial Stability, Financial Services and Capital Markets Union, repeatedly pointed out that EU initiatives on securitization were part of a broader international effort. In fact, in parallel to the discussions on Capital Markets Union and the re-launch of securitization in the EU, the BCBS-IOSCO consulted on criteria for simple and transparent securitization and the BCBS considered how to incorporate these criteria in its revised Securitization Framework. The reforms concerning the criteria for securitization and bank capital requirements for securitization were interlinked, as elaborated in the following section.

One form of leverage that the EU and the UK deployed in their international pace-setting efforts was the argument that international standards on safe securitization and related bank capital rules were needed to protect the levelled playing field and avoid global market fragmentation resulting from different regulatory approaches (*Financial Times*, 6 January 2016).[9] Initially, the EU's plan to boost its securitization market through regulatory changes envisaged that this securitization had to originate in the EU, raising the question of whether European investors would be discouraged from buying products originated elsewhere, in particular those created in the US. Moreover, while the EU legislative proposal would reduce capital requirements for European investors, similar requirements for US-based investors would not be reduced because those standards were set by the US (*Financial Times*, 6 January 2016).[10] Given these premises, the US had then an incentive to support international standards on these matters.

Puzzling and *turf fighting* involved central bankers, banking regulators, and securities markets *regulators*, who sought to understand the risks that securitization entailed as well as how to tackle those risks. In turn, problem-definition and problem-solving concerning securitization depended on the regulatory outlooks, mandates and competences of sectoral regulators. Thus, macro-prudential regulators (generally, central bankers) led the discussion on the financial stability risks related to securitization. Banking regulators dealt with bank capital rules for securitization. Securities markets regulators discussed disclosure and retention requirements. Central bankers also paid attention to the implications of securitization for their monetary policy.

In the wake of the crisis, central bankers and banking regulators called for 'new standards applicable to securitization activities that would better align the incentives faced by market participants involved in the various stages of the securitization process' (Bernanke 2010)—these rules, however, were to be set by securities market regulators. As Paul Tucker (2010) at the Bank of England noted, 'when the music stopped ... investors and savers could not tell sound asset-backed securities from unsound ones. So, one lesson must surely be that securities regulators and exchanges, which admit asset-backed securities to the listing, should set more exacting but also simpler standards for transparency.' The ECB advocated greater transparency and disclosure in securitization markets, noting that investors needed to get access to relevant information to be

[9] *Financial Times*, 'EU and US split over securitisation: Capital markets', by Brunsden, J. and Hale, T., 6 January 2016.

[10] *Financial Times*, 'EU and US split over securitisation: Capital markets', by Brunsden, J., Hale, T., 6 January 2016.

able to exercise the required due diligence. Banking regulators worried about the risk that securitization involved for banks, but also considered securitization as a potential way for banks to diversify risks. Thus, they were aware of the trade-off between the risk posed by securitization and its function as an important tool for bank funding and liquidity (*Financial Times*, 19 December 2012).[11]

Securities market regulators called for more transparency, disclosure, and better underwriting standards in securitization. In the wake of the crisis, the SEC noted that US securities laws were outdated and new legislation was needed on securitization (*Financial Times*, 27 October 2009).[12] Mary Schapiro (2010), the Chair of the SEC, pointed out that two things had to change after the crisis: investors needed better information about the pooled assets that backed securities; and the interests of organizations that issued and sponsored these securities had to be better aligned with the interests of investors. In a later speech, she noted that 'many originators were not accountable for the loans they made, loosening underwriting standards and passing off the entire credit risk to investors through securitization' (Schapiro 2011).

Among US regulatory agencies, there were some disagreements on retention requirements. Thus, the Federal Deposit Insurance Corporation supported the 5% risk retention requirement and Michael Krimminger, the Deputy to the Chairman for Policy at the Federal Deposit Insurance Corporation, argued that retaining some of the risks of the loan on the balance sheet would realign incentives. By contrast, John Dugan, a senior official at the Office for the Comptroller of the Currency, suggested that a better approach would be for regulators to set minimum loan standards (*Wall Street Journal*, 29 March 2010).[13] Whereas the SEC, as a whole, supported the introduction of retention requirements, some SEC commissioners disagreed with this choice, which was portrayed as a tool favoured by prudential banking regulators. For instance, Commissioner Piwowar (2016a) noted that:

> Rather than carefully examining the attributes of specific types of securitization to determine an optimal credit risk retention rate for each asset class, prudential regulators simply set it at the maximum statutory rate. Perhaps the prudential bureaucrats had their own conflict of interest in setting these

[11] *Financial Times*, 'Banks face stricter capital rules for securitisations', by Masters, B., 19 December 2012.

[12] *Financial Times*, 'The SEC head urges fresh securities laws', by Scholtes, S. and van Duyn, A., 27 October 2009.

[13] *Wall Street Journal*, 'Securities debate is all about trust', by Simon, R. and Scannell, K., 29 March 2010.

> requirements because prudential bureaucrats have a strong interest in self-preservation. Will a prudential bureaucrat get credit if optimally tailored risk retention rates increase economic growth and provide additional opportunities to families and businesses? No. Will a prudential bureaucrat take the blame if the next financial crisis – and there will be one eventually – relates at all to securitizations? Probably. Hence, what better way to side step responsibility than to refrain from using reasoned judgment and rely solely on the most risk-averse interpretation of statute instead?'

The epistemic debate on securitization evolved over time, and had different nuances across jurisdictions. Initially, securitization was framed as a problem that required more precise and stringent rules. Five years or so after the 2008 crisis, securitization came to be framed by regulators in the EU and the UK (as well as by the financial industry) as a potential solution to economic problems (Engelen 2018). The European Commission, the EBA, the ECB, the Bank of England noted that during the crisis defaults and losses associated with securitization varied substantially across asset classes and regions. Hence, the 'trick' was to get the 'right type' of securitization.

Central bankers in Europe were also keen to revive securitization because they partly relied on it for the conduct of their monetary policy (Braun, Gabor, and Hübner 2018; Braun 2020; Braun and Hübner 2018; Braun and Gabor 2020). The ECB was particularly interested in the asset-backed securities market, which acted as one of the transmission channels of the monetary policy of the ECB.[14] Thus, the ECB's support for favourable capital treatment for safe securitization was seen as necessary to restore the liquidity of this market. The ECB was also keen on relaunching securitization to transfer risk away from the banking sector, freeing up bank capita to extend new credit to the real economy. As early as 2010, José Manuel González-Páramo (2010), a member of the Executive Board of the ECB, gave a speech entitled 'Re-starting securitization', calling for the development of transparent, comparable, and simple securitization structures, based on high-quality standards of underlying assets.

Like the ECB, a few years after the crisis, the Bank of England sponsored the relaunch of securitization on the ground that banks could use securitization to diversify their funding and transfer risk on underlying loans and non-banks could also finance lending through securitization (Rule 2015; Bank of England

[14] Asset-backed securities were an important component of the collateral framework of the Eurosystem.

and ECB 2015). A senior official at the Bank of England and co-chair of the BCBS-IOSCO Task Force on Securitization, David Rule (2015) noted that banks and non-banks could use securitization to help match the maturity of their liabilities to their assets. However, this market needed to be 'based on genuine risk transfer, not regulatory arbitrage, such as synthetic sales of thin mezzanine tranches intended to maximize the reduction in regulatory capital at minimum cost'.

An early intuition of the Bank of England and the ECB was that lack of transparency acted as an obstacle to the revitalization of the securitization market (Mersch 2017). In a nutshell, the Bank of England and the ECB (2014a)[15] argued that the potential benefits of securitization depend on its purposes: it could be used to fund assets, to transfer risk, or both. Hence, this market had advantages, but also posed potential risks to financial stability. For these reasons, the involvement of regulators was 'desirable' to 'support its revitalization in a more robust form'. Both the Bank of England and the ECB argued in favour of lowering capital requirements for safe securitization on the grounds of its lower risk (see, for instance, Rule 2015). Yves Mersch, a member of the ECB's Executive Board, was critical of the high capital requirements for securitization set in the wake of the 2008 crisis, which was calibrated on the worst-performing securitized products. He likened this move to 'calibrating the price of flood insurance on the experience of New Orleans for a city like Madrid' (*Financial Times*, 1 October 2014).[16]

Braun (2020) points out that the infrastructural entanglement between the ECB and the securitization market was due to the ECB's decision to integrate asset-backed securities into its collateral-eligibility framework in 2000. Afterward, in the wake of the failure of Lehman Brothers, the ECB assumed the role of 'dealer of last resort' for asset-backed securities. By taking illiquid asset-backed securities onto its balance sheet, the ECB gained leverage over the securitization market, but became more dependent on it (Braun 2020). Yet, while the ECB and the Bank of England sought to revive the securitization market, other central bankers, notably, those in the US, where the post-crisis securitization market was buoyant, warned that the industry had not yet learnt the lessons of the crisis. For instance, Adam Ashcraft, head of credit risk management at the Federal Reserve Bank of New York, cautioned that 'We haven't

[15] https://www.ecb.europa.eu/pub/pdf/other/ecb-boe_case_better_functioning_securitisation_marketen.pdf

[16] *Financial Times*, 'Back from disgrace: Asset-backed securities', by Jones, C. and Thompson, C., 1 October 2014.

done anything meaningful to prevent the securitization market from doing what it just did' (*Financial Times,* 5 June 2014).[17]

Internationally, banking regulators took the lead in setting bank capital rules for securitization. In doing so, they were facilitated by the fact that capital rules had been set internationally since 1989 and were within the remit of the BCBS, which was the most well-established standard setter in finance. Securities markets regulators agreed on the need for better information disclosure and market transparency, but the international standard-setting on these matters remained very thin initially. Instead, rules were set at the domestic level with minimal international coordination. This was because the IOSCO was a less well-established standard-setter as compared to the BCBS and no previous international standards on securitization existed. Only subsequently, criteria for safe securitization were jointly issued by the BCBS-IOSCO, given the fact that the expertise of both banking and securities regulators was needed.

The third factor that influenced the international governance of securitization was *lobbying cum venue shopping*—across jurisdictions and international standard-setters—by the financial industry. In the wake of the 2008 crisis, private financial actors were on their back foot and even though they mobilized extensively against higher bank capital rules on securitized products and retention rules for issuers, they were only partly successful in limiting the regulatory backlash. A few years after the crisis, the financial industry worldwide, but especially in the EU, contributed to the relaunch of securitization, by articulating a persuasive narrative about the benefits of securitization, arguing that the pre-crisis problems caused by securitization were due to how it was used, not to securitization per se (Dorn 2016; Engelen and Glasmacher 2018; Montalbano 2020).

Private actors skilfully engaged in vertical venue shopping, seeking to revive securitization in the EU to revive this market globally by setting international standards that would brand most securitized products as safe, and then lowering bank capital requirements for these products. The 'political entrepreneurship' of the cross-border securitization industry was crucial in explaining the emergence of the Capital Markets Union agenda on the reform of securitization regulation in the EU (Montalbano 2020; see also Ringe 2015; Dorn 2016; Engelen and Glasmacher 2018). Like in the case of the governance of the repo markets (see Chapter 6), private financial actors were able to forge

[17] *Financial Times,* 'Sliced and diced debt deals make a comeback', by Alloway, T. and Thompson, C., 5 June 2014.

Table 7.1 International governance of securitization: actors, pathways, and outcome

States	Regulators	Industry	Outcome
Initially, *no pace-setters* for securitization standards, but US-led trading up of bank capital rules for securitization Belated *pace-setting* by EU and UK on safe securitization and lower capital rules	*Puzzling* among regulators, some disagreement along jurisdictional lines	*Infrastructural power* and *lobbying* by financial industry, forging coalition with (EU) central bankers and non-financial groups	Not very precise, stringent, and consistent rules by IOSCO and BCBS

an alliance with firms in the real economy (Montalbano 2020) as well as with central bankers, because repo and securitization provided the infrastructure through which central banks, in particular, the ECB, but also the Bank of England, implemented their monetary policy. 'This entanglement makes central bankers, who seek to maximize their economic steering capacity, dependent on bankers, giving the latter *infrastructural power*.... which constitutes a distinct source of financial-sector power' (Braun 2020, emphasis added) (for an overview of the main explanations, see Table 7.1).

International Standards for Securitization

In the wake of the crisis, the G20 Leaders (2008) called for a review of the scope of financial regulation with special emphasis on institutions, instruments, and markets that were unregulated. At around the same time, at a US conference on securitization, representatives of the SEC, the Federal Reserve, and the British Financial Services Authority all identified securitization as an area of concern *Financial Times*, 6 February 2008).[18] At the Pittsburgh summit in 2009, following *pace-setting* first and foremost by the US, the G20 agreed that 'securitization sponsors or originators should retain a part of the risk of the underlying assets, thus encouraging them to act prudently'.

The IOSCO set up the Task Force on Unregulated Financial Markets and Products, co-chaired by the Autorité des Marchés Financiers of France and

[18] 'Regulators pledge greater scrutiny of debt products', by Stacy-Marie, I., *Financial Times*, 6 February 2008

the Securities and Investments Commission of Australia. In 2009, the IOSCO's Task Force issued a report that chose securitization and credit default swaps as examples of unregulated markets and products (IOSCO 2009b). Concerning securitization, three key recommendations were put forwards. The first concerned the requirement that originators and/or sponsors should retain long-term economic exposure to securitized products. The second recommendation required transparency through disclosure by issuers to investors. The third recommendation required the independence of service providers engaged by issuers (notably, credit rating agencies), if opinions or services provided by service providers could influence investors' decision to acquire a securitized product. At about the same time, the BCBS (2009a) revised its Securitization Framework by issuing the so-called Basel 2.5 accord, increasing bank capital requirements for 're-securitization' (that is to say, collateralized debt obligations comprised of asset-backed securities), which were more highly correlated with risk than traditional securitization. In December 2012, the BCBS proposed a revised ratings-based approach and a modified supervisory formula approach, both of which were intended to create a 'more risk-sensitive' and 'prudent' calibration.

The responses from the financial industry were very critical. The International Banking Federation (2013b) worried about the 'unintended negative consequences' of the proposed rules, noting that the calibration of the proposed approaches failed to produce capital requirements that were commensurate with the 'true riskiness of the securitization exposures'. In particular, the proposed capital floor level (i.e. 20% risk-weight) was 'excessively high' and would eliminate the capital savings from securitization. The Institute of International Finance (2013) noted that the calibration of the proposed approaches did not reflect the quality and performance of the underlying assets. It required significantly more capital to hold securitized assets compared to holding the same underlying assets directly, which eliminated banks' economic incentive to use securitization. The Global Financial Markets Association (2013) submitted a response letter of more than 120 pages, arguing, inter alia, that the proposed rules would result in much higher capital requirements for most securitization, including high-quality senior tranches, while reducing capital requirements for some lower quality securitization. The proposals did not increase risk sensitivity, rather decreased it, by increasing the risk weight floor and increasing risk weights overall.

In December 2013, the BCBS (2013c) issued a revised consultation paper. In comparison to the first consultation paper, the BCBS significantly reduced capital requirements, although they remained more stringent than under the existing framework. The draft framework included a minimum risk weighting of 15%—less than the 20% that had been previously proposed by the BCBS, but more than bank lobbyists were bidding for—and a simpler method of determining capital requirements than previously proposed. The Basel Committee stated that the new draft standards would lead to 'meaningful' reductions in capital requirements compared with initial proposals.

Moreover, Stefan Ingves, the Swedish central banker who was the Chair of the BCBS, argued that the stringent capital rules on securitization, which had been introduced in 2009, could be softened. He noted that 'securitizations need not in any sense be bad ... Risk weights are not forever. We need to review them. We need to look at the appropriateness of various structures and pass judgment on them' (*Financial Times*, 30 September 2013).[19] Thus, in an attempt to revive the securitization market, under the pace-setting efforts of the EU and the UK, the BCBS undertook further work on securitization. These instruments had been blamed for passing US subprime mortgage losses around the world and their perceived risks had prompted regulators to impose sharp increases in risk weightings, pushing up capital requirements as part of Basel 2.5 reforms in 2009 (BCBS 2009a). Yet, five years or so after the 2008 crisis, a reappraisal was necessary.

As early as 2013, Mario Draghi, the President of the ECB, noted that the 'asset-backed securities market is dead and has been dead for a long time' and launched an initiative to revive this market as a way to finance an economic recovery (*Financial Times*, 9 May 2013).[20] Given limited bank lending in Europe, asset-backed securities were no longer seen as dangerous instruments, but rather an alternative source of finance for small companies, particularly in southern Europe, where credit conditions were very tight. At the Bank of England, Andy Haldane remarked that securitization was potentially the 'financing vehicle for all seasons' and that it should no longer be treated as a 'bogeyman'. The shift in the international regulatory discourse in favour of revamping securitization, rather than trading up its regulation, as it had been done in the aftermath of the crisis, reflected the *pace-setting* efforts of the EU and the UK.

In 2014, the ECB and the Bank of England released two documents on securitization. The first document (Bank of England—ECB 2014a) was prepared for the G20 meeting in March 2014. It noted that securitization, if appropriately structured and regulated, could complement other funding sources

[19] *Financial Times*, 'Watchdog to retreat from strict capital rules', by Jenkins, P., 30 September 2013.
[20] *Financial Times*, 'ECB's Draghi in drive to revive slicing and dicing', Atkins, R., 9 May 2013.

for the real economy, including for small and medium-sized enterprises. Furthermore, it could provide a diversified funding source for banks and, potentially, transfer credit risk to non-bank financial institutions, thereby providing capital relief that could be used by banks to lend to the real economy. A particular focus was on the promotion of simple structures and transparent underlying asset pools with predictable performance (so-called 'high-quality' securitization), while preventing the resurgence of the complex and opaque structures that contributed to the financial crisis. In May 2014, the Bank of England and the ECB (2014b) issued a longer document, *The Case for a Better Functioning Securitization Market in the European Union*, which was subject to public consultation.

Similarly, the EBA (2014), which issued a *Discussion Paper on Simple Standard and Transparent Securitizations*, argued that a 'well-functioning and prudentially sound' securitization market would provide an 'alternative funding channel to the real economy and enhanced risk-sharing'. The European Banking Authority acknowledged that a one-size-fits-all regulatory approach to securitization was no longer appropriate, as it could result in a lenient treatment of risky securitization and conservative treatment of less risky, simple, and transparent transactions. Consequently, the regulatory approach to securitization should incorporate a distinction between high-quality (i.e. 'qualifying') securitization and other securitization. The regulatory definition of qualifying securitization should follow a two-stage approach, whereby to qualify for a different treatment, a securitization transaction should first meet a list of criteria ensuring simplicity, standardization, and transparency and, as a second step, the transaction should meet the criteria of the minimum credit quality of the underlying exposure (EBA 2014).

Internationally, the BCBS and the IOSCO established a joint Task Force on Securitization, which was asked by the FSB to identify the factors that hindered the development of securitization, and develop criteria for simple and transparent securitization. The Task Force was co-chaired by David Rule, a senior official at the Bank of England, and Greg Medcraft, the Chair of the IOSCO. The aims of the criteria proposed by the Task Force were threefold. First, to assist investors, according to the 'what you see is what you get' principle. Second, to assist issuers by making risk transfer more robust. Third, to assist regulators to set risk-sensitive capital requirements for securitization on the basis of a differentiation based on criteria to identify safe securitization (Rule 2014). In December 2014, the BCBS and the IOSCO published for consultation 14 criteria to identify simple, transparent, and comparable securitization. The content of this document was very similar to those of the joint documents produced by the Bank of England and the ECB (2014a, b) and the one issued by the EBA (2014). Hence, it had a marked 'European flavour'.

While the BCB-IOSCO worked on criteria for safe securitization, the BCBS, under the pace-setting efforts of the EU and the UK, began work to lower bank capital requirements for safe securitization. The ECB had pushed for reform for more than a year, but the BCBS did not discuss the issue until when, in mid-2014, the ECB and the Bank of England joined forces to push for the relaxation of capital rules on securitization. At a meeting of the International Monetary Fund in Washington, the ECB and the Bank of England jointly intervened to make their case. Yves Mersch explained that these central banks had a 'common analysis and a common suggestion... We have agreement on the main thrust of a policy line to propose.... We call on those who do those rules to reassess their past position, and to take [our views] into account.' If new rules failed to gain traction in international bodies, such as the Basel Committee, an EU-specific approach would be needed. 'Either we do it at the global level, [or] if that has no prospect of going through any time quickly, we should take into account the needs of the EU and the differences we have in the EU and adjust our regulation to the environment of the EU' (cited in *Financial Times*, 7 April 2014).[21] Finally, Mersch argued that international proposals did not take account of the fact that European securitization performed better than US equivalents during the international financial crisis. Thus, the ECB felt that EU asset-backed securities were treated inappropriately by existing regulation.

The *financial industry* adopted a two-pronged *lobbying* strategy on securitization. It supported the revival of securitization, seeking to make the criteria for simple, transparent, and comparable safe securitization as 'light-touch' as possible. It lobbied the BCBS-IOSCO to this end. At the same time, the industry called for a reduction of bank capital requirements for safe securitization, lobbying the BCBS on this matter, and sought to avoid additional (Basel only) criteria for safe securitization for regulatory capital purposes. To begin with, the industry spearheaded the relaunch of securitization,[22] but wanted to avoid criteria for safe securitization that were too prescriptive and granular. For instance, the trade associations that represented the financial actors most involved in securitization, namely, Global Financial Markets Association, the International Swaps and Derivatives Association, the Institute of International

[21] *Financial Times*, 'Europe's top two central banks seek to revive 'toxic' assets, 7 April 2014.

[22] The *Financial Times* noted that 'For years, bankers sought to persuade regulators and politicians that mortgage-backed securities had a minimal cumulative default rate. Most of this campaigning took place behind closed doors in Brussels and Washington, making it difficult to ascertain the extent to which the decision of the BCBS was a victory for banks' ('Bank lobbying takes the bite out of Basel watchdog's rules', by Alloway, T., 12 January 2013).

Finance, and the International Capital Markets Association (2015) submitted a joint response to the BCBS-IOSCO, calling for 'sensibly calibrated' criteria for simple, transparent, and comparable securitization, avoiding the 'harsh and inappropriate' 'one-size-fits-all regulatory approach of the past'. They also called for favourable bank capital requirements for safe securitization, and the inclusion of synthetic securitization within the scope of the new rules (see also European Banking Federation 2015a).

With reference to bank capital requirements for securitization, which were the remit of the BCBS, in a 'jumbo' joint response of the main trade associations, namely, the Commercial Real Estate Finance Council, the Commercial Real Estate Finance Council Europe, the Global Financial Markets Association,[23] the Institute of International Finance, the International Association of Credit Portfolio Managers, the International Swaps and Derivatives Association, the Securitisation Forum of Japan and the Structured Finance Industry Group (2014) argued that the BCBS's proposed capital requirements for securitization exposures, especially for high-quality exposures, remained much higher than justified by historical losses, or in relation to the capital requirements of the underlying asset pools.

Since the BCBS was also in the process of adopting additional criteria to label certain securitization as safe and, therefore, subject to lower capital rules, the financial industry lobbied against precise and stringent criteria. For instance, the Global Financial Markets Association, International Swaps and Derivatives Association, Institute of International Finance, and International Capital Market Association (2015) noted that some criteria proposed by the BCBS were specific to particular jurisdictions, or asset classes, making it hard to apply those criteria across the board, and undermining the purpose of having international criteria. According to the above named financial associations, the criteria should be articulated in a principle-based manner and synthetic securitization should be included. In general, private financial actors believed that the additional criteria proposed by the BCBS were too burdensome, whereas the (less stringent) BCBS-IOSCO *Simple, Transparent and Comparable Securitization Criteria* 'were sufficiently rigorous to differentiate between low-risk and high-risk securitization'.

The financial industry mobilized at the international and EU levels, engaging in a distinctive form of vertical and horizontal *venue shopping*, seeking to connect and influence regulatory processes at both levels. For instance, in

[23] This transnational association included the Association for Financial Markets in Europe, the Asia Securities Industry & Financial Markets Association, and the Securities Industry & Financial Markets Association.

its response to the consultation of the Bank of England and the ECB on the relaunch of securitization in Europe, the Association for Financial Markets in Europe (2014a, b) noted the consultation of the BCBS-IOSCO on broadly similar themes, albeit at a more general level. While the joint initiative of the Bank of England and the ECB was more 'likely to produce concrete results in Europe in the near to medium term', the BCBS-IOSCO initiative was 'likely to influence the long-term direction of regulation at a global level'. The Association for Financial Markets in Europe remarked that the work undertaken by the Bank of England and the ECB should be coordinated with other workstreams dealing with securitization in the EU and internationally, including the European Banking Authority's work on defining 'qualifying securitization', the BCBS's revisions to the Securitisation Framework, the BCBS's work on liquidity rules (especially, the eligibility of securitization for the Liquidity Coverage Ratio), and the FSB's work on shadow banking (particularly, its securitization workstream). The European Banking Federation (2014) argued that 'Europe should take the lead' internationally in the definition of safe securitization and the review of related bank regulation, playing an influential role in the design of policies at the global level, including those in the domain of the BCBS and the IOSCO.

The British Bankers Association (2014) argued that a globally harmonized approach was paramount and therefore it urged the Bank of England and the ECB to pursue this goal 'robustly' in the BCBS, which was in the process of revising its Securitization Framework. If, however, international harmonization was not feasible in the near future, then a 'Europe only' approach' should be pursued. This association was also concerned by the high-risk weights for securitization proposed by the BCBS. Similarly, the Deutsche Bank (2014) argued that since securitization markets were global, the Bank of England and the ECB should seek to promote criteria for safe securitization in international fora, such as the BCBS and IOSCO. It also noted that:

> The capital charges for securitisation held in the trading book, need to be calibrated in a way that does not discourage trading of securitisation. Unfortunately, the recent BCBS Review of the Trading Book discussion paper proposed significant increases in risk weights for securitisation positions as well as inconsistent treatment and would result in materially higher capital compared to the latest proposals for the regulatory banking book. We hope that the Bank of England and ECB will ensure that the BCBS works to the same guiding principles at the international level that are being used at the EU level. Calibration of both, banking book and trading book capital

> requirements for securitisation is due to be finalised in the coming months and will be of crucial importance to viability of securitisation markets, not just in Europe, but globally.

In 2015, the BCBS-IOSCO issued the *Criteria for Identifying Simple, Transparent and Comparable Securitizations*, however, noting that additional criteria, such as those related to the credit risks of the underlying securitized assets, were necessary for regulatory capital purposes. The BCBS proposed to supplement the criteria issued by the BCBS-IOSCO with additional criteria to differentiate the capital treatment of simple, transparent, and comparable from that of other securitized transactions. The financial industry opposed the additional (more precise and stringent) criteria proposed by the BCBS, arguing that the criteria issued by the BCBS-IOSCO would suffice. Hence, there was a veiled attempt to pit the BCBS against the IOSCO. At the same time, the BCBS proposed to reduce minimum capital requirements for simple, transparent, and comparable securitization by reducing the risk weight floor for senior exposures, and by rescaling risk weights for other exposures. Eventually, the BCBS revised capital requirements for securitization exposures in 2016, including the regulatory capital treatment for simple, transparent, and comparable securitization, and set additional criteria for differentiating the capital treatment of simple, transparent, and comparable securitization from other forms of securitization.

The same process just described was then repeated, under the impulse of EU and UK regulators, with reference to short-term securitization. Therefore, the BCBS-IOSCO (2018) issued *Criteria for Identifying Simple, Transparent and Comparable Short-Term Securitisations,* and then the BCBS opened consultations on the revision of the Securitization Framework for short-term securitization.[24] The Australian Securitisation Forum, the Global Financial Markets Association, the International Capital Market Association, and the Institute of International Finance (2017) submitted a joint response, which was suggestive of the positions of the financial industry. These associations encouraged 'regulators to strive to build a viable consensus among their constituent members regarding the simple, transparent, and comparable securitization criteria to apply to short-term securitizations'. In 2018, the BCBS set additional requirements for the application of lower capital requirements to banks engaged in simple, transparent, and comparable short-term securitization. Eventually, simple, transparent, and comparable short-term securitization

[24] See https://www.bis.org/bcbs/publ/comments/d413/overview.htm

Table 7.2 International standards for securitization

IOSCO	2009	Report on unregulated financial markets and products
Joint Forum	2011	Asset securitization incentives
IOSCO	2012	Report on global developments in securitization regulation
BCBS-IOSCO	2015	Criteria for identifying simple, transparent, and comparable securitization
BCBS	2016	Revised securitization framework (including capital treatment for simple, transparent, and comparable securitization)
BCBS-IOSCO	2018	Criteria for identifying simple, transparent, and comparable short-term securitization
BCBS	2018	Capital treatment for simple, transparent, and comparable short-term securitization

received the same reduction in capital requirements as simple, transparent, and comparable securitization (BCBS 2018) (for an overview of the main standards issued, see Table 7.2).

Conclusion

In the aftermath of the 2008 international financial crisis, new rules on securitization were issued in the main jurisdictions, whereas the international standards issued by the IOSCO remained very thin. By contrast, international bank capital rules for securitization exposures issued by the BCBS were traded up. Less than a decade after the crisis, the regulatory pendulum swung back: criteria for safe (or high quality) securitization were introduced at the international and domestic levels (notably, in the EU), while bank capital rules for securitization became less stringent internationally and domestically.

The relaunch of securitization was mainly promoted by the EU (including the UK), which wanted to make the financial system in Europe less bank-based and considered the US as a potential model to follow. Thus, securitization became the first step in the establishment of Capital Markets Union. By contrast, the US, where capital markets were quite well developed, were somewhat less interested in relaunching securitization, as suggested by the lack of policy initiatives in this area. Whereas the US did not oppose the EU's and UK's efforts, the relaunch of securitization is one of the few instances of international standards that came to light and were sponsored by the Europeans and not the US.

The regulatory community was ambivalent about securitization, but it was mainly divided along jurisdictional lines, whereby regulators in Europe were more well disposed towards securitization than regulators in the US, as illustrated above. Although sectoral regulators had different priorities concerning securitization, this did not result in open epistemic and bureaucratic disagreements because the division of competences was rather clear and the priorities of regulators were compatible. Securities market regulators were responsible for setting rules on securitization, often in collaboration with bank regulators, given that banks were the main originators and traders of securitized products. Banking regulators worried about the risk that securitization involved for banks, but also considered securitization as a potential way for banks to diversify risks. Central bankers, who were generally responsible for financial stability, worried about the risks that securitization entailed. Yet, they also relied on the functioning of this market for the conduct of their monetary policy.

The financial industry resisted more precise and stringent rules on securitization and bank capital requirements for securitized products. Initially, the industry, which was on its back foot in the wake of the crisis, met with limited success. However, over time, private financial actors were instrumental in promoting the narrative of safe securitization to foster economic growth by unlocking alternative sources of funding for the real economy, in addition to traditional bank lending. Furthermore, the transnational financial industry, as well as financial companies based in the US, rallied behind the European efforts to revamp securitization by setting (not very stringent) international criteria for safe securitization and by lowering bank capital rules on securitized products. Only a few (non-financial) groups, such as Finance Watch (2015), and academics (e.g. Gabor and Vestergaard 2015) expressed their concerns about the risks of reinvigorating securitization.

8

Bank Exposure to Shadow Banking

Dangerous Liaisons?

The securitization of the off-balance-sheet activities of banks (in particular, loans and mortgages) and their short-term liabilities due to refinancing on the repo market and through MMFs—which were key aspects of shadow banking discussed in the previous chapters—played a major role in the building up of the international financial crisis of 2008. After the crisis, the indirect regulation of shadow banking was pursued by tightening up international banking regulation, which is the topic of this chapter. Whereas post-crisis bank capital and liquidity rules were tightened up, building on pre-existing international standards (the Basel accords), other banking rules issued post-crisis, notably, those on large exposures, equity investment in funds, and step-in risk, lacked any real bite. Eventually, bank capital rules for 'safe' securitization were also revised downwards.

This empirical pattern is explained by the preferences of the main jurisdictions and the mobilization of the financial industry. To begin with, the US and the UK, which were eager to sponsor stringent international bank capital and liquidity rules in the wake of the 2008 crisis, acted as pace-setters. The EU was a partial foot-dragger initially and, as time went by, the EU and the UK became pace-setters in promoting a reduction of capital requirements for safe securitization. Other banking rules, notably, those on large exposures, equity investment in funds, and step-in risk, lacked major 'sponsor' jurisdictions. Only one set of regulators, banking regulators, were involved. They agreed on the need to tighten up capital and liquidity rules post-crisis, but, initially, they did not agree on the new level—the lines of division mostly run along jurisdictional lines. That said, the setting of rules for safe securitization also required the collaboration between banking regulators and securities markets regulators and their respective international standard-setting bodies, as explained in the previous chapter.

Lobbying by the financial industry contributed to rolling back bank capital requirements for securitization and prevented precise and stringent standards

The Perils of International Regime Complexity in Shadow Banking. Lucia Quaglia, Oxford University Press.
 DOI: 10.1093/oso/9780192866523.003.0008

on bank's large exposures, equity investment in funds, and step-in risk. Private financial actors mobilized at multiple levels of governance: they lobbied 'their' national regulators; they also made the case for the relaunch of securitization in the EU and the UK and prompted these jurisdictions to take the lead in sponsoring safe (and less highly capitalized) securitization in the relevant international fora. The financial industry also pointed out the cumulative effects of banking rules as well as the risk of regulatory arbitrage out of the banking system to the benefit of the shadow banking system. Finally, financial firms sought to forge an alliance with non-financial firms, strategically pointing out that bank capital and liquidity rules had implications for the flow of funding to the real economy.

Main Issues in the International Governance of Banks and Shadow Banking

The 2008 international financial crisis revealed that banks were strongly undercapitalized and lacked sufficient liquidity (Brunnermeier et al. 2009; De Larosière et al. 2009; Financial Services Authority 2009; Group of Thirty 2009). With specific reference to the interaction between banking and shadow banking, several problems came to the fore. The first problem concerned the use of special purpose entities or conduits by banks—these entities were de facto shell companies controlled by banks. Before the crisis, asset-backed securities and other forms of securitization were transferred into special purpose entities or conduits, which were kept off the banks' balance sheets and were not subject to capital requirements. Hence, banks reduced securitized assets on their balance sheets, reducing their capital needs without changing their risk exposure (Thiemann 2018, 2014). However, banks, mainly for reputational reasons, stepped in to provide financial support to these shell companies when they ran into trouble during the crisis (Adrian and Ashcraft 2012; Luck and Schempp 2014), and the impaired assets held by these entities returned onto the balance sheets of banks (Kamin and Pounder De Marco 2010).

International standards on bank capital, specifically, the Basel I accord (1989), which set capital requirements for internationally active banks, de facto accelerated the development of securitization that enabled banks to circumvent capital rules (Thiemann 2018). Furthermore, since Basel I applied the same capital charge on all assets, regardless of the credit quality of the borrower, it gave banks an incentive to remove high-quality assets from their books by securitizing them. However, the originating banks often held on to the riskiest first-loss positions to help support their deals (Fabozzi, Davis, and Choudhry 2006). So, even though banks reduced their capital requirements, they did not reduce their risk exposure (Thiemann 2018).

Basel II(2005) sought to close some regulatory loopholes by introducing the 'Securitization Framework' for bank exposures to securitization. The accord reduced the incentives for banks to securitize loans to high-quality borrowers by applying higher capital charges on junior securitization tranches, so that banks would face higher costs if they retained them on their books. As initially proposed, Basel II was expected to have a significant impact on securitization, but this was less evident once the final rules were issued because their content was watered down during the standard-setting process (Lall 2012; Goldbach 2015a).[1] At any rate, Basel II was in the process of being implemented when the international financial crisis began in 2007. Although the Securitization Framework was tightened up in the wake of the crisis, it was revised again downwards, after the BCBS-IOSCO issued criteria for safe securitization in 2015 and 2018 (see also Chapter 7). Another weak point of pre-crisis international banking regulation was the trading book, which had been agreed in 2005. Traditional banking products were kept in the banking book, where capital requirements were higher, whereas products that were securitized (and followed the originate-to-distribute model) were kept in the trading book, which was subject to lower capital charges. This encouraged regulatory arbitrage by moving financial instruments from the banking book to the trading book (PricewaterhouseCoopers 2017). But, the major losses for banks during the crisis came from the trading book, where complex structured financial instruments and securitized products were held (Lee 2015).

Two other parts of the Basel III package had implications for shadow banking: the leverage ratio and liquidity rules. Basel III introduced a minimum leverage ratio, which was a non-risk-based ratio and was calculated by dividing the Tier 1 capital of the bank (mainly equities) by the bank's average total consolidated assets (the sum of the exposures of all assets and non-balance sheet items). It affected shadow banking because the leverage ratio included both on-balance-sheet exposures as well as off-balance-sheet exposures, such as undrawn amounts on credit lines and derivative transactions. The Liquidity Coverage Ratio, which was part and parcel of Basel III, was to ensure that banks had an adequate stock of high-quality liquid assets (BCBS

[1] In one of its preparatory documents the BCBS (2004b) noted 'the Committee has made several modifications to the internal ratings-based approach to securitization exposures to address industry concerns raised during consultations related to complexity of the securitization proposal and potential operational burden related to its implementation'.

2013a). It extended to special purpose entities set up by banks, which were also required to hold a buffer of high-quality liquid assets when using securities financing transactions. Thus, the Liquidity Coverage Ratio made it more costly for banks to obtain short-term repo funding. Another liquidity rule, the Net Stable Funding Ratio, was intended to encourage banks to extend the duration of their liabilities to reduce dependence on short-term wholesale funding sources, including those in the shadow banking system.

Besides capital and liquidity requirements for bank exposures to shadow banking, other issues that needed to be addressed were banks' large exposures, their equity investment in funds and the step-in risk. Last but not least, it is useful to provide some data about the size of the global banking system and its intersection with the shadow banking system. In 2019, total financial system assets were $379 trillion. Bank financial assets were $147 trillion,[2] OFIs assets were $114 trillion, and the narrow measure of shadow banking was $51 trillion. Banks were the largest single sector of the financial system in 22 jurisdictions of the 29-Group (21 non-euro area states plus 8 euro area states). However, MUNFI represented more than 50% of the financial system in 11 of those jurisdictions, with OFIs typically comprising the largest share. Investment funds and MMFs remained the largest OFI sub-sectors that provided credit to banks. Banks were the single largest source of lending, accounting for 83% of global loan assets and lending by banks was $80 trillion, whereas OFI lending assets were $14 trillion (FSB 2020a).

Main Actors in the International Governance of Banks

The *pace-setters* of the Basel III accord, including the provisions concerning shadow banking, were the US and the UK. In the wake of the 2008 crisis, the Secretary of the US Treasury, Timothy Geithner, pointed out that 'the top three things to get done are capital, capital, and capital' (*Washington Post*, 25 March 2010). Daniel Tarullo (2011) of the Federal Reserve Board argued that strong capital standards were central to the overall reform agenda for financial regulation because 'the crisis confirmed that capital standards had been wholly inadequate: the required capital levels were much too low, particularly trading book capital requirements'. In the UK, the so-called Turner Review published by the British Financial Services Authority (2009) called for an increase in 'the

[2] https://www.statista.com/statistics/421221/global-financial-institutions-assets-by-institution-type/

quality and quantity of capital … significantly above existing Basel rules … a maximum gross leverage ratio…. and liquidity regulation and supervision'.

The US and, especially, the UK, had a very internationalized banking sector—meaning that they were home and host to large cross-border banks. During the 2008 international financial crisis, the US authorities had to bail out several US banks and the Federal Reserve had to provide a substantial amount of emergency funding to the subsidiaries and branches of foreign undercapitalized banks operating in the US. Foreign subsidiaries and branches, in turn, transferred part of that funding to their parent companies in Europe (McDowell 2012). In the UK, the three largest domestic banks had to be bailed out by the government using taxpayer money, whereas about 40% of the banking sector was foreign-owned.

Domestic unilateral action (i.e. national capital rules) would not have sufficed to deal with the low capital level of foreign banks operating in the US and the UK and would have subjected domestic banks to comparative disadvantages in international competition—international harmonization was needed. Furthermore, the adjustment costs deriving from tighter international capital and liquidity standards were low in the US and the UK (James and Quaglia 2020). The massive government-led recapitalization of ailing US and UK banks during the crisis left them relatively well-capitalized afterward. In terms of domestic regulatory templates, US banks already complied with the leverage ratio, which had been in place in the US since the 1990s. Furthermore, capital markets in the US provided the bulk of funding to the real economy. Similarly, the banking sector, especially wholesale investment banking in the City of London, did not provide substantial funding to the real economy. Hence, the impact of higher international capital requirements on economic growth in the US and the UK was expected to be lower than in continental Europe (Howarth and Quaglia 2016).

The EU was in favour of tightening up capital requirements for banks, albeit not to the same extent as the US and the UK. Mario Draghi, President of the ECB, in his former capacity as chairman of the FSB, called the loopholes in Basel II 'one of the major factors of the crisis' (Draghi 2008). Yet, continental countries were less exposed to negative externalities than the US and the UK because most of the EU cross-border banking was intra-EU (i.e. to and from other EU countries) and, on average, foreign penetration by non-EU headquartered banks was below 10% in the EU as a whole. In 'core' EU countries, such as France and Germany, foreign (EU and non-EU) bank penetration was the lowest in the EU (Schoenmaker 2013). At the same time, the adjustment costs to more stringent international capital standards were high for banks in continental Europe, which were significantly undercapitalized. Furthermore, banks provided most of the credit to the real economy in continental Europe, and, consequently, stricter capital rules would be detrimental to economic growth. Thus, whereas the EU supported the revision of Basel II, it was a *partial foot-dragger* in the making of Basel III as it worried about the stringency of the new rules (Quaglia and Spendzharova 2017).

Continental countries in the EU faced a trilemma concerning financial stability, the international competitiveness of their financial industry, and economic growth (interviews, see Howarth and Quaglia 2016). The trilemma became more acute following the sovereign debt crisis in the EU, which further depressed economic growth and, indeed, the EU initially did not comply with Basel III domestically (Quaglia 2019; Young 2014). The priority for the EU became to improve the flow of credit to non-financial companies, also through the relaunch of securitization, as explained in the previous chapter, by reducing capital requirements for safe securitization. Hence, from 2014 onwards, the EU, together with the UK, acted as a *pace-setter* internationally to set new rules for safe securitization through the joint work of the BCBS-IOSCO and lower capital rules for securitization in the BCBS.

Banking *regulators* gathered in the BCBS were in the driving set in the international policy discussions on banking rules. However, the work of the BCBS intersected with that of the IOSCO on the issue of securitization. The IOSCO and the BCBS workstreams on securitization had different remits—the former focused on assessing and aligning incentives associated with securitization (for example, by imposing risk retention rules), while the latter focused on the calculation of capital requirements for banks' securitization exposures. Yet, there were some interlinkages, given that capital requirements influenced banks' incentives to engage in securitization as originator, sponsor, investor, etc. Hence, the BCBS and the IOSCO worked jointly to set criteria for safe securitization.

Regulators in the US and the UK were the main sponsors of more robust post-crisis international rules for bank exposure to shadow banking. Daniel Tarullo (2014a) pointed out the need to address the financial stability risks posed by the use of large amounts of short-term wholesale funding by banks—the liquidity rules in Basel III were instrumental to this end. The Federal Reserve[3] also favoured a fundamental review of the trading book, exploring possible standardized capital requirements for market risk as a back-up for internal model-derived risk weights, as it had been done for credit risk in the

[3] Tarullo (2012c) argued that the Federal Reserve 'provided significant leadership in the Basel discussions' at the international level, while at the domestic level it spent a considerable amount of time in 'interagency negotiations that eventually yielded agreement or compromise on individual points'.

banking book (Tarullo 2012c). Similarly, the British Financial Services Authority (2009) noted the inadequate focus on liquidity risks in Basel I and II and the flaws in the trading book.

The ECB, which had only observer status in the BCBS when Basel III was discussed, was particularly interested in securitization, which had implications for the transmission channels of the monetary policy of the ECB. A few years after the crisis, after the ECB had acquired responsibility for banking supervision in the euro area, the ECB advocated the relaunch of securitization to transfer risk away from the banking sector, and provide extra credit to the real economy. To this end, the ECB supported a favourable capital treatment for safe securitization. Likewise, the Bank of England sponsored the relaunch of securitization on the ground that banks could use securitization to diversify their funding and transfer risk on underlying loans, whereas non-banks would be able to raise funding through securitization (Rule 2015). In comparison to the international governance of shadow banking entities and transactions, *puzzling* and *turf fighting* among sectoral regulators were limited in setting international standards for bank exposure to shadow banking because one set of regulators, banking regulators prevailed. However, securities market regulators were involved in setting the criteria for safe securitization, working jointly with banking regulators, which entailed the quest for epistemic common ground and the management of turf fighting, as detailed in the previous chapter.

The *financial industry* lobbied against rigorous post-crisis capital and liquidity rules, forging a broad coalition with non-financial actors, especially in the EU (Howarth and Quaglia 2013) and engaging in *venue-shopping* across levels of governance (Young 2014, 2013). Thus, financial and non-financial companies in the EU (for instance, the Motor Industry Associations in France, Germany, and the UK issued a joint document)[4] argued that the international capital requirements proposed by the Basel Committee were too high—particularly, for high-quality securitization—and, therefore, there was an imbalance between capital requirements for securitized loans and non-securitized ones. Private financial actors, which were instrumental in relaunching securitization in the EU (Montalbano 2020), noted that the proposed international rules, 'appear to allow, either by design or otherwise, for the very high-quality European securitization markets to be impaired' and would 'negatively impact a form of financing that was essential to the health of the European economy' (European Banking Federation 2015b).

[4] https://www.ecb.europa.eu/pub/pdf/other/141013-abs-joint-responses.en.pdf

Table 8.1 International governance of bank exposure to shadow banking: actors, pathways, and outcomes

States	Regulators	Industry	Outcome
Pace-setting by US and UK Partial *foot-dragging* by EU	Some disagreement along jurisdictional lines	*Lobbying* at the domestic and international levels, coalitions with non-financial groups	Precise and stringent rules by BCBS, partly watered down for securitization, reducing consistency
No 'sponsor' for rules on bank step in risk and equities investment in funds	Ditto	Ditto	Other bank rules remained vague

At the international level, the main transnational players, such as the International Banking Federation and the IIF, pointed out that the BCBS should consider the compounded effects of the various elements of Basel III, including the leverage ratio and liquidity rules, the revision of the securitization framework and the trading book review. These associations (and their members) stressed the interlinkages between the revisions of the Securitization Framework by the BCBS and the IOSCO's Workstream on Securitization. The industry also lamented the fact that the trading book and securitization framework were dealt with by different workstreams of the BCBS, whereas it would have been better to include the treatment of securitization in the trading book in the consultation concerning the securitization framework. Finally, private financial actors articulated powerful counter-narratives, arguing that more stringent capital and liquidity rules would disrupt the flow of credit to the real economy (for a rebuttal of these arguments, see Admati and Hellwig 2013) and, with specific reference to shadow banking, that the international regulatory tightening concerning securitization was based on losses associated with US subprime residential mortgage-backed securities during the financial crisis. This event was not regarded by financial institutions as representative of the performance of securitization globally and was unlikely to recur in light of post-crisis regulatory reforms (for an overview of the main explanations, see Table 8.1).

International Standards for Bank Capital and Liquidity

In the wake of the 2008 crisis, the BCBS, under the pace-setting of the US and the UK, and the partial foot-dragging of the EU, revised the Basel II accord in 2009 (the so-called Basel 2.5) and, then, replaced it with the Basel III accord (BCBS 2010). Other parts of the Basel III package (for example, rules on liquidity, securitization, and the trading book) were issued afterward. The accord and its subsequent revisions had major implications not only for the banking sector, but also for shadow banking because these rules established more stringent capital and liquidity requirements for banks that engaged in shadow banking.

Within the BCBS, the US and UK supported higher capital requirements, a more restrictive definition of what counted as bank capital, and precise and stringent liquidity rules. By contrast, the main continental European countries, notably, France and Germany, supported a smaller increase in capital requirements, a less restrictive definition of bank capital, and less precise and stringent liquidity rules (interviews, see Howarth and Quaglia 2016). The outcome of these negotiations, the Basel III accord, was a compromise between the positions of these two groups (see Goldbach 2015a, b; Howarth and Quaglia 2016; Young 2012). The BCBS was also deeply divided about what should count as liquid assets beyond cash, sovereigns, and high-rated corporate bonds (*Financial Times*, 20 December 2013).[5] Some European regulators, as well as politicians, feared that stricter rules would exacerbate the continent's economic problems, hence they favoured a broad definition of liquid assets, set a rather low level. Other regulators preferred a narrower definition of liquid assets, set at a rather high level, pointing out that liquidity dried up in the market in 2008 (*Financial Times*, 25 September 2012).[6]

Eventually, with reference to bank capital requirements and shadow banking, Basel III increased from 0% to 20% the credit conversion factor for bank commitments with an original maturity of one year (or less) that were not unconditionally cancellable (BCBS 2010). With reference to bank liquidity rules, the Liquidity Coverage Ratio, which was agreed three years after the first part of the Basel III accord, assigned a 100% drawdown rate to undrawn amounts of credit and liquidity facilities extended by banks to special purpose entities (BCBS 2013a). The Liquidity Coverage Ratio also required banks to hold a buffer of high-quality liquid assets when they used securities financing transactions. The Net Stable Funding Ratio required banks to maintain a stable funding profile in relation to the composition of their assets and off-balance sheet activities (BCBS 2014a).

[5] *Financial Times*, 'Capital rules eased for bundled loans', by Fleming, S., 20 December 2013.
[6] *Financial Times*, 'Basel naysayers delve into detail in battle to dilute reforms', by Masters, B., 25 September 2012.

Lobbying by the financial industry sought to dilute particular portions of the Basel III package. Industry's efforts become more sophisticated over time, after the BCBS dismissed exaggerated claims from the big global banks that Basel III would lead to 10 million fewer jobs (James and Quaglia 2020). Subsequently, industry groups commissioned—or, in some cases, carried out—targeted research projects to show how certain parts of the proposed rules could have deleterious effects. For instance, a Harvard University study sponsored by the American Securitisation Forum focused on the Liquidity Coverage Ratio, arguing that a tight liquidity definition could prove self-defeating and that accepting a broader range of assets would lead to greater stability (cited in *Financial Times*, 24 September 2012).[7] These studies dovetailed with positions taken by some European regulators and politicians. Eventually, the BCBS decided to loosen the new bank liquidity rules. According to the original definition of the Liquidity Coverage Ratio, banks could only count sovereign bonds, cash, and top-quality corporate bonds. The final rules allowed banks to fill 15% of their buffer with some equities, some mortgage-backed securities, and almost all investment-grade corporate bonds (*Financial Times,* 8 January 2013).[8]

A second set of banking rules that had direct implications for shadow banking regarded the trading book. Norah Barger, a senior official at the Federal Reserve, questioned whether it was appropriate to keep securitization exposures on the trading book. 'It's very clear sticking exposures in the trading book was seen as a great way to avoid all manner of sins' (reported in *Financial Times*, 6 February 2008).[9] The *Financial Stability Report* of the Bank of England (2009a), noted that major UK banks suffered substantial write-downs across the trading book. In a subsequent report, the Bank of England (2009b) high lighted the 'deep-seated potential fault-lines in the regulatory framework for dealing with traded assets also need to be mitigated. The boundary between trading and banking books was a source of arbitrage ahead of the crisis. Banks classified as part of their trading books a growing range of illiquid assets, such as structured credit products, that would have received much higher capital charges under banking book rules.' In July 2009, the BCBS (2009b) revised the Basel II market risk framework, increasing capital requirements against

[7] *Financial Times*, 'Basel naysayers delve into detail in battle to dilute reforms', by Masters, B., 24 September 2012.

[8] *Financial Times*, 'Regulators to face new risks', by Masters, B., 8 January 2013.

[9] *Financial Times*, 'Regulators pledge greater scrutiny', by Ishmael S-M., 6 February 2008.

market risk. However, the appropriate capital treatment of traded assets was to be considered by the BCBS as part of a fundamental review of the trading book.

In 2012, the BCBS issued the first consultative paper on the trading book review, followed by a second consultative paper in 2013. The rules, which were sponsored by the US and UK, sought to limit the switching between the trading book and the banking book, also reducing the differences in capital requirements against similar types of risk on either book, especially for securitization. Eventually, the BCBS finalized the minimum capital requirements for market risk in January 2016, incorporating changes that were made following the previous consultative documents and several quantitative impact studies. The key features of the revised framework included: a revised boundary between the trading book and banking book; a revised internal model approach for market risk; a revised standardized approach for market risk; the incorporation of the risk of market illiquidity.

Rules on Large Exposures for Banks

The FSB (2011b) noted that limiting banks' exposures to individual shadow banking entities would help to reduce the interconnection between the regular banking system and the shadow banking system. Furthermore, it would also reduce the size and leverage of individual shadow banking entities whose funding depended on banks. International guidance on large exposure had been issued by the BCBS in 1991, but necessitated improvements (e.g. the level of the limits needed to be revised), and greater international harmonization was needed. The FSB asked the BCBS, the competent standard-setting body, to review the large exposure standards with an additional focus on shadow banking. In turn, the BCBS asked its Large Exposures Group to work on this matter.

The Group drew three main lessons concerning large exposures: banks did not consistently measure and control exposures to counterparties; major losses in one systemically important financial institution could trigger contagion effects; and banks were exposed to shadow banks (BCBS 2013e). To address these issues, the BCBS (2014d) issued the *Supervisory Framework for Measuring and Controlling Large Exposures*, substantially revising the version issued in 1991. The purpose of large exposure limits was to constrain the maximum loss that a bank could face in the event of the failure of a counterparty or a group of connected counterparties (i.e. counterparties that were interdependent and likely to fail simultaneously).

The large exposure standard included a limit of 25% of a bank's Tier 1 capital applied to all bank exposures to a single counterparty (or groups of connected counterparties). A tighter limit (15%) was applied to exposures between banks that were global systemically important banks. The framework contained provisions concerning the treatment of exposures to funds and securitization. It included requirements for banks to apply a 'look-through' approach, which was applicable for exposures to structures with underlying assets, such as securitization vehicles and a 'substitution approach', which required banks to limit both direct and indirect exposures to counterparties (e.g. whenever a counterparty provided a guarantee for exposure to another counterparty).[10] Once these risks were identified, bank exposure would be subject to the large exposure limit (BCBS 2014d). The new standard supplemented the existing Basel III accord discussed in the previous section.

Capital Requirements for Banks' Equity Investments in Funds

The BCBS also worked on risk-based capital requirements for banks' exposures to investment in funds. The original scope of the BCBS's work covered the regulatory capital treatment of banks' exposures to funds acting as shadow banking entities, but the Committee decided to expand its work to cover the capital requirements that applied to banks' investments in the equity of all types of funds. The draft international standards were issued for public consultation in July 2013 and only a handful of responses were received. The joint response submitted by the Institute of International Finance, the International Banking Federation, the Global Financial Markets Association (2013) was indicative of the position of the financial industry. These associations supported the BCBS's decision to look at all types of funds rather than shadow banking funds, but urged the BCBS to differentiate between specific types of funds, which had very diverse characteristics and risks. Hence, the regulatory treatment of banks' equities in investment funds should be 'targeted and proportionate to the risks'. These trade associations also warned about potential overlaps with other regulatory initiatives, particularly the work of the IOSCO on investment funds, discussed in Chapter 5.

[10] If a bank has a large exposure to a certain counterparty and also holds investments in a securitization vehicle that holds assets of that counterpart, it is important to look through the structure to ensure all exposures to that counterparty are correctly captured. Similarly, if a bank has an exposure to a certain counterparty, which is guaranteed by another counterparty, it is important that the bank recognizes the indirect exposure to the second counterparty (Chapman et al 2020).

In December 2013, the BCBS (2013d) issued *Capital Requirements for Banks' Equity Investments in Funds*, revisiting its Basel II policy framework for the prudential treatment of banks' investments in the equity of funds that were held in the banking book. The revised policy framework applied to investments in all types of funds (e.g. hedge funds, managed funds, and other investment funds). It tightened up the existing framework by considering the leverage of a fund in determining risk-based capital requirements associated with banks' investments in a fund and reflecting the risk of a fund's underlying investments, including the use of a 1250% risk weight if there was not sufficient transparency regarding the investment activities of a fund (BCBS 2013d).

Rules on Step-in Risk for Banks

The FSB (2011b) recommended restricting banks' ability to stand behind shadow banking entities that were not included in the consolidated balance sheets of banks by applying a stricter regulatory treatment of 'implicit support'. This would also help to reduce the interconnectedness between banks and shadow banking entities. The FSB asked the BCBS, which was the competent standard-setter, to work on the identification and management of step-in risk for banks that sponsored special purpose entities. Step-in risk refers to the risk that a bank will provide financial support to an entity beyond, or in the absence of, its contractual obligations, should the entity experience financial stress. The BCBS asked its Standards Implementation Group to examine this issue and the group proposed *Guidelines on the Identification and Measurement of Step-in Risk* in 2015.

The objective was to mitigate spillovers from the shadow banking system to banks. Thus, the focus was on the identification of unconsolidated entities to which a bank could provide financial support, to protect itself from adverse reputational risk. Initially, the BCBS was unsure about how the proposals would fit into the existing regulatory framework, including whether they would fall within Pillar 1 (mandatory requirements) and/or pillar 2 (supervisory discretion) (BCBS 2015: 5). This suggests that there were some disagreements among regulators: US and UK regulators preferred the inclusion of the proposed rules under Pillar 1, rather than Pillar 2, continental European countries preferred the opposite (interviews).

The responses of the financial industry to the first consultation document of the BCBS were very critical.[11] The Institute of International Finance and

[11] For an overview, see https://www.bis.org/bcbs/publ/comments/d349/overview.htm

International Banking Federation (2016) issued a joint response, arguing that the proposal ignored the fact that step-in during the financial crisis had been largely limited to certain investment structures. Hence, the proposed framework was too broad—its indicators had the potential to 'scope in nearly any unconsolidated entity with which a bank transacted or acted as a sponsor'. These associations asked the BCBS not to proceed with its proposal, and if the BCBS decided to proceed anyway, a major rethinking of the proposed rules was needed. Similarly, the Global Financial Markets Association, the Commercial Real Estate Finance Council, Commercial Real Estate Finance Council Europe and the Real Estate Roundtable (2016) submitted a critical joint response. They believed that the post-crisis changes to accounting standards as well as the new capital and liquidity rules had already addressed step-in risks. Hence, the BCBS should set its proposed guidelines aside. Should the Committee decide to proceed with new rules, it should not follow the 'blunt, risk-insensitive, and pre-emptive approach' set out in the consultation paper, which 'vastly overestimated the scale of the step-in risk'. The American Bankers Association (2016) believed that a global capital standard to address step-in risks was 'unnecessary, redundant, and potentially disruptive'. Other national banking associations, such as the French Banking Federation (2016) and the German Banking Industry Committee (2016), were equally critical of the proposal.

The BCBS issued a revised consultation paper in 2017, recognizing the need for a 'tailored approach' rather than a 'standardized one'. Hence, the framework did not entail automatic Pillar 1 capital or liquidity charges in addition to the existing Basel standards. The BCBS also expanded the identification criteria to take into account the risk characteristics of the entities involved in addition to the banks' relationships with them (2017a: 3). The revised proposal was relatively well-received by the industry,[12] which noted that the hearing hosted by the BCBS in April 2016 was important to foster mutual understanding between the industry and regulators concerning the development of this new approach. Thus, the Institute of International Finance, the International Banking Federation, the Global Financial Markets Association, and the Commercial Real Estate Finance Council (2017) appreciated the change in the overall regulatory approach.

The final *Guidelines on the Identification and Management of Step-in Risk* adopted in 2017 (BCBS 2017a) looked very different from what the BCBS had initially proposed in 2015 (BCBS 2015). The proposals had been significantly

[12] For an overview, see https://www.bis.org/bcbs/publ/comments/d398/overview.htm

Table 8.2 International standards for bank exposures to shadow banking

International standard-setting body	Date of issuance	Standards (framework, guidance, etc)
BCBS	2009	Enhancements to the Basel II framework (Basel 2.5)
BCBS	2010	Basel III
BCBS	2013	Capital requirements for banks' equity investments in funds
BCBS	2014	Supervisory framework for measuring and controlling large exposures
BCBS	2014	Basel III: Revision to the securitization framework
BCBS	2016	Basel III: Revision to the securitization framework (amended to include the 'Capital treatment for simple, transparent, and comparable" securitization')
BCBS	2017	Guidelines on the identification and measurement of step-in risk
BCBS	2018	'Capital treatment for short-term simple, transparent, and comparable securitization

watered down. A 'flexible' and 'tailored' approach was introduced, mostly based on bank self-assessment.[13] The guidelines did not prescribe any automatic Pillar 1 capital or liquidity charge. Furthermore, they focused on residual step-in risk (i.e. the step-in risks after considering the risk mitigants). Although the guidelines aimed for consistency across jurisdictions, they acknowledged the 'idiosyncratic nature of step-in risk' and, therefore, allowed for 'banks' one-off assessments of each case and for the supervisory evaluation of such assessments' (BCBS 2017a) (for an overview of the main standards, see Table 8.2).

Conclusion

To sum up, after the 2008 crisis, bank prudential rules were tightened up to ensure that banks' exposures to shadow banking were adequately captured.

[13] In particular, banks define the entities to be evaluated for potential step-in risk; banks identify entities that are immaterial and exclude them from the evaluation. Banks assess all remaining entities against the step-in risk indicators provided in the guidelines. For entities where step-in risk is identified, banks estimate the potential impact on liquidity and capital and report their self-assessment to their supervisor. After reviewing the bank's self-assessment, the supervisor decides whether additional measures were needed (BCBS 2017a).

Basel III and its subsequent additions and revisions contained provisions that enhanced capital and liquidity requirements for banks' exposures to shadow banking activities, such as securitization and securities financing; banks' exposures to shadow banking entities, including step-in risk for special purpose entities and investments in the equity of funds; as well as a standard for measuring and controlling banks' large exposures. The combined effects of these measures were to reverse the pre-crisis trend of growing interconnectedness between the banking and shadow banking system. Indeed, such interconnectedness gradually declined after the 2008 crisis, but it remained higher than the pre-crisis period, partly due to interconnectedness between banks, MMFs, investment funds, and broker-dealers (FSB 2017a).

On the one hand, the reduction of potential direct negative spillovers from shadow banks to banks by tightening up banking rules was one of the main successes of the post-crisis regulatory overhaul (Griffith-Jones 2017). And, in fact, banks coped reasonably well with the covid-related economic crisis (Cunliffe 2020; FSB 2020b), as discussed in the concluding chapter. On the other hand, it is telling that one of the main regulatory reforms of *shadow banking* concerned the regulation of the *banking* sector (Griffith-Jones 2017), which increased the risk of regulatory arbitrage. For instance, Daniel Tarullo (2013), a member of the Federal Reserve Board, noted that bank regulation would apply only to banks that were already within the perimeter of prudential regulation. However, it was unclear whether this would be enough to address systemic risk and whether new banking regulation would encourage regulatory arbitrage. Hence, it was necessary to complement prudential bank regulation with regulatory tools that could be applied on a market-wide basis, focusing on particular kinds of transactions, as discussed in Chapters 6 and 7 and as well as non-bank entities, as discussed in Chapter 5. Similarly, Adair Turner, Chairman of the British Financial Services Authority, noted that although the BCBS was responsible for setting capital standards for banks, the reduction of the risks posed by the broader non-bank sector was only feasible by regulating the products, such as securitization, on which banks relied, rather than the institutions themselves (cited in *Financial Times*, 27 April 2012).

The US and the UK pushed for more precise and stringent bank capital and liquidity rules after the 2008 crisis to deal with the traditional dilemma between financial stability and the competitiveness of the financial industry. The EU faced a trilemma, which added a third objective, economic growth, to the dilemma, because banks provided credit to the real economy in Europe, which was therefore reluctant to tighten up banking rules too much. The Basel III accord was a compromise between these positions and evolved over time. On the one hand, liquidity rules were added and the regulation of the trading book was tightened up. On the other hand, the EU, with the support of the UK, managed to lower capital rules on safe securitization, to revive this financial activity. The tug of war between the US and the EU re-emerged when the so-called Basel IV accord was negotiated, but this accord is not discussed in this chapter because it did not have major implications for the regulation of shadow banking.

Regulators often disagreed along jurisdictional lines—oversimplifying, the US, and the UK versus continental Europe—for most parts of the Basel III package, with the main exception of securitization. On this matter, British and Continental regulators, especially, the Bank of England and the ECB, were on the same page, keen to revive securitization from 2014 onwards. Epistemic disagreements and turf fighting among sectoral regulators did not come to the fore because regulatory agencies other than banking regulators gathered in the BCBS were not directly involved in the international governance of banking. Unlike for shadow banking entities and activities, where regulators, at times, could not even agree on whether certain entities and activities were part of the shadow banking system or the risk they posed for financial stability, there was shared professional knowledge and consolidated experience in international cooperation among banking regulators. Yet, negotiations were at times difficult, in particular on new topics, such as securitization and step in risk, which involved both banking and securities market regulators.

The financial industry pushed back against more rigorous international standards on bank capital and liquidity as well as new banking rules, notably, those on step-in risk. The industry used the well-rehearsed narrative that tighter rules for banks would harm the real economy and, therefore, formed a broader coalition with firms in the real economy. This strategy worked better in Europe, where banks did provide considerable funding to non-financial companies, rather than in the US, where many non-financial companies funded themselves in the capital market. At any rate, the financial industry also argued that it was necessary to consider the compounded effects of the various elements of Basel III, including the leverage and liquidity ratios, the revision of the securitization framework, and the trading book review. Private financial actors mobilized at multiple levels and in several regulatory venues: the national level, notably, in Germany and France; the regional level in the EU; and the international level, that is to say, vis à vis the BCBS as well as the IOSCO (for securitization), seeking to exploit divisions among banking regulators across jurisdictions, as well as between banking and securities market regulators.

9

Overall Comparative Assessment

The previous chapters have examined the politics and political economy of international standard-setting concerning shadow banking entities and activities. This penultimate chapter carries out an overall comparison across the elemental regimes that are part of the international shadow banking complex. It then discusses the preferences of the main actors that engage in the game of shadows concerning the definition, measurement, monitoring, and regulation of shadow banking, explaining how their pathways of influence are affected by regime complexity. Finally, this chapter spells out the perils of regime complexity and puts forward some policy recommendations in this respect.

Comparing Elemental Regimes in the Shadow Banking Complex

The post-crisis international regime complex on shadow banking was composed of parallel, nested, and interlinked elemental regimes on a variety of shadow banking entities and activities. The international standards issued as part of these regimes had limited precision, stringency, and consistency, even though there was considerable variation across sets of rules. The *elemental regime for monitoring global shadow banking*, which also encompassed definition, measurement, and data collection, became more detailed over time. However, it did not become more rigorous because the measurement of shadow banking was narrowed down and its definition was eventually changed, acquiring more market-friendly connotations. Indeed, China and other emerging economies first, and the US, the UK, and the EU later, took a somewhat 'revisionist' approach. Moreover, this regime was about monitoring risks, rather than reducing them via regulation. The monitoring efforts were led by the FSB, in collaboration with the BIS and the IMF, especially for data standardization and collection.

The Perils of International Regime Complexity in Shadow Banking. Lucia Quaglia, Oxford University Press.
 DOI: 10.1093/oso/9780192866523.003.0009

The *elemental regime on shadow banking entities*—MMFs, hedge funds, and other investment funds—had limited precision, stringency, and consistency. The FSB and the IOSCO were unable to agree on a methodology to identify G-SIFIs, creating some inconsistency with what had been done for globally systematically important banks and insurers (there is regulatory consistency if various sets of rules are compatible, and work together towards the same purpose, see Quaglia and Spendzharova 2019, 2021b). On the one hand, it is true that shadow banking entities encompassed a variety of different funds: MMFs, hedge funds, and collective investment funds (active and passive, such as mutual funds and exchange-traded funds). On the other hand, these funds represent a very large segment of the financial sector. Some G-SIFIs are bigger than globally systemically important banks. Yet, robust international standards for investment funds were not sponsored by the main jurisdictions, whereas international rules on MMFs were opposed by China, and those on hedge funds were opposed by the US and the UK.

Moreover, there was considerable epistemic and bureaucratic disagreement among sectoral regulators. Specifically, prudential regulators worried about the financial stability risks posed by investment funds and asset management, whereas securities market regulators, which were the direct regulators of these funds, worried less about systemic risks and prioritized investor protection. There was not even a consensus among regulators as to whether investment funds and asset management should be considered as part of the shadow banking system. These divisions were skillfully exploited by the fund industry that engaged in lobbying cum venue shopping, opposing regulation that would be costly for funds and their customers. Private financial actors also took an issue with the inclusion of asset management under the broad umbrella of shadow banking, or 'non-bank finance', arguing instead that it should be called 'market-based finance' (e.g. Blackrock 2018).

The *elemental regime on securities financing transactions* was relatively precise—for instance, the international rules on haircuts were based on quantitative formulae—but had limited stringency and consistency because a large part of the repo market was eventually excluded from the scope of the FSB's rules, whose content was watered down during the standard-setting process. Moreover, the internationally agreed deadline for the domestic implementation of these standards was postponed several times. International standards for securities financing were half-heartedly sponsored by the US and the EU (including the UK), which disagreed on consequential matters and were internally divided. In fact, there were epistemic and bureaucratic tensions concerning the regulation of the repo market among (macro and micro) prudential regulators, securities market regulators, central bankers, and finance ministry officials. These public authorities looked at the repo market from different perspectives and had different priorities, which were strategically exploited by private financial actors. The financial industry opposed the trading up of rules on securities financing by forging an ad-hoc alliance with central banks and finance ministries, which depended on the repo markets for the conduct of monetary policy and the management of the public debt, respectively. Thus, the governance of the elemental regimes of securities financing and securitization (discussed next) brought to the fore the infrastructural power of finance (Braun 2020; Braun and Gabor 2020; Gabor 2016a, 2020).

The *elemental regime on securitization* had limited precision, stringency, and consistency. Initially, international rules for securitization, as such, remained very thin, whereas bank capital requirements for securitized products were tightened up by the BCBS—these two sets of standards were interlinked (meaning that rules in a given elemental regime had direct implications for those in other regimes, Quaglia 2020). Afterward, rather loose criteria for safe securitization were issued by the BCBS-IOSCO, whereas international bank capital standards for this activity were lowered by the BCBS. The US sponsored higher capital requirements on securitization in the wake of the 2008 crisis. However, a few years after the crisis, the EU and the UK sought to revamp securitization via regulation, notably, by promoting international standards for safe securitization as well as by lowering capital for bank exposures to this activity.

Regulators across jurisdictions had somewhat different views concerning the governance of securitization, an explanation that is in line with a state-centric account. Notably, central bankers in Europe were eager to revive this market a few years after the crisis, less so central bankers in the US. Moreover, central bankers, banking regulators, and securities market regulators looked at securitization from different angles, even though this did not result in open confrontation. Securitization had implications for monetary policy, especially its transmission channel, hence it was of concern for central banks. It also affected banks, which were the main originators and traders of securitized products, and, therefore, it impinged upon the stability of banks and the banking system, which are within the remit of banking regulators. Finally, securities regulators were primarily responsible for setting the rules for securitization. The financial industry opposed strict rules for securitization and bank exposures to securitization, forged an ad hoc coalition with non-financial actors (Montalbano 2020) and (European) central bankers (Braun 2020; Braun and

Gabor 2020; Gabor 2016a), and supported the attempt to revitalize this market by the EU and the UK (Quaglia 2021).

Unlike the regimes on shadow banking entities and activities discussed above, the *elemental regime on bank exposures to shadow banking* had considerable precision and stringency, even though the latter was partly traded down over time, producing some inconsistency across banking regulation. Specifically, bank capital and liquidity rules that build on previous reiterations of the Basel accords were tightened up, but capital rules for safe securitization were subsequently watered down. Banking regulators gathered in the BCBS, prompted by US and UK regulators, were able to resist (in part) lobbying from the financial industry. By contrast, the financial industry was relatively more successful in opposing new rules on bank step-in risk and bank investment in funds, on which there was no agreement among regulators.

In the shadow banking complex, the elemental regime on global shadow banking monitoring, which measured the size of this part of the financial sector, was interlinked with the elemental regimes of shadow banking entities and activities, which, in turn, were parallel to one another. The elemental regimes on securities lending and securitization, which were activities undertaken also by banks, were interlinked with the elemental regime on bank exposures to shadow banking, which in turn, was nested into the broader regime on bank capital and liquidity regulation. More generally, the regulation of shadow banking had implications for banks, which engaged in shadow banking activities and interacted with shadow banking entities. At the same time, banking regulation had implications for shadow banking activities and entities, which was also referred to as the 'indirect regulation' of shadow banking. Hence, inconsistency between these two regimes could encourage regulatory arbitrage away from the banking sector.

The international governance of shadow banking failed to restrain the growth of this part of the financial sector after the international financial crisis of 2008. In 2019, the broad measure of global shadow banking had more than doubled from the pre-crisis period and the narrow measure of shadow banking had also increased, albeit not to the same extent (FSB 2020a). In the same period (2007–2019), across the five economic functions used to identify and measure global shadow banking (see Chapter 4), the first economic function that related to investment funds and asset management almost tripled. The second economic function that involved loan provisions dependent on short-term funding (primarily, finance companies) surpassed the pre-crisis level and the fifth economic function, related to securitization, almost reached the pre-crisis level in 2019. Moreover, as explained above, several shadow banking entities and activities were not subject to more rigorous international standards. Thus, several risks connected to the shadow banking system remained undetected and unaddressed, posing a potential threat to financial stability, as elaborated in the concluding chapter.

To be fair, initially, in the wake of the 2008 crisis, international standard-setters, as well as domestic regulators, worked in the shadows themselves—trying to piece together disparate and incomplete data to see what systemic risks were associated with the various entities and activities that comprised the shadow banking system (Kodres 2017). Yet, international standards on various aspects of shadow banking did not become more robust over time, nor did they tackle controversial issues that had initially been side-stepped. Moreover, there was not really a process of 'learning by doing' because several rules on shadow banking, for example, on securitization, were watered down over time and major regulatory gaps remained. For instance, there are no international standards to identify non-bank non-insurer G-SIFIs, unlike in the banking and insurance sectors.

Three sets of actors—states, regulators, and the financial industry—affected the game of shadow concerning the definition, measurement, and regulation of global shadow banking after the 2008 crisis. Whereas these actors were at play in each shadow banking elemental regime, their influence on the policy output varied across regimes (see Table 9.1). Thus, interstate competition and, notably, foot-dragging by recalcitrant states, was the main hindrance to tightening up regulation whenever specific shadow banking entities—such as MMFs and hedge funds—were mainly located in few jurisdictions, which were, therefore, eager to defend the competitiveness of that specific sector. In these instances, private financial actors were able to forge an alliance with their

Table 9.1 Main hindrances in international governance of shadow banking across elemental regimes

Main hindrance	Elemental regimes
States	Defining, measuring, and monitoring shadow banking
	MMFs and Hedge funds
	Bank capital and liquidity rules
Regulators	Investment funds and asset management
	Repos
Financial industry	Securitization
	Securities financing

respective national regulators. Puzzling and turf fighting among technocrats were the main hindrances to the tightening up of regulation whenever a variety of public authorities were involved and the new rules directly impinged upon their mandates, competences and regulatory outlooks, as in the case of investment funds, or the conduct of their policies, as in the case of repo for monetary policy and public debt management. In these instances, the financial industry sided with the most sympathetic regulators. The push back from the financial industry was the main hindrance to tightening up regulation whenever the industry had infrastructural power, meaning that the public authorities operated through the markets—as in the case of securitization and securities financing—and/or private financial actors were able to exploit divisions among sectoral regulators, as in the case of asset management. Let us elaborate on these points in more detail, also spelling out how regime complexity affected the ways in which various actors influenced the outcomes at the international level.

States: Pace-setting and Foot-dragging

The main jurisdictions, namely, the US, the EU, and, on some matters, China, influenced international shadow banking governance through pace-setting and foot-dragging in the regime complex, even though their preferences and influence varied across cases. States were at the same time pacesetters, foot-draggers (or neither, hence, they were 'fencesitters') across elemental regimes, which weakened their overall influence in the regime complex. Moreover, jurisdictions were not unitary actors and were often unable to coordinate effectively at the domestic level (among a variety of semi-independent regulatory agencies) as well as across elemental regimes at the international level (for instance, among international standard-setting bodies).

The US acted as a disjointed and half-hearted pacesetter in the shadow banking regime complex, promoting certain post-crisis regulatory reforms, while opposing others. On the one hand, since the US had a large shadow banking system, this jurisdiction had an incentive to limit the systemic risks of this part of the financial system by establishing a sound post-crisis regulatory framework domestically and internationally. On the other hand, the US was reluctant to promote substantially stricter rules on shadow banking, which would have implied major adjustment costs for its domestic financial industry. Moreover, the potential negative externalities of certain shadow banking entities and activities, notably, MMFs, hedge funds and securitization, were limited for the US. If anything, negative externalities went the other way round, as suggested by the spreading of the 2008 international financial crisis, which originated from the securitization of sub-prime mortgages in the US, and then hit the UK and the rest of Europe, which were also heavily affected by the problems experienced by US MMFs and hedge funds. For all these reasons, the US opposed international rules on hedge funds, and did not sponsor rules on MMFs, other investment funds, and securitization. Yet, the trading up of bank capital and liquidity requirements was pursued by the US authorities at the international level to preserve the levelled playing field and prevent negative externalities deriving from loosely regulated foreign banks.

Domestically, US sectoral regulators had different views on several shadow banking issues. Indeed, the SEC was rather slow and timid in issuing new rules on MMFs, hedge funds, and investment funds, including non-bank non-insurer systemically important financial institutions, as auspicated, instead, by the FSOC, the Treasury and the Federal Reserve. The Federal Reserve, together with market actors, undertook a major reform of the domestic tri-party repo market, but the methodologies and haircuts for repo transactions were pursued at the international level because these rules had major competitive implications. Yet, the US Treasury worried about the potential negative side-effects of haircuts on repos for the management of the public debt. Finally, domestic rules on securitization and capital rules on bank exposure to shadow banking were traded up, respectively, by the SEC and US prudential banking regulators. Among regulators, the Federal Reserve was the one that worried the most about shadow banking and in fact, it sponsored considerable research on this matter (Thiemann, Birk, Friedrich2018). According to Daniel Tarullo (2013) at the Federal Reserve

> First, we need to increase the transparency of shadow banking markets so that authorities can monitor for signs of excessive leverage and unstable maturity transformation outside regulated banks.... gaps still exist. For example, many repurchase agreements and securities lending transactions can still only be monitored indirectly. Improved reporting in these areas would better enable regulators to detect emerging risks in the financial system. Second, we need to reduce further the risk of runs on money market mutual funds ... Third, a major source of unaddressed risk emanates from the large volume of short-term securities financing transactions in our financial system, including repos, reverse repos, securities borrowing, and lending transactions.

The EU had different preferences across the international shadow banking regime complex, acting as a timid pacesetter in certain elemental regimes (e.g. hedge funds and MMFs), a partial footdragger in others (e.g. bank capital requirements), or neither (e.g. asset management). Moreover, the EU was internally divided concerning the regulation of certain shadow banking entities (notably, hedge funds and MMFs), which weakened the EU's influence internationally. Indeed, these types of funds were concentrated in the UK, Luxembourg and Ireland, which strenuously opposed new EU and international rules. After heated intra-EU debates, the EU issued rather stringent legislation on hedge funds in 2011 and MMFs in 2017—it was the first time these entities were regulated at the EU level. Other investment funds and the asset management industry were already tightly regulated in the EU, even though, from the point of view of investor protection, rather than macroprudential risks. New EU legislation was also issued on shadow banking activities, such as the Securities Financing Transactions Regulation in 2015 and the Regulation on Securitisation in 2017. Yet, the EU rules on securities financing concerned only data reporting and disclosure, whereas the EU rules on securitization and related bank capital requirements were traded down over time. Initially, the EU was also partly non-compliant with international bank capital rules, the Basel III accord (Quaglia 2019).

The EU's zeal in regulating shadow banking was mitigated by the fact that the EU had a large shadow banking system, which increased considerably after the 2008 crisis. Consequently, the stricter regulation of shadow banking implied adjustment costs for this industry in the EU. Furthermore, when the post-crisis economic recession kicked in and was followed by the sovereign debt crisis in the euro area, shadow banking—reframed as market-based banking—was seen as a way to provide funding to the real economy and foster economic recovery in Europe. Hence, the EU toned down its rules on securitization, to be precise, the regulation of simple and transparent securitization, and successfully sought to trade down these rules also at the international level (Quaglia 2021). The revamp of securitization in the EU was also an attempt by the EU to follow the US model for the development of financial markets, as part of the broader project of Capital Markets Union.

Besides ambivalent pacesetters, there were also footdraggers, notably, certain emerging countries, which believed that the international regulatory framework developed post-crisis was mainly suitable for advanced countries and that a 'wait-and-see approach' was advisable for countries where shadow banking was evolving rapidly (Liansheng 2015). Thus, initially, China was a fencesitter because it was a newcomer in key international financial regulatory bodies, notably, the FSB and the BCBS, and, therefore, it did not actively engage in the international policy debate. Then, China became a footdragger, criticizing the FSB's definitions of shadow banking and refusing to fully participate in the global monitoring exercise between 2012 and 2017 (Gruin and Knaack 2020). It was difficult for China to agree on the regulation concerning non-bank credit entities and activities because trust companies and securities brokerages in China were quite different from those of advanced economies. China was also a footdragger concerning the international regulation of MMFs. As Liansheng (2015) notes, China was unable or unwilling to accept international standards that required domestic reforms for which it was not yet ready (see also, Foot and Walter 2011).

From 2017 onwards, China abandoned its foot-dragging at the international level because of shifting domestic priorities, that is to say, policy failures in the shadow banking system due to regulatory arbitrage and capture, favoured by an outdated regulatory system. Following a master plan from Politburo's study group on national financial security, all financial agencies coordinated their regulations more closely and a wave of regulatory reforms ensued from 2017 onwards (Gruin and Knaack 2020). The new Financial Stability and Development Committee set up under the State Council was housed at the People's Bank of China, which expanded its macroprudential assessment framework to shadow banking and online lending. The China Securities Regulatory Commission imposed tighter requirements on MMFs that could be listed as systemically important, as later confirmed by the People's Bank of China. There was a regulatory crackdown on wealth management products, whereby the People's Bank of China, the China Securities Regulatory Commission, the China Banking and Insurance Regulatory Commission and the State Administration of Foreign Exchange published rules on the asset management industry (Gruin and Knaack 2020). This regulatory crackdown affected China's asset management industry: its growth slowed from 35.6% in 2016 to 3.5% in 2017 (*China Daily*, 1 January 2018). Yet, the trend picked up again and China's banking-asset-management sector alone is projected to exceed $5 trillion by 2021, while the total asset management sector, which also includes insurers and trust companies, will surpass $22 trillion by 2021.[1]

Regulators: puzzling and turf fighting

Puzzling and turf fighting among technocrats was detrimental to the governance of the shadow banking regime complex, which involved different public

[1] https://www.mckinsey.com/featured-insights/china/chinas-70-billion-opportunity-an-interview-with-cheng-hye-cheah

authorities that were often unable to coordinate effectively and offered multiple access points to private financial actors. Puzzling concerned problem definition and problem-solving and, indeed, the very definition of shadow banking was controversial and shifted over time in the international debate. This was not simply a semantic exercise, but, rather, it implied the framing and reframing of what shadow banking was and the risks it entailed (Engelen 2018; Gabor 2018). After the 2008 crisis, there was a collective puzzling on shadow banking by financial regulators. For instance, Paul Tucker (2010) pointed out the need to think through what really comprised shadow banking, and how to regulate its different manifestations by 'avoiding seeing shadow banking everywhere and in all capital market innovations'.

The challenge was to maximize the benefits of shadow banking for the economy, while minimizing systemic risks (Tucker 2010). Similarly, Tarullo (2016a) stressed the need to 'disaggregate all the activities that might be characterized as shadow banking in order to regulate those that pose risks to the financial system, while not unduly burdening forms of credit extension that help to meet the savings and investment needs of households and businesses.' The complication was that shadow banking came in different shades in different jurisdictions. Thus, activities that in one context were called shadow banking, in other contexts were called market-based financing. Moreover, shadow banking evolved over time. Tarullo (2016a) drew attention to 'the constantly changing, and largely unrelated, set of intermediation activities pursued by very different types of financial market actors… Indeed, the very rigor of new regulations applicable to firms within the prudential perimeter may well incentivize more innovation outside that perimeter'.

Epistemic disagreement among regulators involved fundamental issues, such as the definition and measurement of shadow banking—the very term shadow banking was contentious and there was no agreement about which entities and activities were part of the shadow banking system. In contrast to shadow banking, in other financial sectors, such as banking and insurance, there was a well-established body of technical knowledge that provided some common ground to regulators as well as the availability of relevant data, which contributed to evidence-based regulation. Thus, banking and insurance regulators negotiating in their respective international standard-setting bodies were often able to find workable compromises. Unlike in the case of banking and insurance, where only one set of sectoral regulators was involved and a silos-like model of governance prevailed, in shadow banking a variety of public authorities were involved in different ways, which complicated the quest for common ground among technocrats.

The puzzling on shadow banking was due to two reasons. First, it was a relatively new financial phenomenon and, hence, there was limited technical knowledge on this matter as well as a scarcity of relevant data because this part of the financial system had remained in the shadows. Several interviewees pointed out the need for more and better data. After 2008, more data were generated, but sometimes they were of bad quality, unlike for instance, in banking and insurance, and, on certain matters, such as asset management, data availability remained limited, which was a concern especially for 'data-driven' prudential regulators. As one interviewee (see James and Quaglia 2022) noted 'central bankers and banking regulators want numbers, but they don't have access to the relevant numbers in asset management. That leaves them frustrated and they tend to fall back on speculation and hypothetical scenarios about potential risk.'

Second, a variety of regulators—(macro and micro) prudential regulators, securities market regulators and central banks—are involved in shadow banking governance, but they have different remits, powers and epistemic views. Macroprudential regulators have the objectives to protect financial stability and reduce systemic risk. To this end, they engage in macroeconomic analyses, paying attention to the economic cycle, and focus at the systemic level. The main macroprudential instruments are system-wide capital and liquidity requirements, such as counter cyclical capital buffers and sectoral capital requirements. Microprudential (banking) regulators have the objectives to protect the soundness of individual banks as well as the resilience of the entire banking system. To this end, they use entity-based prudential instruments, notably capital and liquidity requirements, and conduct in-depth analyses of bank balance sheets.

Securities regulators have the objectives to protect investors as well as market transparency and integrity. Their instruments, which focus on transactions and markets, include rules of conduct, information disclosure, financial reporting and benchmarks. Securities regulators monitor market conduct, investor treatment, and engage in litigation, as well as back and forth discussions with the supervisees. Central bankers are responsible for the conduct of monetary policy, but often have also macroprudential responsibilities. Central bankers and prudential regulators tend to have training in economics, whereas securities markets regulators tend to have legal training and/or are financial professionals. It is not just a matter of formal qualification (economists vs lawyers), but also mindsets. As one interviewee noted, 'prudential regulators and securities regulators do not speak the same language, they have not found common ground or a common taxonomy' (interviews, see James and Quaglia 2022).

After the crisis, central bankers started to develop a macroprudential outlook, also because of their mandate to safeguard system-wide financial stability, and, therefore, began to pay considerable attention to the financial stability risks posed by shadow banking (Woyames Dreher 2019). Central bankers were eager to extend some forms of prudential regulation to shadow banking entities and activities. As explained by Daniel Tarullo (2016b) in an instructive speech entitled 'Pedagogy and scholarship in a post-crisis world', the post-crisis approach that was chosen to regulate shadow banking examined significant forms of credit intermediation outside the banking system to determine whether some type of prudential regulation was needed.[2] However, this bank-like approach for shadow banking was not shared by securities market regulators, whose mandate mainly concerned market functioning and investor protection, rather than system-wide financial stability. For instance, prudential regulators wanted to extend bank-like regulation to investment funds, whereas there was a consensus among securities regulators that investment funds should not be regulated like banks.

Part of the problem was that sectoral regulators looked at shadow banking entities and activities through the prisms of their regulatory outlooks and worried about the aspects of shadow banking that directly affected their mandate and policies. For instance, with reference to investment funds, 'prudential regulators see big firms that can pose systemic risks and quote a long list of non-banking numbers, by contrast, securities regulators see thousands of discreet funds, which are not interconnected, have no leverage or arbitrage and which are ringfenced'. 'Prudential regulators, especially central bankers, worry about the systemic implications of falling prices in asset management, whereas securities regulators consider this a matter of transparency and equal treatment of customers, basically, investor protection, not systemic financial stability.' 'For prudential regulators, the answer to everything is capital, but this lever does not work, for instance, for asset management because asset managers do not have capital. Thus, the tools used for banks, notably capital, are not effective for asset management' (interviews, see James and Quaglia 2022). The regulation of the repo market also brought to the fore the different epistemic

[2] For instance, 'regulators look at a particular form, such as MMFs. If no significant risks to financial stability are identified, or if some regulation to counteract those risks is implemented, the form of intermediation may then be thought of as relatively safe (at least from a systemic perspective) market-based finance' (Tarullo 2016b).

views and policy priorities of financial regulators, central banks, and finance ministries, as explained in Chapter 7.

Epistemic puzzling among technocrats intersected with bureaucratic turf fighting among sectoral regulatory agencies. Prudential regulators were eager to regulate and supervise shadow banking entities and activities outside their purview, which, in turn, caused bureaucratic clashes with securities markets regulators, which were the direct regulators for several shadow banking entities (i.e. MMFs, hedge funds, and collective investment funds) and activities (asset management, securities financing, and securitization). As one securities market regulator put it, 'prudential regulators have their tanks on the lawn of securities regulators and the squabbling is still going on. Some of it is about territory.' The protection of financial stability was principally within the mandate of central banks, which were generally responsible for macroprudential regulation, although that varied across jurisdictions. At the same time, banking regulators (within or without the central banks) were involved in the regulatory process both directly, due to bank exposures to shadow banking, and indirectly, due to the interconnections between banks and shadow banking. Hence, as Paul Tucker (2010) noted 'banking supervisors cannot sleep safely solely on the basis of their own work' and, therefore, the goal was to make the core banking system safe, avoiding the problems of the past replicating themselves beyond the perimeter of the regulated banking sector (i.e. in the shadow banking system).

At the international level, the FSB, where central banks and prudential regulators considerably outnumber securities market regulators, pointed out the risks posed by asset management and the need to identify (and, eventually, regulate more strictly) globally systemic non-bank non-insurer financial institutions. However, this approach was not shared by securities market regulators in the IOSCO, which resisted the application of a prudential mindset and bank-like tools to investment funds. At the domestic level, epistemic disagreements coupled with bureaucratic turf fights came to the fore in the US, which has a very fragmented institutional architecture for financial regulation and supervision. This fragmentation also meant that a more comprehensive and radical approach to the post-crisis regulation of shadow banking was not adopted. As Tarullo (2016a) remarked, an alternative approach could have been to adopt a 'broad definition of shadow banking', with 'specified regulatory consequences that ensued more or less automatically'. Yet, it was not clear that the authority existed to take this approach, either by an individual regulatory agency or even collectively (Tarullo 2016a).

The Federal Reserve, which had considerable expertise and resources, sought (with mixed success) to take the lead, but on specific issues, such as MMFs and investment funds, the SEC was the relevant regulatory agency. As critically argued by the SEC Commissioner Michael Piwowar (2016a), the 'SEC's tripartite mission is to protect investors, maintain fair, orderly, and efficient markets, and facilitate capital formation… The fact-based approach of the SEC on the regulation of the securities market does not fit the so-called "shadow banking" view of jurisdictional grabbing prudential regulators.' One senior regulator noted 'micro and macroprudential regulation in the US are not well coordinated and there was a disagreement between the SEC and the Federal Reserve. The FSOC was greatly weakened by bad relations between US agencies… Checks and balances are not "games of gentlemen", they are designed to keep you in check.' Domestic disagreement and bureaucratic turf fight at times spilled over to the international level because the SEC is a heavyweight in the IOSCO and the Federal Reserve in the FSB. For instance, 'the FSB was thinking in US terms when moving forward the discussion on G-SIFIs. The IOSCO, which was dominated by thinking of the SEC, completely opposed this idea. Hence, the tug of war IOSCO-FSB was an extension to Madrid and Basel of the discussion (tug of war) in Washington' (interviews, see James and Quaglia 2022).

In the EU, the ECB, the ESMA, and the ESRB did not always sing from the same script (Endrejat and Thiemann 2020; Thiemann, Birk, and Friedrich 2018), although in the EU the disagreements among sectoral regulators were underplayed, mainly due to the institutional weakness of ESMA and the ESRB vis-à-vis the ECB-centric Single Supervisory Mechanism. Moreover, the multi-level architecture for financial governance in the EU made national supervisors more vulnerable to pressure from 'their' financial industry, opting for lenient approaches that would not disadvantage domestic firms in the international competition (Vestergaard and Quorning 2019; Thiemann 2018). In the UK, which had a less fragmented architecture for financial regulation and supervision, the powerful Bank of England was in the driving sea. This domestic institutional set up reduced open disputes with other regulatory agencies, even though the Bank, occasionally, disagreed with the Financial Conduct Authority.

It is noteworthy that epistemic disagreements coupled with bureaucratic turf fights also occurred in China, making international cooperation on this matter more difficult. After the financial crisis, the Chinese Central Bank (the People's Bank of China) paid greater attention to financial stability and tried to build up a macroprudential policy framework, generating the potential for conflict with other domestic financial regulators, such as the China Banking Regulatory Commission and the China Securities Regulatory Commission. These regulators were able to agree on general principles, but not on specific policy recommendations and tools (Gruin and Knaack 2020). To improve the co-ordination amongst the domestic authorities and pursue the tightening up of shadow banking regulation, the Financial Stability and Development Committee was established in 2017 at the People's Bank of China, which expanded its macroprudential assessment framework to shadow banking and online lending. In turn, this improved the interactions of Chinese authorities with their counterparts at the international level, notably in the FSB (Gruin and Knaack 2020).

Private Financial Actors: Lobbying cum Venue Shopping

The financial industry affected international shadow banking governance by lobbying at multiple governance levels and in several policy venues as well as by forging coalitions with financial and non-financial actors and the public authorities. The shadow banking regime complex provided a multiplicity of access points and opportunities for vertical and horizontal venue shopping, magnifying the influence of private financial actors. On the one hand, as one policy stakeholder noted, the shadow banking system is very variegated, even 'investment funds are very different among themselves and have dissimilar investment strategies. This confronts regulators with different risks. Lobbying is also different. For instance, small funds do not go and talk to regulators, mainly the big funds do so. But the smaller funds tend to be represented by the trade associations.' On the other hand, as one regulator noted 'When several players in the financial industry go to regulators to explain that there is not a problem with something, it is the cartesian proof that the problem exists because lobbying is very costly' (interviews, see James and Quaglia 2022).

The leitmotiv articulated by various parts of the financial industry was that *they* were not part of the shadow banking system. Thus, according to the narrative articulated by private financial actors, shadow banking was 'somewhere else' (see Palan and Nesvetailova 2014), or 'somewhat else'.[3] The private financial actors that were unable to make the case to be excluded from the scope of shadow banking, for instance, hedge funds, argued that they had already

[3] In their article 'Elsewhere, Ideally Nowhere: Shadow Banking and Offshore Finance', Palan and Nesvetailova (2014) used the concept of 'elsewhere' and 'nowhere', which are well established in the study of off shore finance in international political economy, with reference to shadow banking.

been subject to more stringent post-crisis rules, or that they posed no systemic risk. Similarly, banks that interacted with shadow banks resisted more stringent rules, arguing that banking regulation had already been tightened up after the crisis.

Furthermore, banks, investment funds, and other financial actors exploited knowledge gaps and limited data availability to warn about the unintended or unexpected effects of new rules, overplaying the concerns of the public authorities. Hence, the financial industry argued that more precise and stringent rules on repos would impinge upon the ability to refinance public debts on the markets, which was a priority for finance ministry officials; the transmission mechanism of monetary policy, which was a priority for central banks. Likewise, securitization was presented by the financial industry as an additional source of funding for non-financial firms. Yet, repos and securitization were also clear instances of the infrastructural power of the financial industry and its entanglement with key policy areas (monetary and fiscal policies) which were the competence of central banks and finance ministries, respectively.

Various types of financial actors deployed strategic narratives to fend off regulation. To begin with, banks pushed back against precise and stringent regulation of securitization, repos, and bank exposures to shadow banking. Banks argued that banking regulation had been traded up considerably after the 2008 crisis, hence, higher capital and liquidity requirements for bank exposures to shadow banking were unwarranted and would have detrimental cumulative effects. Moreover, more precise and stringent rules for banks would encourage regulatory arbitrage outside the traditional banking sector and would restrict lending to the real economy. Investment funds, especially, collective funds, argued that asset management was not part of shadow banking and was different from traditional banking. On these grounds, investment funds opposed regulatory constraints on the leverage and liquidity of asset management. The large funds also put up a fight whenever regulators sought to devise methodologies to identify G-SIFIs. Thus, the big transnational players lobbied securities market regulators at the domestic level (e.g. the SEC) and the international level (e.g. the IOSCO) to be excluded from the definition of non-bank non-insurance systemically important financial institutions, which could have subjected them to additional regulation and supervision.

Private financial actors engaged extensively in venue shopping in the shadow banking regime complex. For example, investment funds tended to 'cling on' securities market regulators. This was because these regulators were seen as having a better understanding of the industry they supervised and were likely to be sympathetic to the concerns of that industry. At the same time, securities regulators saw as part of their remit to explain to prudential regulators how asset management works. As one senior securities market regulator quipped 'if you put a fund manager in front of a prudential regulator, that is not very helpful'. In turn, a prudential regulator argued that 'the question is whether large funds lobby regulators, or whether the regulators are the lobbyists for the public good', noting that the shadow banking sector is very different from banking. 'Banks tend to be tied to sovereigns, whereas, for instance, investment funds, are more global: they are often registered in the Cayman Islands, but investing everywhere. So the politics are very different.... Many banks and governments depend on central banks, Blackrock and other large funds do not. They are more liquid and solvent than many governments. They are free to make investment choices without the constraints that exist for parliaments. Large investment funds have the financial instruments to de facto define economically what is going on' (interviews, see James and Quaglia 2022).

The Perils of International Regime Complexity in Shadow Banking

On the one hand, interstate conflicts, disagreements among technocrats, and the power of the financial industry are endemic in the regulation of global finance. On the other hand, compared to other financial sectors, the reform of post-crisis governance of shadow banking is underwhelming. The main reason for this outcome is regime complexity, which generates a multi-dimensional chessboard in which various actors play, compounding problems, while splintering solutions. In a regime complex, the conflicts discussed above and which characterize the governance of global finance, pile up. Thus, jurisdictions pursue different preferences and compete with each other; sectoral regulators disagree on consequential matters involving competences and regulatory outlooks; and the financial industry resists regulation by engaging in venue-shopping and coalition-building. At the same time, the resolution of these conflicts is made more difficult by the fragmentation of regulatory authority across elemental regimes, meaning that no actor is in the driving seat, several of them work at cross purposes and have quasi veto powers, whereas a focal coordinating institution is missing (for an overview, see Table 9.2). Let us elaborated upon these points by comparing policy dynamics in traditional silos-like regimes and regime complexes.

Table 9.2 Actors, pathways, and the perils of regime complexity

Actors	Perils of regime complexity
States *Pace-setting and foot-dragging*	• A state can have multiple roles (pacesetter and footdragger) in the regime complex, sometimes working at cross purposes across elemental regimes • States are not unitary actors: problems in coordinating domestic semi-independent regulatory agencies • Disjointed international leadership in the regime complex
Regulators *Puzzling and turf fighting*	• Multiplicity of sectoral regulators in the regime complex increases puzzling and turf fighting • Different mandates, competences, and regulatory outlooks: problems of coordination among international standard setters • No focal institution in the regime complex
Financial industry *Lobbying cum venue shopping*	• Multiple access points and selective choice of lobbying venues for private actors in the regime complex • Opportunities to forge coalitions with sectoral regulators and other interest groups across elemental regimes • Fragmentation of regulatory authority facilitates divide et impera by industry in the regime complex

In an international *silos-like regime*, the 'hegemon' (Simmons 2001; Helleiner 2014; Oatley 2015), that is, the US, or the 'great powers' (Drezner 2007), that is, the US and the EU, might take the lead in promoting international cooperation, acting as pacesetters, exploiting issue-linkages (or de-linkages) and offering side payments (Oatley and Nabors 1998). For instance, the US and the UK took the lead in promoting post-crisis international standards to resolve ailing banks (Germain 2016; James and Quaglia 2020), whereas other jurisdictions, including the EU (Quaglia 2017a), were first fencesitters and then followers, that is to say, they implemented the relevant international rules at the domestic level. In the case of standards on loss-absorbing capacity for banks, the US and the UK also acted as pacesetters (James and Quaglia 2020), linking the issue of bank capital to the issue of bank resolution. Moreover, they were able to overcome some foot-dragging by China, which was offered some side payments in the form of temporary exemptions for Chinese G-SIBs. The EU and, within it, the UK, successfully promoted embryonic international solvency standards for insurers (Quaglia 2014), despite some foot-dragging by the US, by linking these regulatory measures in the insurance sector to what had already been done in the banking sector.

In an international *regime complex*, it is more difficult for either the hegemon or the great powers to take the lead and steer the regulatory process for three reasons. First, states can be pacesetters in some elemental regimes of the complex and footdraggers in others, weakening their overall influence. In fact, states do not have an incentive to push hard for more robust rules in a given elemental regime, overruling opposition from other states, because they are aware that they will be the ones resisting more robust rules in other elemental regimes of the complex. For instance, the UK advocated international rules on MMFs, but resisted those on hedge funds, whereas the US and the UK called for tighter capital rules for banks, but opposed capital requirements for hedge funds. Second, states would need to spend considerable resources in pursuing their preferences by playing the multi-dimensional game of the complex, coordinating their actions across elemental regimes and reacting to the moves of other relevant players. Third, a variety of domestic semi-autonomous regulatory agencies are involved across elemental regimes, often with limited coordination at the national level, as elaborated below. The scholarly works that point out the ability of states, in particular, the great powers or the hegemon, to promote international cooperation and the effective management of a regime complex tend to assume that states act as unitary actors, with complete information. Whereas not only states can have inconsistent preferences across the regime complex as well as incomplete information, but also domestic regulatory agencies that negotiate in international bodies have distinct regulatory preferences and do not necessarily coordinate with one another.

In an international *silos regime*, financial regulators, for instance, banking and insurance regulators, agree on fundamental epistemic issues, such as the definition of what banks and insurers are, how to measure banking and insurance business, and the main tools to regulate banks and insurers. Despite their shared technical knowledge, and similar sectoral regulatory outlooks and mandates, banking regulators and insurance regulators across jurisdictions, at times, disagree on certain issues, such as the calibration of instruments. Yet, building on their shared professional knowledge, they are often able to reach workable technical compromises. For instance, in setting international standards for banks and insurers, there were disagreements concerning the prescribed level of capital for banks and insurers (e.g. Quaglia 2014a; Singer 2007, 2004), but sectoral regulators gathered in their respective international standards-setting bodies (such as the Basel Committee or the International Association of Insurance Supervisors) were instrumental in hammering out a deal.

In an international *regime complex*, which involves a variety of regulators that have different mandates, competences, and regulatory outlooks, it is more difficult to do so, especially if there is not a focal institution to promote cooperation among technocratic bodies and there are no formal or informal mechanisms for cooperation among international standard setters. To be sure, the FSB attempted to emerge as a focal institution in the shadow banking regime complex, but it had limited success because it had neither the resources nor the mandate to do so, whereas other international bodies, notably, the IOSCO and, to a lesser extent, the BCBS, defended their competences. Moreover, the fragmentation of competences among various international and domestic regulatory bodies makes technocrats more vulnerable to pressure from the financial industry and facilitates venue shopping by private actors.

Third, in a traditional *silos regime*, the financial industry can mobilize at various levels (domestic, regional, and international), but in a limited number of horizontal venues, hence, basically, facing the same regulators (e.g. banking or insurance regulators) and, not infrequently, the same officials (as these are small policy communities). By contrast, in a *regime complex*, the financial industry can engage extensively in vertical and horizontal venue shopping, forging alliances with sympathetic sectoral regulators, public authorities (such as central banks and finance ministries), and other private actors (for instance, firms in the real economy). Hence, compared to a silos regime, a regime complex offers multiple channels of access and lobbying opportunities to the financial industry. For example, investment funds lobbied securities regulators to fend off more stringent rules advocated by prudential regulators. Banks lobbied treasury officials and central bankers to exempt the repo market on sovereign bonds from haircuts, overplaying the potential implications of haircuts for the management of the public debt and the conduct of monetary policy.

Policy Recommendations for Managing Regime Complexity in Shadow Banking

Since international regime complexity has hindered the reform of shadow banking governance after the international financial crisis of 2008, how could the shortcomings spelled out in the previous section be addressed?

The 'first best' solution to the problems at hand would be the creation of a world financial authority with a mandate to write new shadow banking rules. Yet, this proposal would not be feasible in practice for several reasons. First, nowadays, there is little appetite among elected officials and public opinion for the establishment of new international institutions, within and without finance. On the contrary, international institutions have increasingly been criticized by politicians and public opinion in various jurisdictions and this debate has become very politicized (De Vries, Hobolt, and Walter 2021; Zurn 2019). Unlike, for example, in the case of the International Monetary Fund and the World Trade Organization, the political backlash has not directly targeted international financial standard setters so far (Zaring 2020), except for some criticisms of the Basel Committee in the EU and the US (Quaglia 2019; Young 2014). However, at the domestic level, there has been some backlash against central banks and other regulatory agencies in finance (e.g. Tortola 2020). Second, there are already many international standard-setting bodies in finance, generating an overcrowded regulatory space—adding one more standard-setting body would complicate things further. Finally, previous proposals for a world financial authority (e.g. Eatwell and Taylor 2000; Lastra 2014) made very little inroads, as the idea was ostracized not only by elected officials, but also by regulators.

Given these circumstances, the 'second best' option to reform the international governance of shadow banking would be amore pragmatic incrementalist approach by improving the existing international financial architecture, with two important twists. To begin with, the FSB should be given a leading role in steering the work of other international standard-setters on various aspects of shadow banking and, therefore, the competences and resources of the FSB should be enhanced. In fact, the FSB still has a relatively small secretariat and limited budget (Donnelly 2012; Gadinis 2014). Most of its work is carried out by ad hoc working groups that bring together domestic regulators of member jurisdictions, which also chair these groups (Pagliari 2013a). The FSB offers the advantage of including representatives of other international standard setters (such as the BCBS, the IOSCO, the CPMI) as well finance ministry officials, which can put some political weight behind the FSB's effort to define, monitor, and regulate shadow banking.

Secondly, in order to strengthen the international governance of shadow banking, it is necessary to improve the formal and informal mechanisms for cooperation between sectoral regulators at the international level. Some formal mechanisms to enhance cooperation among international standard-setting bodies are the cross-referencing of standards and institutional deference (Pratt

2018); semi-formal mechanisms are joint studies, joint working groups, and co-chairing of these groups; and informal mechanisms are the exchange of information (through phone calls and meetings) as well as the secondment of officials, to develop a better understanding of their respective regulatory outlooks (Quaglia and Spendzharova 2021b).

Thirdly, the main jurisdictions can play an important role in managing regime complexity if they value the collective goods produced by the complex (Gehring and Faude 2014; Johnson and Urperleinen 2012). Yet, to do so, these jurisdictions would need to act as unitary actors, or, at least, they should be able to project coherent views concerning the governance of a regime complex. In finance, unlike in other policy areas where domestic regulatory agencies have limited autonomy, a variety of semi-independent domestic regulatory agencies are involved, often with inadequate domestic coordination. At times, bureaucratic rivalries between sectoral financial regulators at the domestic level get transmitted to the international level and vice versa, impinging upon international standards-setting, as it happened in the US during the policy debate on non-bank non-insurer G-SIFIs and investment funds more generally, or in China concerning the (initially delayed and partial) provision of national data on shadow banking entities and activities to the FSB. Thus, mechanisms to foster cooperation between financial regulatory agencies at the national level are instrumental to improving coordination among international financial standard setters (and vice versa). They are also instrumental to enabling the main jurisdictions to manage regime complexity.

Finally, of particular importance is the alignment of preferences of the great powers and the strategies they deploy across the regime complex (Drezner 2007). For instance, in the case of derivatives, the US, the EU, and, within it, the UK (before Brexit), which have by far the largest derivatives markets in the world, had strong incentives to promote relatively precise, stringent, and consistent international rules on various aspects of derivatives, whereas there was no major opposition from other countries, including raising powers (Quaglia 2020). In the case of shadow banking, the main jurisdictions were much less forthcoming in sponsoring more stringent regulation after the 2008 crisis and they did not see eye to eye on important matters.

To improve the global governance of shadow banking, greater transatlantic and, after Brexit, transchannel cooperation is needed, whereby the US, the UK, and the EU should throw their weights behind the development of a more effective international regime for shadow banking, similar to what they did in the case of derivatives (Quaglia 2020). However, unlike in the case of derivatives, where raising powers, including China, were not crucial players, it would be crucial to have these jurisdictions on board in the case of shadow banking regulation, given the importance of certain forms of shadow banking in China and other emerging economies. Recently, China has become more aware of and sensitive to the risks posed by shadow banking and has tightened up domestic rules. It has also indicated its willingness to be a rule maker rather than a rule-taker in finance.

Conclusion

This penultimate chapter has brought together the main themes discussed in the previous chapters that focused on the individual elemental regimes on shadow banking entities and activities. First, by comparing elemental regimes across the shadow banking complex, it has shown that the post-crisis international standards issued lacked precision, stringency, and consistency, although there was variation across elemental regimes. Second, these empirical patterns have been explained by focusing on the actors that influenced the international governance of shadow banking. Certain actors and the conflicts they generate, such as interstate competition, were more important in certain elemental regimes, notably, the definition and measurement of shadow banking, the regulation of MMFs, hedge funds, and bank capital rules. Other actors and the conflicts they generate, such as disagreement among regulators, were paramount in other elemental regimes, namely, the regulation of investment funds, asset management, and repos. The power of the financial industry was at play in all elemental regimes, but was greater whenever private financial actors were able to form an alliance with sectoral regulators and non-financial firms, as in the cases of securitization and securities financing. Third, the chapter has spelled out the perils of regime complexity, which generates a multi-dimensional game with a variety of players, and what could be done about it to strengthen the international governance of shadow banking.

10

Conclusions

Shadow Banking and Finance

This research began with an empirical puzzle concerning the international governance of shadow banking, which, before the international financial crisis of 2008, was subject to limited public regulation and oversight, notwithstanding the risks that this variegated system entailed. After 2008, the international governance of shadow banking entities and activities was reformed, but, overall, it remained relatively thin, despite the important role of this part of the financial system in the playing out of the crisis, its massive size, cross-border nature, and systemic risk. Whereas pre-crisis international standard-setting in finance took place in a silos-like structure, post-crisis international standards concerning shadow banking entities and activities were issued jointly, or separately, by a variety of international bodies, without a clear hierarchical structure—it was a regime complex.

This book explains the perils of regime complexity, which facilitated the game of shadows played by states, regulators, and private actors concerning the definition, measurement, and regulation of global shadow banking. This chapter first summarizes the main theoretical and empirical findings of the research and then details the book's broader contributions to the field. It also engages with some alternative explanations, discussing their analytical leverage and limitations. Finally, it carries out a policy-relevant assessment of the post-crisis international reforms of shadow banking, highlighting some open issues concerning the governance of shadow banking, also in light of the economic crisis that ensued from the Covid-19 pandemic.

Main Findings of the Research

This research argues that the international governance of shadow banking after the 2008 crisis was a game of shadows that unfolded in three consecutive and reiterated steps concerning the definition, monitoring, and regulation of

The Perils of International Regime Complexity in Shadow Banking. Lucia Quaglia, Oxford University Press.
 DOI: 10.1093/oso/9780192866523.003.0010

shadow banking. The definition of shadow banking influenced its measurement and monitoring. The use of a narrow measure of shadow banking led to the underestimation of the overall size of this system and its various components, which, in turn, affected monitoring, especially, the assessment of the risks posed by shadow banking and the regulatory measures that were deemed to be necessary to deal with these risks. Eventually, the very term shadow banking disappeared in the shadow and was replaced by a more neutral definition—market-based finance, which, in turn, affected its regulation, because market-based finance was seen in a rather positive light. Moreover, the change of terminology contributed to giving the impression that the entities and activities in the shadow banking system were no longer in the shadow, and therefore precise and stringent rules were not needed.

The game of shadows involved states, regulators, and private actors. All these players were eager to define shadow banking in a way that would strategically exclude certain entities and activities. Jurisdictions were keen on excluding from the definition of shadow banking the types of financial entities and activities that were important for their national economy. Similarly, various parts of the financial industry mobilized at the domestic and international levels to be left outside the perimeter of shadow banking. At times, sectoral regulators were also reluctant to include in the definition of shadow banking the financial entities and activities that were under their direct oversight. Whenever new international rules were proposed, they were generally watered down during the standard-setting process. Moreover, the rules issued were not well-coordinated, generating regulatory gaps and inconsistencies. The game of shadow unfolded recursively over time. An emblematic instance of this game was securitization, which was initially considered as one of the main culprits of the crisis, and was, therefore, subject to more stringent bank capital requirements in line with other post-crisis reforms of capital rules for banks. However, after being redefined as 'simple and transparent securitization' (hence, 'safe'), international bank capital rules on securitization were relaxed, producing some inconsistency with other capital rules.

The game of shadow that forms the leitmotiv of this book was facilitated by international regime complexity, which generated a multi-dimensional chessboard in which there was no steering authority, several players worked at cross purposes and there was no focal institution to coordinate the reform efforts at the international level. In certain elemental regimes, such as the definition, measurement, and monitoring of global shadow banking and the governance of MMFs and hedge funds, the main hindrance to stringent regulation was interstate competition. In other elemental regimes, such as asset management and repos, the main hindrance to stringent regulation was disagreement among financial regulatory agencies, central banks, and finance ministries. In other elemental regimes, notably, securitization and securities financing, the pushback came from the financial industry, which deployed its infrastructural power. Furthermore, the financial industry was able to engage in venue shopping not only across jurisdictions and governance levels, but also horizontally, pitting sectoral regulators against one another and forging coalitions with actors in the real economy.

Alternative Explanations

It is also insightful to discuss the analytical leverage of alternative explanations for the outcome of interest, namely, the week international governance of shadow banking after the 2008 global financial crisis. The main alternative explanations can be grouped into two main camps: those that centre only on *one* of the three approaches used in this book—namely, inter-state competition, transgovernmental networks, and financial industry power—and other mainstream approaches that have been used in the literature to explain the politics of regulating global finance and global markets more generally, namely: US 'hegemony' and the 'new interdependence'; the 'rational design' of international institutions and 'experimentalist governance'; and domestic politics and 'political salience'.

To begin with, as elaborated in the previous chapter, a *state-centric* approach accounts for the weak regulation of certain shadow banking elemental regimes—such as MMFs, hedge funds, bank capital, and liquidity—where conflicts among states were strong. Yet, this approach does not have much explanatory power with reference to other shadow banking elemental regimes—such as investment funds, repos, securities lending, and securitization—where interstate competition was limited. The *transgovernmental* approach accounts for the weak regulation of investment funds and repos, where bureaucratic and ideational conflicts among regulators were noticeable. Yet, it does not have much explanatory power concerning MMFs, hedge funds, securitization, securities lending, bank capital, and liquidity, where conflicts among types of regulatory agencies were minimal. The explanation centred on the *power of the financial industry* crops up in every shadow banking elemental regime, but does not account for the variation of the regulatory outcomes across elemental regimes (e.g. bank rules on shadow banking were more robust than rules on investment funds). Also, it does not explain why other financial services (e.g. banks, derivatives, etc.) were more stringently regulated after the 2008 crisis, despite lobbying from the financial industry.

Another explanation would focus on *US hegemony* (Helleiner 2014; Simmons 2001), arguing that the US structural power, in addition to its market size and regulatory capacity (Drezner 2007), allows this jurisdiction to set international standard and/or export its rules worldwide—the so-called *Washington effect*. A similar explanation could also be extended to the other main jurisdiction in finance, the EU—the *Brussels effect* (Bradford 2020, 2015). The key jurisdictions in shadow banking are the US and the EU, which account for the bulk of shadow banking assets (FSB 2019a). As such, both jurisdictions had powerful incentives to seek more stringent international standards for shadow banking to safeguard financial stability at home, whilst maintaining a level playing field internationally (Kapstein 1989; Singer 2007, 2004). Yet, there was little evidence of them trading up international rules or the Washington effect and Brussels effect. Moreover, neither the US nor the EU were eager to export their domestic shadow banking rules or apply them extraterritorially, unlike, for example, for some aspects of derivatives regulation (see, for example, Gravelle and Pagliari 2018; Knaack 2015). The *new interdependence* approach (Farrell and Newman 2014, 2016, 2018, see also Büthe and Mattli 2011) postulates, among other things, the risk of rule overlap between the main jurisdictions, leading to clashes over whose rules should apply. Yet, there were no major transatlantic regulatory clashes on shadow banking.

A second explanation would focus on the international institutional architecture. Some authors point out the *rational design of international institutions*, which are described as 'explicit arrangements, negotiated among international actors, that prescribe, proscribe, and/or authorize behavior' and argue that 'many institutional arrangements are best understood through "rational design" among multiple participants' (Koremenos et al. 2001: 766; see also Johnson and Urpelainen 2012; Urpelainen and van de Graaf 2015). Yet, this book has shown that the rational pursuit of interest-driven goals by states resulted in a less than rational institutional design for governing shadow banking. Other authors draw attention to *experimentalist governance* (De Burca, Keohane, and Sabel 2013, 2014; Kalyanpur and Newman 2017; Posner 2015; Zeitlin 2015), which is based on a recursive process of provisional goal-setting at the international level and subsequent revisions based on learning from the comparison of alternative approaches in different local contexts. The findings of this book suggest that experimentalist governance was at play, but produced unsatisfactory learning concerning the post-crisis governance of shadow banking.

A final explanation would focus on *domestic politics* and *public salience* of financial regulation (Culpepper 2011; Pagliari 2013b), whereby in the aftermath of crises, finance gains high public salience, which leads politicians and regulators to put in place more stringent rules. As the memories of a crisis fade away, public salience decreases and regulation becomes less stringent. This approach would lead us to expect proposals for tougher shadow banking regulation at the height of the crisis as salience peaked—but that these would be significantly diluted or abandoned as political attention declined over time. Yet, this explanation fails to explain why stricter rules on several aspects of shadow banking were not issued in the wake of the crisis, while some of the most significant reforms only developed years later.

Contributions to the Literature

This book makes three contributions to the literature. To begin with, it demonstrates that the post-crisis governance of global shadow banking was feeble: international standards had limited precision, stringency, and consistency. Instead of becoming more robust over time, the governance of global shadow banking was partly hollowed out through the game of shadows concerning the definition, measurement, and regulation of various aspects of shadow banking, to the detriment of financial stability. This finding speaks to an ongoing controversy in the literature about the scope of the reforms of financial regulation after the international financial crisis of 2008.

A first body of works has considered the international financial crisis of 2008 as a 'Bretton Wood moment' (Helleiner 2010), which was to sanction the 'end of liberal finance' (Nesvetailova and Palan 2010). These works have detected more stringent post-crisis regulation due to the weakened power of the financial industry (Pagliari and Young 2014; Young 2012, 2014) and the political salience of financial regulation (Culpepper 2011; Pagliari 2013b, 2012)—at least in the aftermath of the crisis. Other works have stressed the ideational turn, hence, the development of a 'macroprudential paradigm' (Baker 2013a, b, 2014, 2015) and the coming to the fore of a 'market-shaping' approach, rather than the pre-crisis 'market-making' approach (Quaglia 2012). In practice, after the crisis, new macroprudential regulation was developed (Borio 2003, 2012), bank capital requirements were increased—although not as much as some academics (e.g. Admati and Hellwig 2013) and policymakers (e.g. Haldane 2012) would have liked—and the regulation of derivatives was also substantially tightened up (Helleiner et al. 2018; Quaglia 2020).

By contrast, a second stream of literature has pointed out the incremental nature of the post-2008 crisis regulatory reforms (Maynz 2012, 2015; Moschella and Tsingou 2013a, b; Tsingou 2015b), arguing that the market-friendly approach to financial regulation continued after the crisis, which was a 'status quo crisis' (Helleiner 2014). The limited regulatory change was attributed to the preferences of the US (Helleiner 2014), the resurgent power of the financial industry (Baker 2010; Bell and Hindmoore 2014, 2015), its transnational nature (McKeen-Edwards and Porter 2013; Porter 2014a, b) and the involvement of private actors in the regulatory process, which led to the selection of those ideas that suited their interests (Baker and Underhill 2015; Underhill 2015). By illustrating the limited scope and extent of post-crisis regulatory reforms concerning shadow banking, which constitutes a large part of the global financial system, this book concurs with and reinforces the assessment that regulatory changes were incremental and only partly tackled systemic risk.

Second, this book points out the perils of international regime complexity, which combines and magnifies problems that plague the governance of global finance, while hindering problem-solving. To begin with, there was interstate conflict, whereby the financial 'great powers' (Drezner 2007), namely, the US and the EU, half-heartedly supported more robust regulation of shadow banking and, sometimes, they did not agree with one another. Thus, the US, the EU (and within it, the UK) were reluctant to act as pacesetters in trading-up shadow banking regulation and as managers of the regime complex. A transatlantic consensus was missing on important aspects of shadow banking. At the same time, an emerging financial great power, China, which had a burgeoning shadow banking system, often disagreed with the views of developed countries, acting as a footdragger and resisting certain regulatory reforms, notably those on MMFs (Gruin and Knaack 2020; Knaack and Gruin 2020), but not others, such as hedge funds and securitization, which would have only marginally affected the prevailing forms of shadow banking in China.

This book also highlights the lengthy and challenging process of finding some ideational common ground among technical experts, which sometimes did not agree on the problems that needed to be address and the most appropriate regulatory solutions. The sectoral regulatory agencies involved in the shadow banking regime complex had different epistemological views about what shadow banking was, the risks it entailed, and how it should be regulated (Nesvetailova 2018). This epistemic discrepancy (Thiemann, Birk, and Friedrich 2018), as well as bureaucratic turf fighting at the domestic and international levels, weakened the ability of transgovernmental networks to manage regime complexity (Bach and Newman 2010, 2014; Newman and Posner 2018; Zaring 2020). From time to time, controversies emerged amongst regulators at the domestic level (for instance, between the SEC and the Federal Reserve in the US) as well as at the international level, that is to say, amongst international standards-setting bodies, notably, between the IOSCO and the FSB—this resulted in a sui generis bureaucratic two-level game.

Finally, the financial industry exerted structural power (Bell and Hindmoor 2014, 2016; Woll 2016), which reflected the economic importance of the financial sector for the world economy and national economies; instrumental power (Pagliari and Young 2014), related to the resources (of various type) available to private financial actors; ideational power, ensuing from the ability to generate congenial policy narratives (Baker and Wigan 2017) and infrastructural power (Braun 2020; Braun, Gabor, and Hubner 2018). Financial actors lobbied with considerable success at different levels (international, regional, and domestic) and in multiple venues (for example, vis-à-vis various international standard-setting bodies) across the regime complex to avoid a major regulatory overhaul. The power of the private financial actors was enhanced by the archipelago architecture of the regime complex, which facilitated the strategy of divide et impera as well as the formation of ad-hoc coalitions.

The third contribution of this book is to provide the first comprehensive account of the post-crisis 2008 international reforms of global shadow banking governance. It maps the over-crowded regulatory space in shadow banking by identifying the elemental regimes that compose the regime complex and by highlighting gaps and inconsistencies. It demonstrates that, overall, the post-crisis international regulation of shadow banking was feeble, albeit there was variation across the elemental regimes on shadow banking entities and activities. These findings have real-world relevance because shadow banking constitutes a large and increasing part of the global financial system. Thus, the weak governance of shadow banking has implications for financial stability tout court, as elaborated next.

Contributions to the Policy Debate

This book also contributes to the policy debate on the reforms of the governance of global finance after the international financial crisis of 2008. Like in the academic debate, in the real-world policy debate, two contrasting assessments of the post-crisis reforms of shadow banking governance have been put forward. The positive view, which tends to coincide with the 'official' assessment of the reforms undertaken, points out that whereas shadow banking was mostly unregulated before the crisis, it was not so afterward. The FSB's *Shadow Banking Monitoring Report* set the global standards for data specification, collection, and interpretation. Its regional consultative groups conducted annual monitoring exercises and published the results that named and shamed laggards. Thus, the FSB set in place system-wide monitoring, designed to track down the building up of systemic risks and adopt corrective measures, if necessary (Ban et al. 2016).

Furthermore, the FSB's decision to move away from the conception of sectoral financial regulation—whereby banks, securities dealers, or insurance groups were supervised by the respective regulatory agencies—in favour of financial regulation that aligned with economic functions—whereby the same regulatory requirements applied to entities with similar economic functions, irrespective of their legal form or market—had far-reaching implications for financial regulation and supervision. 'Across markets, financial entities are supervised along sectoral boundaries, either by separate agencies or by separate departments in consolidated regulatory agencies. To discard these structures, if only in theory, resembled a momentous departure from precedent' (Woyames Dreher 2019: 575).

Besides the monitoring of global shadow banking, post-crisis international standards were adopted on MMFs, investment funds, securities financing, securitization, and bank exposures to shadow banking, as discussed in the previous chapters. In 2017, the G20 asked the FSB to assess whether the post-crisis policies and monitoring efforts concerning shadow banking were adequate to contain the financial stability risks that this system posed. The FSB (2017e) *Assessment of Shadow Banking Activities, Risks and the Adequacy of Post-crisis Policy Tools to Address Financial Stability Concerns* concluded rather optimistically that the aspects of shadow banking that contributed to the financial crisis had 'declined significantly'. To be fair, the FSB noted that on the one hand, regulatory reforms had contributed to a reduction of vulnerabilities in areas such as MMFs and repos. On the other hand, a rise in assets held in investment funds had increased the risks related to liquidity transformation and structural vulnerabilities in asset management (FSB 2017e) (see Chapter 4). The G20 Leaders at their Hamburg Summit (G20 2017) endorsed the FSB's assessment and emphasized the 'considerable progress made towards transforming shadow banking into resilient market-based finance'.

The rather optimistic assessment outlined above contrasts with the more sombre assessment of the post-crisis reforms of international shadow banking governance put forward in this book. To be sure, the glass is half empty:

a global monitoring system was set in place and a panoply of soft laws was issued to mitigate the risks posed by shadow banking. Yet, the post-crisis regulatory reforms of shadow banking failed to restrain the growth of this part of the financial sector: whereas the broad measure of shadow banking increased considerably, the narrow measure did not increase to the same extent, underestimating the potential risks that shadow banking entailed and, thus, the need for regulation. In turn, several shadow banking entities and activities were not subject to more rigorous international standards, which did not tackle some controversial issues and left important regulatory gaps. Thus, several risks connected to the shadow banking system remain undetected and unaddressed, posing a potential threat to financial stability.

Open Issues in International Shadow Banking Governance

The game of shadows in the international governance of shadow banking has left several issues unaddressed and has kept others in the shadow. Thus, there is the need to 'shine a light' on shadow banking, as argued by Richard Portes (2019), co-chair of the ESRB Committee on Shadow Banking (see also Lane 2013). To begin with, the shadow banking system has continued to grow in size globally as well as in many jurisdictions. In advanced economies, which have the largest shadow banking systems, the narrowly defined shadow banking measures indicate stagnation, while broader measures display a rising trend. In emerging market economies, the growth of shadow banking has been strong, overtaking that of the banking sector. Over time, some financial activities—such as lending to firms—have migrated from traditional banks to the nonbank sector (Adrian 2017). In the US, the shadow banking sector is roughly the same size as the traditional banking sector, and accounts for 31% of global shadow banking assets. In the EU, where the banking sector is larger relative to the economy as a whole than in the US, the shadow sector represents 30–40% of total financial intermediation, and accounts for 26% of global shadow banking. In China, where the banking sector is larger relative to the economy as a whole than in the US, shadow banking accounted for approximately 16% of global shadow banking assets.[1]

Furthermore, shadow banking entities and activities have many linkages to the rest of the global financial system. Some non-bank financial entities, such as Blackrock, are huge. Pension funds have entered the business of making

[1] http://www.chinadaily.com.cn/a/201801/12/WS5a587e52a3102c394518ee54.html.

direct loans, acting as banks—but lacking both the regulatory oversight to which banks are subject and their experience in loan making and risk evaluation. Banks remain vulnerable to shadow banking: approximately 60% of European banks' exposure to shadow banking is to institutions outside the EU, with approximately 27% of the total exposures to US-domiciled shadow banking entities. 'That's risky—or, to be more accurate, it's doubly risky, since we can't be sure just how risky it' (Portes 2019).

At the same time, shadow banking takes different forms across countries. In advanced economies, shadow banking typically involves a chain of financial entities and activities that decompose the process of credit intermediation between lenders and borrowers. Thus, in the US, the UK, and the EU, shadow banking activities mainly concern securitization, securities lending, and repos. By contrast, in developing economies, shadow banking takes the form of credit intermediation between lenders and borrowers, whereas market-based instruments play a rather limited role. In China, which has the largest shadow banking system among emerging economies, shadow banking mainly includes wealth management and trust products. Banks are the dominant players in China's shadow banking system, which is why it is sometimes dubbed the 'shadow of the banks' (Ehlers, Kong, and Zhu 2018).[2] Whereas retail investors are the dominant investor group in China, the main actors in advanced economies are institutional investors operating in capital markets (Elliott, Kroeber, Qiao 2015; Gruin and Knaack 2020; Knaack and Gruin 2020). On the one hand, the risks posed by shadow banking vary depending on the domestic context, and, therefore, a 'one-size-fits-all approach' to shadow banking regulation is not likely to work (Adrian and Jones 2018). On the other hand, the drivers of shadow banking growth have been similar across countries and types of activities (albeit, to different degrees). This suggests the need for an encompassing policy framework to 'minimize the scope for regulatory circumvention induced by the so-called boundary problem' (IMF 2014), to avoid regulatory arbitrage.

Finally, in the wake of the covid-19 pandemic, whereas the banking sector and derivatives markets coped rather well with the ensuing economic crisis (FSB 2020b; Cunliffe 2020), several parts of the shadow banking system did not. To begin, there was a run on MMFs and real estate investment funds, which had invested in mortgage-backed securities (Sengupta and Xue 2020). Moreover, MMFs and hedge funds amplified financial market instability once

[2] Moreover, non-bank credit intermediation in China is also a means for financial development and inclusion (Knaack and Gruin 2020).

the pandemic began (FSB 2020b; Cunliffe 2020). Several investment funds experienced liquidity problems, an issue that had been stressed by central bankers before the covid crisis. Notably, the Governor of the Bank of England, Mark Carney (*Reuters*, 26 June 2019) argued that mutual and exchange-traded funds had no access to central bank money nor fiscal backing, hence they relied heavily on market liquidity. A particular type of securitization, Collateralized Loan Obligations,[3] came under stress during the pandemic. The creation of Collateralized Loan Obligations had been partly a response to high financial inflows into mutual funds, which were also the main investors in Collateralized Loan Obligations, even though the most-senior Collateralized Loan Obligations were owned by banks, pension funds, and insurers (*Wall Street Journal*, 10 June 2021). Before the covid pandemic, the FSB (2019d) had assessed the financial stability risks of Collateralized Loan Obligations, pointing out the decline in the quality of debt coverage covenants and the fact that these unsecured loans were potentially exposed to much larger losses than the historical average (Perotti 2020).

During the unfolding of the covid crisis, securitization and repo markets were propped up by the extraordinary monetary policy measures taken by central banks, notably, the Federal Reserve, the ECB, and the Bank of England (Hauser 2020), (Gabor 2020), which, inter alia, provided liquidity to investment funds.The fiscal authorities worldwide intervened massively in the economy by piling up large amounts of public debt. There is no counterfactual of what would have happened to the shadow banking system in the absence of these extraordinary interventions on the monetary and fiscal sides, given that the international governance of this part of the financial system was not substantially traded up after the international financial crisis of 2008.

[3] These are vehicles that buy loans, usually those issued by highly leveraged large companies, and fund them by selling debt to investors that carry varying levels of return and risk.

References

Abbott, K. W., Genschel, P., Snidal, D., and Zangl, B. (2015) *International Organizations as Orchestrators*, Cambridge: Cambridge University Press.

Admati, A. and Hellwig, M. (2013) *The Bankers' New Clothes: What's Wrong with Banking and What to Do about It*, Princeton: Princeton University Press.

Adrian, T. (2017) 'Shadow banking and market-based finance – Speech', International Monetary Fund, 14 September, Washington, available at https://www.imf.org/en/News/Articles/2017/09/13/sp091417-shadow-banking-and-market-based-finance

Adrian, T. and Ashcraft, A. (2012) 'Shadow banking regulation', *Federal Reserve Bank of New York Staff Report*, N. 559, April, New York, available at https://www.newyorkfed.org/medialibrary/media/research/staff_reports/sr559.pdf

Adrian, T., Ashcraft, A., Breuer, B., and Cetorelli, N. (2019) 'Shadow banking', in Berger, A.N., Molyneux, P. and Wilson, J.O. (eds), *The Oxford Handbook of Banking*, Oxford: Oxford University Press. DOI: 10.1093/oxfordhb/9780199688500.013.0016

Adrian, T. and Jones, B. (2018) 'Shadow banking and market-based finance', International Monetary Fund, Washington, available at https://www.imf.org/~/media/Files/Publications/DP/2018/45663-dp1814-shadow-banking.ashx

Adrian, T. and Shin, H. S. (2009) 'The shadow banking system: Implications for financial regulation', *Federal Reserve Bank of New York Staff Report*, N. 382, New York, available at https://www.newyorkfed.org/medialibrary/media/research/staff_reports/sr382.pdf

Ahdieh, R. (2015) 'Coordination and conflict: The persistent relevance of networks in international financial regulation', *Law and Contemporary Problems* 78 (4): 75–101.

Alter, K. (2022) 'The Promise and Perils of Theorizing International Regime Complexity in an Evolving World', *Review of International Organisations*, 17: 375–396.

Alter, K. J. and Meunier, S. (2006) 'Nested and overlapping regimes in the transatlantic banana trade dispute', *Journal of European Public Policy* 13 (3): 362–382.

Alter, K. J. and Meunier, S. (2009) 'The politics of international regime complexity', *Perspectives on Politics* 7 (1): 13–24.

Alter, K. J. and Raustiala, K. (2018) 'The rise of international regime complexity', *Annual Review of Law and Social Sciences* 14: 329–349.

Alternative Investment Management Association (AIMA) (2013) *Response to Consultation on Framework for Addressing Shadow Banking Risks in Securities Lending and Repos*, 20 November, London, available at https://www.fsb.org/wp-content/uploads/c_131220a.pdf

American Bankers Association (2016) *Response to Consultation on Identification and Measurement of Step-in Risk*, 17 March, Washington, available at https://www.bis.org/bcbs/publ/comments/d349/amba.pdf

Amundi (2017) *Response to Consultation on Liquidity Recommendations for Investment Funds*, 18 September, Paris, available at https://www.iosco.org/library/pubdocs/573/pdf/Amundi%20-%20Liquidity%20Recommendations.pdf

Arner, D. W. and Taylor, M. V. (2009) 'The global financial crisis and the financial stability board: Hardening the soft law of international financial regulation', *University of New South Wales Law Journal* 32 (2): 488–513.

Association for Financial Markets in Europe (AFME) (2014a) *High-quality Securitization for Europe*, June, London, available at https://www.afme.eu/portals/0/globalassets/downloads/publications/afme-high-quality-securitisation-for-europe-the-market-at-a-crossroads.pdf

Association for Financial Markets in Europe (2014b) *Response to the Consultation on Securitisation of the Bank of England and the European Central Bank*, 7 July, London, available at https://www.ecb.europa.eu/pub/pdf/other/141013-abs-joint-responses.en.pdf

Association of Alternative Investment Fund Managers (AIMA) (2009) *Response to IOSCO's Consultation on Hedge Fund Regulation*, 30 April, London, available at blob:resource://pdf.js/e70a7888-f595-4466-955f-39b34049647e#filename=Alternative%20Investment%20Management%20Association%20-%20AIMA.pdf

Australian Securitisation Forum, Global Financial Markets Association, International Capital Market Association, and Institute of International Finance (2017) *Response to Consultation on the Criteria for and Capital Treatment of Simple, Transparent and Comparable Short-Term Securitisation*, 5 October, Basel, available at https://www.bis.org/bcbs/publ/comments/d413/giia.pdf

Bach, D. and Newman, A. L. (2010) 'Transgovernmental networks and domestic policy convergence: evidence from insider trading regulation', *International Organization* 64: 505–528.

Bach, D. and Newman, A. L. (2014) 'Domestic drivers of transgovernmental regulatory co-operation', *Regulation & Governance* 8 (4): 395–417.

Bach, T., De Francesco, F., Maggetti, M., and Ruffing, E. (2016a) 'Special Issue: Symposium: Transnational regulatory networks as means of EU governance: The administrative dimension of multilevel coordination', *Public Administration* 94 (1).

Bach, T., De Francesco, F., Maggetti, M., and Ruffing, E. (2016b) 'Transnational bureaucratic politics: An institutional rivalry perspective on EU network governance', *Public Administration* 94 (1): 9–24.

Baker, A. (2010) 'Restraining regulatory capture? Anglo-America, crisis politics and trajectories of change in global financial governance', *International Affairs* 86: 647–663.

Baker, A. (2013a) 'The new political economy of the macroprudential ideational shift', *New Political Economy* 18 (1): 112–139.

Baker, A. (2013b) 'The gradual transformation? The incremental dynamics of macroprudential regulation', *Regulation & Governance* 7 (4): 417–434.

Baker, A. (2014) 'Macro-prudential regulation', in Muegge, D. (ed.), *Europe and the Governance of Global Finance*, Oxford: Oxford University Press, pp. 172–188.

Baker, A. (2015) 'Varieties of economic crisis, varieties of ideational change: How and why financial regulation and macroeconomic policy differ', *New Political Economy* 20 (3): 342–366.

Baker, A. and Underhill, G. R. (2015) 'Economic ideas and the political construction of the financial crash of 2008', *British Journal of Politics and International Relations* 17 (3): 381–390.

Baker, A. and Wigan, D. (2017) 'Constructing and contesting City of London power: NGOs and the emergence of noisier financial politics', *Economy and Society* 46 (2): 185–210.

Baklanova, V., Copeland, A., and McCaughrin, R. (2015) 'Reference guide to US repo and securities lending markets', *Federal Reserve Bank of New York Staff Reports*, N. 740,

New York, available at https://www.newyorkfed.org/medialibrary/media/research/staff_reports/sr740.pdf

Ban, C. and Gabor D. (2016) 'The political economy of shadow banking', *Review of International Political Economy* 23 (6): 901–914.

Ban, C., Seabrooke, L., and Freitas, S. (2016) 'Grey matter in shadow banking: International organizations and expert strategies in global financial governance', *Review of International Political Economy* 23 (6): 1001–1033.

Bank of England (2009a) *Financial Stability Report*, June, London, June available at https://www.bankofengland.co.uk/financial-stability-report/2009/june-2009

Bank of England (2009b) *Financial Stability Report*, December, London, available at https://www.bankofengland.co.uk/-/media/boe/files/financial-stability-report/2009/december-2009.pdf

Bank of England (2019a) *Response to Consultation on Investment Funds Leverage*, London, available at https://www.iosco.org/library/pubdocs/615/pdf/Bank%20of%20England.pdf

Bank of England and European Central Bank (2014a) *The Impaired Securitization Market*, January, London, available at https://www.ecb.europa.eu/pub/pdf/other/ecb-boe_impaired_eu_securitisation_marketen.pdf

Bank of England and European Central Bank (2014b) *The Case for a Better Functioning of the Securitisation Market in the European Union*, May, London, available at https://www.ecb.europa.eu/pub/pdf/other/ecb-boe_case_better_functioning_securitisation_marketen.pdf

Bank of England and European Central Bank (2015) *Response to Consultation on a Framework for Simple, Transparent and Standardised Securitisation*, 27 March, London, available at https://www.ecb.europa.eu/pub/pdf/other/ecb-boe_response_ec_consultation_on_securitisation20150327.en.pdf

Bank of New York Mellon Corporation, Northern Trust Corporation, and State Street Corporation (2012) *Response to Consultation on Securities Lending and Repos*, 25 May, New York, available at https://www.fsb.org/wp-content/uploads/c_120806b.pdf

Barr, M. and Miller, G. (2006) 'Global administrative law: The view from Basel', *European Journal of International Law* 17 (1): 15–46.

Basel Committee on Banking Supervision (BCBS) (1991) *Supervisory Framework for Measuring and Controlling Large Exposures*, January, Basel, available at https://www.bis.org/publ/bcbsc121.htm

Basel Committee on Banking Supervision (BCBS) (1999a) *Banks' Interactions with Highly Leveraged Institutions*, January, Basel.

Basel Committee on Banking Supervision (BCBS) (1999b) *Sound Practices for Banks' Interactions with Highly Leveraged Institutions*, January, Basel.

Basel Committee on Banking Supervision (BCBS) (2004a) *Securitisation Framework*, January, Basel, available at https://www.bis.org/publ/bcbs105.pdf

Basel Committee on Banking Supervision (BCBS) (2004b) *Press Release: Continued Progress Toward Basel II*, 15 January, Basel, available at https://www.bis.org/press/p040115.htm

Basel Committee on Banking Supervision (BCBS) (2009a) *Enhancements to the Basel II Framework*, July, Basel, available at https://www.bis.org/publ/bcbs157.htm

Basel Committee on Banking Supervision (BCBS) (2009b) *Revisions to the Basel II Market Risk Framework*, July, Basel, available at https://www.bis.org/publ/bcbs158.pdf

Basel Committee on Banking Supervision (BCBS) (2010) *Basel III: A Global Regulatory Framework for More Resilient Banks and Banking Systems*, December, Basel, available at https://www.bis.org/publ/bcbs189_dec2010.pdf

Basel Committee on Banking Supervision (BCBS) (2013a) *Basel III: The Liquidity Coverage Ratio and Liquidity Risk Monitoring Tools*, January, Basel, available at https://www.bis.org/publ/bcbs238.pdf

Basel Committee on Banking Supervision (BCBS) (2013c) *Revisions to the Securitisation Framework*, December, Basel, available at https://www.bis.org/publ/bcbs269.htm

Basel Committee on Banking Supervision (BCBS) (2013d) *Capital Requirements for Banks' Equity Investments in Funds*, December, Basel, available at https://www.bis.org/publ/bcbs266.htm

Basel Committee on Banking Supervision (BCBS) (2013e) *Consultation on Measuring and Controlling Large Exposures*, April, Basel, available at https://www.bis.org/publ/bcbs283.htm

Basel Committee on Banking Supervision (BCBS) (2014a) *Basel III: the Net Stable Funding Ratio*, October, Basel, available at https://www.bis.org/bcbs/publ/d295.pdf

Basel Committee on Banking Supervision (BCBS) (2014d) *Supervisory Framework for Measuring and Controlling Large Exposures*, April, Basel, available at https://www.bis.org/publ/bcbs283.htm

Basel Committee on Banking Supervision (BCBS) (2015) *Consultative Paper on Guidelines on the Identification and Measurement of Step-in Risk*, December, Basel, available at https://www.bis.org/bcbs/publ/d349.pdf

Basel Committee on Banking Supervision (BCBS) (2017a) *Consultative Paper on Guidelines on the Identification and Measurement of Step-in Risk*, March, Basel, available at http//www.bis.org/bcbs/publ/d398.htm

Basel Committee on Banking Supervision (BCBS) (2018) *Capital Treatment for Simple, Transparent and Comparable Short-Term Securitisations*, May, Basel, available at https://www.bis.org/bcbs/publ/d442.pdf

Basel Committee on Banking Supervision (BCBS) – International Organization of Securities Commissions (IOSCO) (2015) *Criteria for Identifying Simple, Transparent and Comparable Securitizations*, July, Basel, available at https://www.bis.org/bcbs/publ/d332.htm

Basel Committee on Banking Supervision (BCBS) – International Organization of Securities Commissions (IOSCO) (2018) *Criteria for Identifying Simple, Transparent and Comparable Short-Term Securitisations*, May, Basel, available at https://www.bis.org/bcbs/publ/d441.htm

Baumgartner, F. and Jones, B. (2009) *Agendas and Instability in American Politics*, Chicago: University of Chicago Press.

Bell, S. and Hindmoor, A. (2014) 'Slaves of the market: Bankers and the great financial meltdown', *British Journal of Politics and International Politics* 17 (1): 1–22

Bell, D. and Hindmoor, A. (2015) *Masters of the Universe, Slaves of the Market*, Cambridge, MA: Harvard University Press.

Bell, S. and Hindmoor, A. (2016) 'Structural power and the politics of bank capital regulation in the United Kingdom', *Political Studies* 65 (1): 103–121.

Bernanke, B. (2010) *Implications of the Financial Crisis for Economics: Speech*, Federal reserve, 24 September, Washington, available at https://www.federalreserve.gov/newsevents/speech/files/bernanke20100924a.pdf

Beyers, J. and Kerremans, B. (2012) 'Domestic embeddedness and the dynamics of multilevel venue shopping in four EU Member States', *Governance* 25 (2): 263–290.

Bieling, H-J. (2014) 'Shattered expectations: The defeat of European ambitions of global financial reform', *Journal of European Public Policy* 21 (3): 346–366.

Blackrock (2014) *Response to Consultation on Assessment Methodologies for Identifying Non-Bank Non-Insurer Global Systemically Important Financial Institutions*, 4 April, New York, available at https://www.iosco.org/library/pubdocs/435/pdf/BlackRock.pdf

Blackrock (2015) Response to *Consultation on Assessment Methodologies for Identifying Non-Bank Non-Insurer Global Systemically Important Financial Institutions*, 29 May, New York, available at https://www.iosco.org/library/pubdocs/479/pdf/BlackRock.pdf

Blackrock (2017) *Response to Consultation on Liquidity Risk Management Recommendations*, 18 September, New York, available at https://www.blackrock.com/corporate/literature/publication/iosco-fund-liquidity-risk-management-091817.pdf

Blackrock (2018) *Taking Market-Based Finance Out of the Shadows*, February, New York, available at https://www.blackrock.com/corporate/literature/whitepaper/viewpoint-taking-market-based-finance-out-of-the-shadows-february-2018.pdf

Borio, C. (2003) 'Towards a macroprudential framework for financial supervision and regulation', *BIS Working Papers* N. 128, Bank for International Settlements, Basel.

Borio, C. (2012) 'The financial cycle and macroeconomics: What have we learnt?', *BIS Working Papers* N. 395, Bank for International Settlements, Basel.

Botzem, S. (2013) 'Continuity of expert rule: Global accountancy regulation after the crisis', in Manuela, M. and Tsingou, E. (eds), *Great Expectations, Slow Transformations*, Colchester: ECPR Press, pp. 149–72.

Botzem, S. (2014a) *The Politics of Accounting Regulation: Organizing Transnational Standard Setting in Financial Reporting*, Cheltenham: Edward Elgar.

Botzem, S. (2014b) 'Transnational standard setting in accounting: Organizing expertise-based self-regulation in times of crises', *Accounting, Auditing & Accountability Journal* 27 (6): 933.

Botzem, S. and Quack, S. (2009) '(No) limits to Anglo-American accounting? Reconstructing the history of the International Accounting Standards Committee: A review article', *Accounting, Organizations and Society* 34 (8): 988–999.

Bradford, A. (2015) 'Exporting standards: The externalization of the EU's regulatory power via markets', *International Review of Law and Economics* 42: 158–173.

Bradford, A. (2020) *The Brussels Effect: How the European Union Rules the World*, Oxford: Oxford University Press.

Braun, B. (2020) 'Central banking and the infrastructural power of finance: The case of ECB support for repo and securitization markets', *Socio-Economic Review* 18 (2): 395–418

Braun, B. and Gabor, D. (2020) 'Central banking, shadow banking, and infrastructural power', in Mader, P., Mertens, D., and van der Zwan, N. (eds), *The Routledge International Handbook of Financialization*, London: Routledge, pp. 241–252.

Braun, B., Gabor, D., and Hubner, M. (2018) 'Governing through financial markets: Towards a critical political economy of Capital Markets Union', *Competition and Change* 2 (2): 101–116.

Braun, B. and Hübner, M. (2018) 'Fiscal fault, financial fix? Capital Markets Union and the quest for macro-economic stabilization in the Euro-Area', *Competition and Change* 22 (2): 101–116.

Breen, M., Hodson, D., and Moschella, M. (2020) 'Incoherence in regime complexes: A sentiment analysis of EU–IMF Surveillance', *Journal of Common Market Studies* 58 (2): 419–437.

British Bankers Association (2014) *Response to Consultation on Securitisation Market in the European Union*, 8 July, London, available at https://www.ecb.europa.eu/pub/pdf/other/141013-abs-joint-responses.en.pdf

Broome, A. and Seabrooke, L. (2015) 'Shaping policy curves: Cognitive authority in Transnational capacity building', *Public Administration* 93 (4): 956–972.

Broome, A., Homolar, A., and Kranke, M. (2018) 'Bad science: International organizations and the indirect power of global benchmarking', *European Journal of International Relations* 24 (3): 514–539.

Brummer, C. (2010a) 'How international financial law works (and how it doesn't)', *Georgetown Law Journal* 99: 257–327.

Brummer, C. (2010b) 'Why soft law dominates international finance—and not trade', *Journal of International Economic Law*13 (3): 623–643.

Brummer, C. (2015) *Soft Law and the Global Financial System*, Cambridge: Cambridge University Press.

Brunnermeier, M., Crockett, A., Goodhart, C., Persaud, A. D., and Shin, H. S. (2009) 'The fundamental principles of financial regulation', *Geneva Reports on the World Economy* 11.

Brunnermeier, M. K. and Pedersen, L. H. (2009) 'Market liquidity and funding liquidity', *Review of Financial Studies* 22 (6): 2201–2238.

Buchanan, B. G. (2017) *Securitization and the Global Economy*, New York: Palgrave.

Busch, M. L. (2007) 'Overlapping institutions, forum shopping, and dispute settlement in international trade', *International Organization* 61: 735–761.

Busuioc, M. (2016) 'Friend or foe? Inter-agency cooperation, organizational reputation and turf', *Public Administration* 94 (1): 40–56.

Büthe, T. and Mattli, W. (2011) *The New Global Rulers: The Privatization of Regulation in the World Economy*, Princeton: Princeton University Press.

Carney, M. (2014) 'The need to focus a light on shadow banking is nigh', *Financial Times*, 15 June.

Carney, M. (2019) *Opening remarks*, Bank of England, 11 July 2019, London, available at https://www.bankofengland.co.uk/-/media/boe/files/financial-stability-report/2019/opening-remarks-july-2019

Casu, B., Sarkysian, A. (2019) 'Securitization', in Berger, A. N., Molyneux, P. and Wilson, J. O. (eds), *The Oxford Handbook of Banking*, Oxford: Oxford University Press, pp. 354–377.

Casu, B., Clare, A., Sarkysian, A., and Thomas, S. (2011) 'Does securitization reduce credit risk taking? Empirical evidence from US bank holding companies', *European Journal of Finance* 17(9): 769–788.

Center for the Study of Financial Market Evolution (2011) *FSB Task Force Frames the Regulation of Shadow Banking*, 28 April, available at http://csfme.org/Full_Article/fsb-task-force-frames-the-regulation-of-shadow-banking

Cerny, P. (2010) *Rethinking World Politics: A Theory of Transnational Pluralism*, Oxford: Oxford University Press.

Cetorelli, N., Mandel, B. H., and Mollineaux, L. (2012) 'The evolution of banks and financial intermediation', *Federal Reserve Bank of New York Economic Policy Review*, July, New York, pp. 1–12 available at https://www.newyorkfed.org/medialibrary/media/research/epr/12v18n2/1207cet1.pdf

Chalmers, A. W. (2015) 'Financial industry mobilisation and securities markets regulation in Europe', *European Journal of Political Research* 54 (3): 482–501.

Chapman, D., Miller, H., Pascarella, K. and Withfield, L. (2020) 'Don't put all your eggs in one basket': protecting banks from the failure of individual counterparties', *Bank of England Quarterly Bulletin*, 26 June, London, available at https://www.bankofengland.co.uk/quarterly-bulletin/2020/2020-q2/dont-put-all-your-eggs-in-one-basket-protecting-banks-from-the-failure-of-individual-counterparties

Chen, K., Ren, J., and Zha, T. (2018) 'The nexus of monetary policy and shadow banking in China', *American Economic Review* 108 (12): 3891–3936.

Chey, H-K. (2006) 'Explaining cosmetic compliance with international regulatory regimes: The implementation of the Basle Accord in Japan, 1998–2003', *New Political Economy* 11 (2): 271–289.

Chey, H-K. (2007) 'Do markets enhance convergence on international standards? The case of financial regulation', *Regulation & Governance* 1 (4): 295–311.

Chey, H-K. (2014) *International Harmonization of Financial Regulation? The Politics of Global Diffusion of the Basel Capital Accord*, London: Routledge.

China Securities Regulatory Commission and Chinese Money Market Fund Association (2012) 'Response to consultation on Money Market Funds', Beijing, available at https://www.iosco.org/publications/?subsection=public_reports

Chwieroth, J. M. (2015) 'Professional ties that bind: how normative orientations shape IMF conditionality', *Review of International Political Economy* 22 (4): 757–787.

Coen, D. and Thatcher, M. (2008) 'Network governance and multi-level delegation: European networks of regulatory agencies', *Journal of Public Policy* 28 (1): 49–71.

Collins, S. and Plantier, C. (2015) 'The IMF is entitled to its opinion, but not to its own facts', in *ICI Viewpoint*, 10 April, available at: http://www.ici.org/viewpoints/view_15_imf_gfsr.

Commercial Real Estate Finance Council, Commercial Real Estate Finance Council Europe, Global Financial Markets Association, Institute of International Finance, International Association of Credit Portfolio Managers, International Swaps and Derivatives Association, Securitisation Forum of Japan and Structured Finance Industry Group (2014) *Response to Consultation on Revisions to the Basel Securitisation Framework*', 24 March, Basel, available at https://www.bis.org/publ/bcbs269/jtagcceiiisas.pdf

Committee on the Global Financial System (2017) 'Repo market functioning', *Committee on the Global Financial System Paper* N. 59, April, Basel, available at https://www.bis.org/publ/cgfs59.pdf

Committee on Securities Lending of the Risk Management Association, International Securities Lending Association and Pan Asian Securities Lending Association (2012) *Response to Interim Report of the FSB Workstream on Securities Lending and Repos*, 25 May, Basel, available at https://www.fsb.org/wp-content/uploads/c_120806h.pdf

Constâncio, V. (2012a) *Shadow Banking – and the ECB Perspective – Speech*, European Central Bank, 27 April, Frankfurt, available at https://www.ecb.europa.eu/press/key/date/2012/html/sp120427.en.html

Constâncio, V. (2012b) *Towards an EU Database for Repo Markets and Securities Lending – Speech*, European Central Bank, 3 December, Frankfurt, available at https://www.bis.org/review/r121204b.pdf

Constâncio, V. (2014) *Beyond Traditional Banking: A New Credit System Coming out of the Shadows – Speech*, European Central Bank, 17 October, Frankfurt, available at https://www.ecb.europa.eu/press/key/date/2014/html/sp141017_2.en.html

Constâncio, V. (2016) *Margins and Haircuts as a Macroprudential Tool – Speech*, European Central Bank, 6 June, Frankfurt, available at https://www.ecb.europa.eu/press/key/date/2016/html/sp160606.en.html

Constâncio, V. (2017) *Macroprudential Policy in a Changing Financial System - Speech*, European Central Bank, 11 May, Frankfurt, available at https://www.ecb.europa.eu/press/key/date/2017/html/ecb.sp170511.en.html

Cooper, A. F. and Thakur, R. (2013) *The Group of Twenty (G20)*, London: Routledge.

Copeland, A., Martin, A., and Walker, M. (2011) 'Repo runs: Evidence from the Tri-Party repo market', *Federal Reserve Bank of New York Staff* Report N. 506, July, New York, available at https://www.newyorkfed.org/medialibrary/media/research/staff_reports/sr506.pdf

Culpepper, P. D. (2011) *Quiet Politics and Business Power*, Cambridge: Cambridge University Press.

Culpepper, P. D. and Reinke, R. (2014) 'Structural power and bank bailouts in the United Kingdom and the United States', *Politics and Society* 42 (4): 427–454.

Cunliffe, J. (2020) *Speech given at the Investment Association Webinar*, 9 June 2020, London, available at https://www.bankofengland.co.uk/-/media/boe/files/speech/2020/financial-system-resilience-lessons-from-a-real-stress-speech-by-jon-cunliffe.pdf?la=en&hash=68025EDB90D936B24560429761646BFEAE2D2D74

Davis, C. L. (2004) 'International Institutions and Issue Linkage: Building Support for Agricultural Trade Liberalization', *American Political Science Review* 98(1): 153–169.

De Bièvre, D., Poletti, A., and Thomann, L. (2014) 'To enforce or not to enforce? WTO judicialization, forum shopping and global regulatory harmonization', *Regulation & Governance*8 (3): 269–286.

De Burca, G., Keohane, R. O., and Sabel, C. F. (2013) 'New modes of pluralist global governance', *New York University Journal of International Law& Politics* 45: 723–786.

De Burca, G., Keohane, R. O., and Sabel, C. F. (2014) 'Global experimentalist governance', *British Journal of Political Science* 44 (3): 477–486.

de Guindos, L. (2018) *The Rising Role of the Investment Funds Sector for Financial Stability in the Euro Area: Speech*, European Central Bank, 12 November, Frankfurt, available at https://www.ecb.europa.eu/press/key/date/2018/html/ecb.sp181112.en.html

De Larosière, J., Balcerowicz, L., Issing, O., Masera, R., McCarthy, C., Nyberg, L., Pérez, J., and Ruding, O. (2009) *Report of the High-level Group on Financial Supervision in the EU*, February, Brussels.

Dell'Ariccia, G., Igan, D., and Laeven, L. (2012) 'Credit Booms and Lending Standards: Evidence from the Subprime Mortgage Market', *Journal of Money, Credit and Banking* 44 (2–3): 367–384.

Deutsche Bank (2014) *Response to Consultation on Better Functioning of Securitisation Market in the European Union*, 4 July, Frankfurt, available at https://www.ecb.europa.eu/pub/pdf/other/141013-abs-joint-responses.en.pdf

De Vries, C., Hobolt, S., and Walter, S. (2021) 'Politicizing international cooperation. The mass public, political entrepreneurs, and political opportunity structures', *International Organization.*

Djelic, M.-L. and Quack, S. (eds) (2010) *Transnational Communities: Shaping Global Economic Governance*, Cambridge: Cambridge University Press.

Donnelly, S. (2012) 'Institutional change at the top: From the Financial Stability Forum to the Financial Stability Board', in Maynz, R. (ed.), *Crisis and Control: Institutional Change in Financial Market Regulation*, Frankfurt: Campus, pp. 261–275.

Dorn, N. (2016) 'Capital cohabitation: EU Capital Markets Union as public and private co-regulation', *Capital Markets Law Journal* 11 (1): 84–102.

Draghi, M. (2008) 'A vision of a more resilient global economy', *Financial Times*, 13 November, London.

Drezner, D. W. (2007) *All Politics is Global: Explaining International Regulatory Regimes*, Princeton: Princeton University Press.

Drezner, D. W. (2009) 'The power and peril of international regime complexity', *Perspectives on Politics* 7 (1): 65–70.

Eatwell, J. and Taylor, L. (2000) *Global Finance at Risk: The Case for International Regulation*, London: New Press.

Eckhardt, J. and De Bievre, D. (2015) 'Boomerangs over lac Léman: transnational lobbying and foreign venue shopping in WTO dispute settlement', *World Trade Review*, 507–530.

Ehlers, T., Kong, S., and Zhu, F. (2018) 'Mapping shadow banking in China: Structure and dynamics', *BIS Working Paper* N. 710, Bank for International Settlements, February, Basel, available at https://www.bis.org/publ/work701.htm

Elliott, D., Kroeber, A., and Qiao, Y. (2015) *Shadow Banking in China: A Primer*, Brookings Institution, March, Washington, available at: http://www.brookings.edu/research/papers/2015/04/01-shadow-banking-china-primer-elliott-kroeber-yu.

Endrejat, V. and Thiemann, M. (2020) 'When Brussels meets shadow banking – Technical complexity, regulatory agency and the reconstruction of the shadow banking chain', *Competition and Change*, https://doi.org/10.1177/1024529420911171

Engelen, E. (2018) 'How shadow banking became non banking finance: The conjnctural power of economic ideas', Nesvatailova, A. (ed.), *Shadow Banking: Scope, Origins and Theories*, London: Routledge, pp. 40–53.

Engelen, E., Ertürk, I., Froud, J., Johal, S., Leaver, A., Moran, M., Nilsson, A., and Williams, K. (2011) *After the Great Complacence: Financial Crisis and the Politics of Reform*, Oxford: Oxford University Press.

Engelen, E. and Glasmacher, A. (2018) 'The waiting game: How securitization became the solution for the growth problem of the Eurozone', *Competition and Change* 22 (2): 165–183.

European Banking Authority (EBA) (2014) *Discussion Paper on Simple Standard and Transparent Securitization*, 14 October, London, available at https://eba.europa.eu/sites/default/documents/files/documents/10180/846157/ceefdf3f-58ea-452f-a924-2563410d1705/EBA-DP-2014-02%20Discussion%20Paper%20on%20simple%20standard%20and%20transparent%20securitisations.pdf?retry=1

European Banking Authority (EBA) (2016) *Policy Advice, on the Basel III Reforms: Securities Financing Transactions*, 2 August, London, available at https://eba.europa.eu/sites/default/documents/files/documents/10180/2886865/870bbd5e-ae8f-4933-9f36-784c7183c7f4/Policy%20Advice%20on%20Basel%20III%20reforms%20-%20SFTs.pdf?retry=

European Banking Federation (2014) *Response to Consultation on Functioning of Securitisation Market in the European Union*, 7 July, Brussels, available at https://www.ecb.europa.eu/pub/pdf/other/141013-abs-joint-responses.en.pdf

European Banking Federation (2015a) *Response to Consultation of the BCBS-IOSCO on Criteria for Simple, Transparent and Comparable Securitisations*, 11 February, Brussels, available at https://www.iosco.org/library/pubdocs/467/pdf/European%20Banking%20Federation.pdf

European Banking Federation (2015b) *Response to the European Commission Consultation on Criteria for Simple, Transparent and Comparable Securitisations*, 15 May, Brussels, available at https://www.ebf.eu/wp-content/uploads/2017/01/EBF_014574K-EBF-response-to-Commission-consultation-on-Securitisation-.pdf

European Commission (2009) *Commission Staff Working Document*, 30 April, Brussels, available at https://eur-lex.europa.eu/legal-content/EN/TXT/PDF/?uri=CELEX:52009SC0576&from=EN

European Commission (2012) *Green Paper: Shadow Banking*, 19 March, Brussels, available at https://eur-lex.europa.eu/legal-content/EN/TXT/?uri=CELEX:52012DC0102

European Commission (2015) *Consultation Document: An EU Framework for Simple, Transparent and Standardised Securitization*, 18 February, Brussels, available at https://ec.europa.eu/finance/consultations/2015/securitisation/docs/consultation-document_en.pdf

European Commission (2017) *Report on Transparency of Securities Financing Transactions and Reuse*, 19 October, Brussels, available at https://ec.europa.eu/transparency/regdoc/rep/1/2017/EN/COM-2017-604-F1-EN-MAIN-PART-1.PDF

European Fund and Asset Management Association (2014a) *Response to Consultation on Methodologies for G-SIFIs*, 7 April, Brussels, available at https://www.iosco.org/library/pubdocs/435/pdf/European%20Fund%20and%20Asset%20Management%20Association%20(EFAMA).pdf

European Fund and Asset Management Association (2014b) *Response to Consultation on the Proposed Application of Numerical Haircut Floors to non-bank-to-non-bank transactions*, 15 December, Brussels, available at https://www.fsb.org/wp-content/uploads/European-Fund-and-Asset-Management-Association-EFAMA.pdf

European Fund and Asset Management Association (2015) *Response to Consultation on Assessment Methodologies for G-SIFIs*, 29 May, Brussels, available at https://www.iosco.org/library/pubdocs/479/pdf/European%20Fund%20and%20Asset%20Management%20Association%20(EFAMA).pdf

European Fund and Asset Management Association (2017) *Response to Consultation on Liquidity Risk Management Recommendations*, 3 October, Brussels, available at https://www.iosco.org/library/pubdocs/573/pdf/EFAMA.pdf

European Securities and Markets Authority (ESMA) (2016) *Report on Shadow Banking, Leverage and Pro-cyclicality*, 4 October, Paris, available at https://www.esma.europa.eu/press-news/esma-news/esma-reports-shadow-banking-leverage-and-pro-cyclicality

European Systemic Risk Board (ESRB) (2012) *Occasional Paper on Money Market Funds*, 22 June, Frankfurt, available at https://www.esrb.europa.eu/pub/pdf/occasional/20120622_occasional_paper_1.pdf

European Systemic Risk Board (ESRB) (2015) *Report on the Efficiency of Margining Requirements to Limit Pro-cyclicality*, 28 July, Frankfurt, available at https://www.esrb.europa.eu/pub/pdf/other/150729_report_pro-cyclicality.en.pdf

European Systemic Risk Board (ESRB) (2016) *Opinion to ESMA on Securities Financing Transactions and Leverage*, 4 October, Frankfurt, available at https://www.esrb.europa.eu/pub/pdf/other/20161004_esrbopinion.en.pdf

European Systemic Risk Board (ESRB) (2017) *Macroprudential Use of Margins and Haircuts*, 17 February, Frankfurt, available at https://www.esrb.europa.eu/pub/pdf/reports/170216_macroprudential_use_of_margins_and_haircuts.en.pdf

European Systemic Risk Board (ESRB) (2019) *Response to Consultation on Investment Funds Leverage*, 3 September, Frankfurt, available at https://www.iosco.org/library/pubdocs/615/pdf/ESRB.pdf

Fabozzi, F., Davis, H., and Choudhry, M. (2006) *Introduction to Structured Finance*, London: John Wiley & Sons.

Falleti, G. T. and Lynch, J. (2009) 'Context and Causal Mechanisms in Political Analysis', *Comparative Political Studies* 42 (9): 1143–1166.

Farrell, H. and Newman, A. L. (2014) 'The new politics of interdependence: Cross-national layering in Trans-Atlantic regulatory disputes', *Comparative Political Studies* 48 (4): 497–526.

Farrell, H. and Newman, A. L. (2016) 'The new interdependence approach: theoretical development and empirical demonstration', *Review of International Political Economy* 23 (5): 713–736.

Farrell, H. and Newman, A. L. (2018) 'Linkage politics and complex governance in Transatlantic surveillance', *World Politics* 70(4): 515–554.

Fidelity (2015) *Response to Consultation on Assessment Methodologies for G-SIFIs*, 27 May, Boston, available at https://www.iosco.org/library/pubdocs/479/pdf/Fidelity%20Management%20and%20Research%20Company.pdf

Finance Watch (2015) *Cheat sheet: What Is Securitisation (CMU)?*, 28 February, Brussels, available at https://www.finance-watch.org/publication/cheat-sheet-what-is-securitisation-cmu/

Financial Crisis Inquiry Commission (2011) *Report*, January, Washington, available at https://www.govinfo.gov/content/pkg/GPO-FCIC/pdf/GPO-FCIC.pdf

Financial Services Authority (FSA) (2009) *The Turner Review: A Regulatory Response to the Global Banking Crisis*, March, London, available at http://www.actuaries.org/CTTEES_TFRISKCRISIS/Documents/turner_review.pdf

Financial Stability Board (FSB) (2010) *Reducing the Moral Hazard Posed by Systemically Important Financial Institutions*, November, Basel, available at https://www.fsb.org/2010/11/r_101111a/

Financial Stability Board (FSB) (2011a) *Shadow Banking: Scoping the Issues*, April, Basel, available at http://www.financialstabilityboard.org/2011/04/shadow-banking-scoping-the-issues/

Financial Stability Board (FSB) (2011b) *Report with Recommendations to Strengthen Oversight and Regulation of Shadow Banking*, October, Basel, available at http://www.financialstabilityboard.org/2011/10/r_111027a/

Financial Stability Board (FSB) (2012a) *Report on Securities Lending and Repos: Market Overview and Financial Stability Issues*, April, Basel, available at http://www.fsb.org/wp-content/uploads/r_120427.pdf

Financial Stability Board (FSB) (2012b) *Consultative Document: A Policy Framework for Addressing Shadow Banking Risks in Securities Lending and Repos*, November, Basel, available at https://www.fsb.org/wp-content/uploads/r_121118b.pdf?page_moved=1

Financial Stability Board (FSB) (2012c) *Strengthening Oversight and Regulation of Shadow Banking: An Integrated Overview of Policy Recommendations*, November, Basel, available at http://www.financialstabilityboard.org/2012/11/r_121118/

Financial Stability Board (FSB) (2012e) *Global Shadow Banking Monitoring Report*, November, Basel, available at http://www.financialstabilityboard.org/2012/11/r_121118c/

Financial Stability Board (FSB) (2013a) *Strengthening Oversight and Regulation of Shadow Banking: An Overview of Policy Recommendations*, August, Basel, available at https://www.fsb.org/wp-content/uploads/r_130829a.pdf

Financial Stability Board (FSB) (2013b) *Policy Framework for Strengthening Oversight and Regulation of Shadow Banking Entities* (other than MMFs), August, Basel, available at https://www.fsb.org/wp-content/uploads/r_130829c.pdf?page_moved=1

Financial Stability Board (FSB) (2013c) *Policy Framework for Addressing Shadow Banking Risks in Securities Lending and Repos*, August, Basel, available at https://www.fsb.org/2013/08/r_130829b/

Financial Stability Board (FSB) (2013d) *Global Shadow Banking Monitoring Report of 2013*, November, Basel, available at https://www.fsb.org/wp-content/uploads/r_131114.pdf

Financial Stability Board (FSB) (2014a) *Global Shadow Banking Monitoring Report*, October, Basel, available at http://www.financialstabilityboard.org/2014/11/global-shadow-banking-monitoring-report-2014/

Financial Stability Board (FSB) (2014b) *Progress Report on Transforming Shadow Banking into Resilient Market-Based Financing*, November, Basel, available at http://www.financialstabilityboard.org/2014/11/progress-report-on-transforming-shadow-banking-into-resilient-market-based-financing/

Financial Stability Board (FSB) (2014c) *Regulatory Framework for Haircuts on Non-centrally Cleared Securities Financing Transactions*, October, Basel, available at https://www.fsb.org/wp-content/uploads/r_141013a.pdf

Financial Stability Board (FSB) (2015a) *Global Shadow Banking Monitoring Report of 2015*, November, Basel, available at https://www.fsb.org/wp-content/uploads/global-shadow-banking-monitoring-report-2015.pdf

Financial Stability Board (FSB) (2015d) *Standards and Processes for Global Securities Financing Data Collection and Aggregation*, November, Basel, available at https://www.fsb.org/2015/11/standards-and-processes-for-global-securities-financing-data-collection-and-aggregation-3/

Financial Stability Board (FSB) (2015e) *Regulatory Framework for Haircuts on Non-centrally Cleared Securities Financing* Transactions, November, Basel, available at https://www.fsb.org/2015/11/regulatory-framework-for-haircuts-on-non-centrally-cleared-securities-financing-transactions-3/

Financial Stability Board (FSB) (2016a) *Thematic Review on the Implementation of the FSB Policy Framework for Shadow Banking Entities*, May, Basel, available at https://www.fsb.org/wp-content/uploads/Shadow-banking-peer-review.pdf

Financial Stability Board (FSB) (2016b) *Consultation Paper on Policy Recommendations to Address Structural Vulnerabilities from Asset Management Activities*, June, Basel, available at https://www.fsb.org/wp-content/uploads/FSB-Asset-Management-Consultative-Document.pdf

Financial Stability Board (FSB) (2017a) *Global Shadow Banking Monitoring Report of 2016*, May, Basel, available at https://www.fsb.org/wp-content/uploads/global-shadow-banking-monitoring-report-2016.pdf

Financial Stability Board (FSB) (2017b) *Policy Recommendations to Address Structural Vulnerabilities from Asset Management Activities*, January, Basel, available at https://www.fsb.org/2017/01/policy-recommendations-to-address-structural-vulnerabilities-from-asset-management-activities/

Financial Stability Board (FSB) (2017c) *Rehypothecation and Collateral Re-use: Potential Financial Stability Issues, Market Evolution and Regulatory Approaches*, January, Basel, available at https://www.fsb.org/wp-content/uploads/Re-hypothecation-and-collateral-re-use.pdf

Financial Stability Board (FSB) (2017d) *Non-cash Collateral Re-Use: Measure and Metrics*, January, Basel, available at https://www.fsb.org/2017/01/non-cash-collateral-re-use-measure-and-metrics/

Financial Stability Board (FSB) (2017e) *Assessment of Shadow Banking Activities, Risks and the Adequacy of Post-crisis Policy Tools to Address Financial Stability Concerns*, July, Basel, available at https://www.fsb.org/2017/07/assessment-of-shadow-banking-activities-risks-and-the-adequacy-of-post-crisis-policy-tools-to-address-financial-stability-concerns/

Financial Stability Board (FSB) (2018a) *Compendium of Standards*, Basel, available at https://www.fsb.org/work-of-the-fsb/about-the-compendium-of-standards/

Financial Stability Board (FSB) (2018b) *Securities Financing Transactions: Reporting Guidelines*, March, Basel, available at https://www.fsb.org/2018/03/securities-financing-transactions-reporting-guidelines/

Financial Stability Board (FSB) (2018c) *Global Shadow Banking Monitoring Report of 2017*, Basel,

Financial Stability Board FSB (2019a) *Global Monitoring Report on Non-Bank Financial Intermediation of 2018*, February, Basel, available at https://www.fsb.org/wp-content/uploads/P040219.pdf

Financial Stability Board (FSB) (2019b) *Per Review MMFs implementation*, October, Basel, available at https://www.iosco.org/library/pubdocs/pdf/IOSCOPD640.pdf

Financial Stability Board (FSB) (2019d) *Vulnerabilities of Leveraged Loans and CLOs*, 19 December, Basel, available at https://www.fsb.org/2019/12/fsb-report-assesses-vulnerabilities-of-leveraged-loans-and-clos/

Financial Stability Board (FSB) (2020a) *Global Monitoring Report on Non-Bank Financial Intermediation of 2019*, February, Basel, available at https://www.fsb.org/wp-content/uploads/P190120.pdf

Financial Stability Board (FSB) (2020b) *COVID-19 pandemic: Financial stability implications and policy measures taken*, April 2020, Basel, available at https://www.fsb.org/2020/04/covid-19-pandemic-financial-stability-implications-and-policy-measures-taken/

Financial Stability Board (FSB) Regional Consultative Group for Asia (2014), *Report on Shadow Banking in Asia*, August, Basel, available at https://www.fsb.org/wp-content/uploads/r_140822c.pdf

Financial Stability Board (FSB) and Bank for International Settlements (BIS) (2018) *Securities Financing Transactions: Reporting Guidelines*, March, Basel, available at https://www.fsb.org/wp-content/uploads/P050318-3.pdf

Financial Stability Board (FSB) and International Monetary Fund (IMF) (2009) *The Financial Crisis and Information Gaps*, October, Washington, available at https://www.imf.org/external/np/g20/pdf/102909.pdf

Financial Stability Board (FSB) and International Organization of Securities Commissions (IOSCO) (2014) *Assessment Methodologies for Non-bank Non-Insurer Global Systemically Important Financial Institutions (G-SIFIs)*, January, Basel, available at https://www.fsb.org/2014/01/r_140108-2/

Financial Stability Board (FSB) and International Organization of Securities Commissions (IOSCO) (2015) *Assessment Methodologies for Non-bank Non-Insurer Global Systemically Important Financial Institutions (G-SIFIs)*, March, Basel, available at https://www.fsb.org/2015/03/assessment-methodologies-for-identifying-non-bank-non-insurer-global-systemically-important-financial-institutions/

Fioretos, O. (2010) 'Capitalist diversity and the international regulation of hedge funds', *Review of International Political Economy* 17 (4): 696–723.

Fischer, S. (2015) *Financial Stability and Shadow Banks: What We Don't Know Could Hurt Us - Speech*, Federal Reserve, 5 December, Washington, available at https://www.bis.org/review/r151207b.htm

Foot, R. and Walter, A. (2011) *China, the United States, and Global Order*, Cambridge: Cambridge University Press.

French Banking Federation (2016) *Response to Consultation on Identification and Measurement of Step-in Risk*, 17 March, Paris, available at https://www.bis.org/bcbs/publ/comments/d349/frenchbankingfe.pdf

Gabor, D. (2014) 'The political economy of repo markets', available at https://www.brot-fuer-die-welt.de/fileadmin/mediapool/blogs/Hanfstaengl_Eva/gabor_political_economy_of_repo_markets.pdf

Gabor, D. (2016a) 'The (impossible) repo trinity: The political economy of repo markets', *Review of International Political Economy* 23 (6): 967–1000.

Gabor, D. (2016b) 'A step too far? The European financial transactions tax on shadow banking', *Journal of European Public Policy* 23 (6): 925–945.

Gabor, D. (2018) 'Goodbye (Chinese) Shadow Banking, Hello Market-based Finance', *Development and Change* 49 (2): 394–419.

Gabor, D. (2020) 'Critical macro-finance: A theoretical lens', *Finance and Society* 6 (1): 45–55.

Gabor, D. and Ban, C. (2016) 'Banking on bonds: the new links between states and markets', *Journal of Common Market Studies* 54 (3): 617–635.

Gabor, D. and Vestergaard, J. (2015) 'The Capital Markets Union: Faith in finance restored, contract with finance rewritten?', 23 July, Brussels, available at https://www.finance-watch.org/the-capital-markets-union-faith-in-finance-restored-contract-with-finance-rewritten/

Gabor, D. and Vestergaard, J. (2016) *Towards a Theory of Shadow Money*, available at https://www.ineteconomics.org/uploads/papers/Towards_Theory_Shadow_Money_GV_INET.pdf

Gabor, D. and Vestergaard, J. (2018) 'Chasing unicorns: The European single safe asset project', *Competition & Change* 22 (2): 139–164.

Gadinis, S. (2014) 'The Financial Stability Board: The new politics of international financial regulation', *Texas International Law Journal* 48 (2): 157–176.

Gadinis, S. (2015) 'Three pathways to global standards: Private, regulator, and ministry networks', *American Journal of International Law* 109 (1): 1–57.

Gallagher, M. (2014) *Letter from SEC Commissioner*, 15 May, Washington, available at: https://www.sec.gov/comments/am-1/am1-52.pdf

Gallagher, M. (2015) *Bank Regulators at the Gates: The Misguided Quest for Prudential Regulation of Asset Managers – Speech*, 10 April, Washington, available at https://www.sec.gov/news/speech/041015-spch-cdmg.html

Gebauer, S. and Mazelis, F. (2019) 'Macroprudential regulation and leakage to the shadow banking sector', *Discussion Paper of the German Institute for Economic Research*, July, Berlin, German Institute for Economic Research, available at https://ideas.repec.org/p/diw/diwwpp/dp1814.html

Gehring, T. and Faude, B. (2014) 'A theory of emerging order within institutional complexes: How competition among regulatory international institutions leads to institutional adaptation and division of labor', *Review of International Organizations* 9 (4): 471–498.

Gelzinis, G. (2019) *Strengthening the Regulation and Oversight of Shadow Banks*, 18 July, Washington, available at https://www.americanprogress.org/issues/economy/reports/2019/07/18/471564/strengthening-regulation-oversight-shadow-banks

Germain, R. (2016), 'Locating authority: Resolution regimes, SIFIs and the enduring significance of financial great powers', *Journal of Banking Regulation* 17 (1–2), pp. 34–45.

German Banking Industry Committee (2016) *Response to Consultation on Identification and Measurement of Step-in Risk*, 16 March, Frankfurt, available at https://www.bis.org/bcbs/publ/comments/d349/gbic.pdf

Gerring, J. (2008) 'The mechanismic worldview: Thinking inside the box', *British Journal of Political Science* 38 (1): 161–179.

Global Financial Markets Association (2013) *Response to Consultation on Revisions to the Basel Securitisation Framework*, 18 March, London, available at https://www.bis.org/publ/bcbs236/gfma.pdf

Global Financial Markets Association, Commercial Real Estate Finance Council, Commercial Real Estate Finance Council Europe and Real Estate Roundtable (2016) *Response to Consultation on Identification and Measurement of Step-in risk*, 4 March, Basel, available at https://www.bis.org/bcbs/publ/comments/d349/gccerer.pdf

Global Financial Markets Association, International Swaps and Derivatives Association, Institute of International Finance, International Capital Market Association (2015) *Response to Consultation con Criteria for Identifying Simple, Transparent and Comparable Securitisation*, 13 February, Basel, available at https://www.iosco.org/library/pubdocs/467/pdf/GFMA-ISDA-IIF-ICMA.pdf

Global Financial Markets Association, the International Capital Market Association, and the Institute of International Finance (2017) *Response to Consultation on Criteria for Identifying Simple, Transparent and Comparable Short-Term Securitisations*, 5 October, London.

Goldbach, R. (2015a) *Global Governance and Regulatory Failures*, Basingstoke: Palgrave.

Goldbach, R. (2015b) 'Asymmetric influence in global banking regulation, transnational harmonization, the competition State, and the roots of regulatory failure', *Review of International Political Economy* 22 (6): 1087–1127.

González-Páramo, J. M. (2010) *Re-starting securitisation – Speech*, 16 June, Frankfurt, available at https://www.ecb.europa.eu/press/key/date/2010/html/sp100616.en.html

Goodhart, C. (2011) *The Basel Committee on Banking Supervision: A History of the Early Years 1974–1997*, Cambridge: Cambridge University Press.

Gorton, G. (2010) *Slapped by the Invisible Hand: The Panic of 2007*, Oxford: Oxford University Press.

Gorton, G. and Metrick, A. (2009) 'Securitized Banking and the Run on Repo', *NBER Working Paper* No. 15233, August, Cambridge (MA), available at http://www.nber.org/papers/w15223.pdf

Gorton, G. and Metrick, A. (2010) 'Regulating the Shadow Banking System', *Brookings Papers on Economic Activity*, September, Washington, available at https://www.brookings.edu/wp-content/uploads/2010/09/2010b_bpea_gorton.pdf.

Gravelle, M. and Pagliari, S. (2018) 'Global markets, national toolkits', in Helleiner, E., Pagliari, S., and Spagna, I. (eds), *Governing the World's Biggest Market: The Politics of Derivatives Regulation After the 2008 Crisis*, Oxford: Oxford University Press, pp. 82–106.

Greene, E. F. and Broomfield, E. L. (2013) 'Promoting risk mitigation, not migration: A comparative analysis of shadow banking reforms by the FSB, USA and EU', *Capital Market Law Review* 8 (1): 6–53.

Griffith-Jones, S. (2017) 'Regulating international financial markets', in Schlager, C., Chen, D., Rosenplanter, A., and Zhang, H. (eds), *China And The Group 20: The Interplay between a Rising Power and an Emerging Institution*, Washington: World Century.

Group of Thirty (G30) (2009) *Financial Reform: A Framework for Financial Stability*, Washington, DC.

Group of Twenty (G20) (2009a) 'Communiqué G20 Leaders Summit London', 2–3 April, London.

Group of Twenty (G20) (2010) 'Communiqué G20 Leaders Summit Seoul', 11–12 November, Seoul.

Group of Twenty (G20) (2011) 'Communiqué G20 Leaders Summit Cannes', 3–4 November, Cannes.

Group of Twenty (G20) (2013a) 'Communiqué G20 Leaders Summit St Petersburg', 5–6 September, St Petersburg.

Group of Twenty (G20) (2013b) *Road Map Roadmap towards Strengthened Oversight and Regulation of Shadow Banking*, September, Toronto, http://www.g20.utoronto.ca/2013/G20_Roadmap_towards_Strengthened_Oversight_and_Regulation_of_Shadow_Banking.pdf

Group of Twenty (G20) (2017) G20 'Leaders' Declaration: Shaping an Interconnected World', 8 July, Toronto.

Gruin, J. and Knaack, P. (2020) 'Not just another shadow bank: Chinese authoritarian capitalism and the "developmental" promise of digital financial innovation', *New Political Economy* 25 (3), 370–387.

Haldane, A. G. (2012) *The Dog and the Frisbee – Speech*, Bank of England, 31 August, London, available at https://www.bis.org/review/r120905a.pdf

Haldane, A. (2014) *The Age of Asset Management: Speech*, Bank of England, 4 April, London, available at https://www.bis.org/review/r140507d.pdf

Hardie, I. and Howarth, D. (eds) (2013) *Market-Based Banking and the International Financial Crisis*, Oxford: Oxford University Press.

Hauser, A. (2012) *Shining a Light in the Shadows: Speech*, Bank of England, 21 June, London, available at https://www.bankofengland.co.uk/-/media/boe/files/speech/2012/shining-a-light-in-the-shadows

Hauser, A. (2013) *The Future of Repo: 'Too much' or 'too little: Speech*, Bank of England, 11 June, London, available at https://www.bankofengland.co.uk/speech/2013/the-future-of-repo-too-much-or-too-little

Hauser, A. (2020) *Seven Moments in Spring: Covid-19, financial markets and the Bank of England's balance sheet operations – Speech*, Bank of England, 4 June, London.

Heldt, E. C. and Schmidtke, H. (2019) 'Explaining coherence in international regime complexes: How the World Bank shapes the field of multilateral development finance', *Review of International Political Economy* 26(6): 1160–1186.

Helfer, L. (2009) 'Regime shifting in the international intellectual property system', *Perspectives on Politics* 7 (1): 39–44.

Helleiner, E. (2010) 'The Financial Stability Board and International Standards', *IGI G20 Papers* No. 1, available at https://www.cigionline.org/sites/default/files/g20_no_1_1.pdf

Helleiner, E. (2013) 'Did the financial crisis generate a fourth pillar of global economic architecture?', *Swiss Political Science Review* 19 (4): 558–563.

Helleiner, E. (2014) *The Status Quo Crisis: Global Financial Governance after the 2008 Financial Meltdown*, Oxford: Oxford University Press.

Helleiner, E., Pagliari, S., and Spagna, I. (eds) (2018) *Governing the World's Biggest Market: The Politics of Derivatives Regulation after the 2008 Crisis*, Oxford: Oxford University Press.

Henning, C. R. (2017) *Tangled Governance*, Oxford: Oxford University Press.

Howarth, D. and Quaglia, L. (2013) 'Banking on stability: The political economy of new capital requirements in the European Union', *Journal of European Integration* 35 (3): 333–346.

Howarth, D. and Quaglia, L. (2016) 'The comparative political economy of Basel III in Europe', *Policy and Society* 35 (3): 205–214.

Institute of International Finance (IIF) (2012) *Shadow Banking: A Forward-Looking Framework for Effective Policy*, June, Washington, available at https://ec.europa.eu/finance/consultations/2012/shadow/docs/contributions/individual-others/iif_en.pdf

Institute of International Finance (IIF) (2013) *Response to Consultation on Revisions to the Basel Securitization Framework*, 15 March, Washington, available at https://www.bis.org/publ/bcbs236/iif.pdf

Institute of International Finance (IIF) (2014) *Response to Consultation on Assessment Methodologies for G-SIFIs*, 4 April, Washington, available at https://www.iosco.org/library/pubdocs/435/pdf/Institute%20of%20International%20Finance%20(IIF).pdf

Institute of International Finance, International Banking Federation, Global Financial Markets Association (2013) *Response to Consultation on Capital Requirements for Banks Equity Investments in Funds*, 4 October, Basel, available at https://www.bis.org/publ/bcbs257/jointiifgfmaibf.pdf

Institute of International Finance and International Banking Federation (2016) *Response to Consultation on Identification of Step-in Risk*, 17 March, Washington, available at https://www.bis.org/bcbs/publ/comments/d349/ioifibf.pdf

Institute of International Finance, International Banking Federation, Global Financial Markets Association, Commercial Real Estate Finance Council, Commercial Real Estate Finance Council of Europe (2017) *Response to Consultation on Guidelines for Identification and Measurement of Step-in risk*, 15 March, Washington, available at https://www.bis.org/bcbs/publ/comments/d398/iif.pdf

International Banking Federation (2012) *Response to Report on Securities Lending and Repos*, 20 June, London, available at https://www.fsb.org/wp-content/uploads/c_120806m.pdf

International Banking Federation (2013a) *Response to Consultation on Framework for Addressing Shadow Banking Risks in Securities Lending and Repo*, 29 November, London, available at https://www.fsb.org/wp-content/uploads/c_131220m.pdf

International Banking Federation (2013b) *Response to Consultation on Revisions to the Basel Securitisation Framework*, 20 March, London, available at https://www.bis.org/publ/bcbs236/internationalba.pdf

International Banking Federation (2019) *Response to Consultation on Revisions to Basel 3 and the Treatment of Securities Financing Transactions*, 11 January, London, available at http://www.ibfed.org.uk/wp-content/uploads/2019/01/IBFed-letter-to-BCBS-on-capital-treatment-of-SFTs_11jan19.pdf

International Capital Market Association (2013a) *Understanding the Repo Market*, February, London, available at 'https://www.icmagroup.org/assets/documents/Regulatory/Repo/Repo-FAQs-January-2019.pdf

International Capital Market Association (2013b) *What is the Difference between Repo and Securities Lending*, London, available at https://www.icmagroup.org/Regulatory-Policy-and-Market-Practice/repo-and-collateral-markets/icma-ercc-publications/frequently-asked-questions-on-repo/13-what-is-the-difference-between-repo-and-securities-lending/

International Capital Market Association (2019) *European Repo Market Survey*, 4 December, available at https://www.icmagroup.org/assets/documents/Market-Info/Repo-Market-Surveys/No-36-December-2018/ICMA-European-repo-market-survey-number-36-conducted-December-2018-040419.pdf

International Capital Market Association and European Repo Council (2012a) *Shadow Banking and Repo*, 20 March, London, available at https://www.icmagroup.org/Regulatory-Policy-and-Market-Practice/repo-and-collateral-markets/icma-ercc-publications/icma-ercc-reports/shadow-banking-and-repo/

International Capital Markets Association (ICMA) and European Repo Council (2012c) *Response to Consultation on Securities Lending and Repos*, 22 May, London, available at https://www.fsb.org/wp-content/uploads/c_120806e.pdf

International Capital Market Association and European Repo Council and the International Securities Lending Association (2013) *Response to Consultation on Shadow Banking Risks in Securities Lending and Repos*, 28 November, London, available at https://www.fsb.org/wp-content/uploads/c_131220l.pdf

International Monetary Fund (IMF) (2006) *Global Financial Stability Report*, April, Washington.

International Monetary Fund (IMF) (2014) *Global Financial Stability Report*, October, Washington.

International Monetary Fund (IMF) (2015) *Global Financial Stability Report*, October, Washington.

International Monetary Fund (IMF) (2018) *Global Financial Stability Report*, October, Washington.

International Organization of Securities Commissions (IOSCO) (1999) *Hedge Funds and Other Highly Leveraged Institutions*, November, Madrid.

International Organization of Securities Commissions (IOSCO) (2009a) *Hedge Funds Oversight: Final Report*, June, Madrid, available at https://www.iosco.org/library/pubdocs/pdf/IOSCOPD293.pdf

International Organization of Securities Commissions (IOSCO) (2009b) *Report on Unregulated Financial Markets and Products*, September, Madrid, available at https://www.iosco.org/library/pubdocs/pdf/IOSCOPD301.pdf

International Organization of Securities Commissions (IOSCO) (2012a) *Consultative Report on Money Market Fund Systemic Risk Analysis and Reform Options*, April, Madrid, available at https://www.iosco.org/library/pubdocs/pdf/IOSCOPD379.pdf

International Organization of Securities Commissions (IOSCO) (2012b) *Policy Recommendations on Money Market Funds*, October, Madrid, available at http://www.csrc.gov.cn/pub/csrc_en/affairs/AffairsIOSCO/201210/P020121010500138903810.pdf

International Organization of Securities Commissions (IOSCO) (2012c) *Report on Global Developments in Securitisation Regulation*, November, Madrid, available at http://www.iosco.org/library/pubdocs/pdf/IOSCOPD394.pdf

International Organization of Securities Commissions (IOSCO) (2013) *Principles of Liquidity Risk Management for Collective Investment Schemes*, March, Madrid, available at https://www.iosco.org/library/pubdocs/pdf/IOSCOPD405.pdf

International Organization of Securities Commissions (IOSCO) (2015a) *Peer Review of Regulation of Money Market Funds: Final Report*, September, Madrid, available at https://www.iosco.org/library/pubdocs/pdf/IOSCOPD502.pdf

International Organization of Securities Commissions (IOSCO) (2018a) *Consultative Paper on Leverage*, November, Madrid, available at https://www.iosco.org/library/pubdocs/pdf/IOSCOPD615.pdf

International Organization of Securities Commissions (IOSCO) (2018b) *Recommendations for Liquidity Risk Management for Collective Investment Schemes*, February, Madrid, available at https://www.iosco.org/library/pubdocs/pdf/IOSCOPD590.pdf

International Organization of Securities Commissions (IOSCO) (2018c) *Open-ended Fund Liquidity and Risk Management – Good Practices and Issues for Consideration*, February, Madrid, available at https://www.iosco.org/library/pubdocs/pdf/IOSCOPD591.pdf

International Organization of Securities Commissions (IOSCO) (2019a) *Recommendations for a Framework Assessing Leverage in Investment Funds*, December, Madrid, available at https://www.iosco.org/library/pubdocs/pdf/IOSCOPD645.pdf

International Organization of Securities Commissions (IOSCO) (2019c) *Peer Review of Regulation of Money Market Funds*, October, Madrid, available at https://www.iosco.org/library/pubdocs/pdf/IOSCOPD640.pdf

International Securities Lending Association (2014) *Response to Consultation on Regulatory Framework for Haircuts on Non-Centrally Cleared Securities Financing Transactions*, 15 December, London, available at https://www.fsb.org/wp-content/uploads/International-Securities-Lending-Association-ISLA.pdf

International Securities Lending Association (2019), *Securities Lending Market Report*, February, London, available at https://www.isla.co.uk/assets/smart-pdfs/isla-securities-lending-market-report-february-2020/files/downloads/ISLA_SLReport_Feb2020_spreads.pdf

Investment Company Institute (2013) *Response to Consultation on Regulatory Framework for Haircuts on Non-Centrally Cleared Securities Financing Transactions*, 27 November, Washington, available at https://www.fsb.org/wp-content/uploads/c_131220n.pdf

Investment Company Institute (2014) *Response to Consultation on Assessment Methodologies for Identifying G-SIFIs*, 7 April, Washington, available at https://www.iosco.org/library/pubdocs/435/pdf/Investment%20Company%20Institute%20(ICI).pdf

Investment Company Institute (2015) *Response to Consultation on Assessment Methodologies for Identifying G-SIFIs*, 29 May, Washington, available at https://www.iosco.org/library/pubdocs/479/pdf/Investment%20Company%20Institute%20(ICI).pdf

Investment Company Institute (2016) *Response to Consultation to Policy Recommendations to Address Structural Vulnerabilities from Asset Management Activities*, 21 September, Washington, available at https://www.fsb.org/wp-content/uploads/Investment-Company-Institute-ICI1.pdf

Investment Company Institute (2017) *Response to Consultation on Recommendations for Liquidity Risk Management of Investment Funds*, Washington, available at https://www.iosco.org/library/pubdocs/573/pdf/ICI%20Global%20-%20Liquidity%20Recommendations.pdf

James, S., Pagliari, S., and Young, K. (2021) 'The internationalization of European financial networks: A quantitative text analysis of EU consultation responses', *Review of International Political Economy* 28 (4): 898–925.

James, S. and Quaglia, L. (2020) *The UK and Multi-level Financial Regulation: From the Crisis to Brexit*, Oxford: Oxford University Press.

James, S. and Quaglia, L. (2022) 'Epistemic contestation and interagency conflict: The challenge of regulating investment funds', *Regulation & Governance*, doi.org/10.1111/rego.12457

Jobst, A. (2008) 'What Is Securitization?', *Finance and Development*, September, Washington, available at https://www.imf.org/external/pubs/ft/fandd/2008/09/pdf/basics.pdf

Johnson, T. and Urpelainen, J. (2012) 'A strategic theory of regime integration and separation', *International Organization* 66 (4): 645–677.

JointForum (2011) *Report on Asset Securitisation Incentives*, July, Basel, available at https://www.bis.org/publ/joint26.pdf

Jordana, J. (2017) 'Trans-governmental networks as regulatory intermediaries: Horizontal collaboration and the realities of soft power', *Annals of the American Academy of Political and Social Science* 670: 245–261.

Kacperczyk, M. and Schnabl, C. (2012) 'How safe are money market funds?', April, New York, available at http://pages.stern.nyu.edu/~sternfin/mkacperc/public_html/mmfs.pdf

Kalaitzake, M. (2017) 'Death by a thousand cuts? Financial political power and the case of the European Financial Transaction Tax', *New Political Economy* 22 (4): 709–726.

Kalyanpur, N. and Newman, A. L. (2017) 'Form over function in finance: International institutional design by bricolage, *Review of International Political Economy* 24 (3): 363–392.

Kamin, S. B. and Pounder DeMarco, L. (2010) 'How did a domestic housing slump turn into a global financial crisis', *Board of Governors of the Federal Reserve System International Finance Discussion Paper* N. 994, January, Washington, available at https://www.federalreserve.gov/pubs/ifdp/2010/994/ifdp994.pdf

Kapstein, E. B. (1989) 'Resolving the regulator's dilemma: International coordination of banking regulations', *International Organisation* 43 (2): 323–347.

Kapstein, E. B. (1992) 'Between power and purpose: Central bankers and the politics of regulatory convergence', *International Organization* 46 (1): 265–287.

Karmel, R. and Kelly, C. (2009) 'The hardening of international soft law in finance', Brooklyn *Journal of International Law* 34: 884–950.

Kelley, J. (2009) 'The more the merrier? The effects of having multiple international election monitoring organizations', *Perspectives in Politics* 7(1): 59–64.

Kempthorne, D. (2013) *Governing International Securities Markets: IOSCO and the Politics of International Securities Market Standards*, Doctoral Thesis, University of Waterloo, available at http://hdl.handle.net/10012/7661

Keohane, R. O. and Victor, D. G. (2011) 'The regime complex for climate change', *Perspectives on Politics* 9 (1): 7–23.

Kirton, J. (2013) *G20 Governance for a Globalized World*, Aldershot: Ashgate.

Knaack, P. (2015) 'Innovation and deadlock in global financial governance: Transatlantic coordination failure in OTC derivatives regulation', *Review of International Political Economy* 22 (6):1–32.

Knaack, P. and Gruin, J. (2020) 'From shadow banking to digital financial inclusion: China's rise and the politics of epistemic contestation within the financial stability board', *Review of International Political Economy*, available at https://doi.org/10.1080/09692290.2020.1772849

KnightM. (2008) *Securitisation: was the tail wagging the dog? - Speech*, 29 May, Basel, available at https://www.bis.org/speeches/sp080602.htm

Kodres, L. E. (2017) 'Shadow Banks: Out of the Eyes of Regulators', *Finance and Development*, available at https://www.imf.org/external/pubs/ft/fandd/basics/52-shadow-banking.htm

Koremenos, B., Lipson, C., and Snidal, D. (2001) 'The Rational Design of International Institutions', *International Organization* 55 (4): 761–799.

Kranke, M, (2020) Exclusive Expertise: The Boundary Work of International Organizations. Review of International Political Economy, https://doi.org/10.1080/09692290.2020.1784774

Kranke, M. and Yarrow, D. (2019). 'The global governance of systemic Rrisk: How measurement practices tame macroprudential politics', *New Political Economy* 24(6): 816–832.

Krugman, P. (2009) 'Out of the Shadows', *New York Times*, 18 June.

Lall, R. (2012) 'From failure to failure: The politics of international banking regulation', *Review of International Political Economy* 19 (4): 609–638.

Lall, R. (2014) 'Timing as a source of regulatory influence: A technical elite network analysis of global finance', *Regulation & Governance*9 (2): 125–143.

Lane, T. (2013) *Shedding Light on Shadow Banking - Speech*, 26 June, Basel, available at https://www.bis.org/review/r130628g.pdf

Lastra, R. (2014) 'Do we need a world financial organization?', *Journal of International Economic Law* 17 (4): 787–805.

Lavelle, K. C. (2013) *Money and Banks in the American Political System*, Cambridge: Cambridge University Press.

Lavelle, K. C. (2019) 'US foreign policy and the governance of finance', *Business and Politics*21 (1): 1–26.

Leblond, P. (2011) 'EU, US and international accounting standards: A delicate balancing act in governing global finance', *Journal of European Public Policy* 18 (3): 443–461.

Lee, E. (2015) 'The shadow banking system – why it will hamper the effectiveness of Basel III', *Journal of International Banking Law and Regulation* 30 (7): 373–381.

Lesage, D. and Van de Graaf, T. (2013) 'Thriving in complexity? The OECD system's role in energy and taxation', *Global Governance* 19 (1): 83–92.

Li, L., Li, Y., Macchiavelli, M., and Zhou, X (2020) 'Liquidity Restrictions, Runs, and Central Bank Interventions: Evidence from Money Market Funds', Federal Reserve, December, available at https://papers.ssrn.com/sol3/papers.cfm?abstract_id=3607593

Liansheng, Z. (2015) 'The shadow banking system of China and international regulatory cooperation', *New Thinking and the New G20* Paper N. 6, March, Waterloo, available at https://www.cigionline.org/sites/default/files/new_thinking_g20_no6.pdf

Luck, S. and Schempp, P. (2014) 'Banks, shadow banking and fragility', *ECB Working Paper Series* N. 1726, ECB, August, Frankfurt, available at https://www.ecb.europa.eu/pub/pdf/scpwps/ecbwp1726.pdf

Lysandrou, P. and Nesvetailova, A. (2015) 'The role of shadow banking entities in the crisis: A disaggregated view', *Review of International Political Economy* 22(2): 257–279.

Macartney, H., Howarth, D., and James, S. (2020) 'Bank power and public policy since the financial crisis', *Business and Politics* 22 (1): 1–24.

Mahoney, C. and Baumgartner, F. (2008) 'Converging perspectives on interest group research in Europe and America', *West European Politics* 31(6): 1253–1273.

Maijoor, S. (2014) *Asset Management and the Regulatory Challenges Ahead – Speech*, ESMA, 5 November, Paris, available at https://www.esma.europa.eu/sites/default/files/library/2015/11/2014-1333_steven_maijoor_keynote_speech_at_efama_5_nov_2014.pdf

Maijoor, S. (2019) *Keynote address at the EFAMA Investment Management Forum*, ESMA, 22 November, Paris, available at https://www.esma.europa.eu/sites/default/files/library/esma71-319-157_steven_maijoor_keynote_speech_-_efama_conference_22_nov_2019.pdf

Managed Funds Association (2013) *Response to Consultation on Policy Framework for Addressing Shadow Banking Risks in Securities Lending and Repos*, 28 November, Washington, available at https://www.fsb.org/wp-content/uploads/c_131220s.pdf

Marcacci, A. (2012) 'IOSCO: The world standard setter for globalized financial markets', *Richmond Journal of Global Law and Business* 12: 23–44.

Marcacci, A. (2014) 'IOSCO and the spreading of a US-Like regulatory philosophy around the world', *European Business Law Review* 25 (6): 759–809.

Merkel, A. and Sarkozy, N. (2009) *G20 summit joint statement by Angela Merkel and Nicolas Sarkozy*, 1 April, Berlin.

Maynz, R. (ed.) (2012) *Crisis and Control: Institutional Change in Financial Market Regulation*, Cologne: Max Planck Institute for the Study of Societies.

Maynz, R. (ed.) (2015) *Negotiated Reform: The Multilevel Governance of Financial Regulation*, Frankfurt: Campus Verlag.

McCully, P. (2007) 'Teton reflections', *Pimco: Global Central Bank Focus*, 7 September, Newport (CA).

McDowell, D. (2012) 'The US as "sovereign international last-resort lender": The Fed's currency swap programme during the Great Panic of 2007–09', *New Political Economy* 17 (2): 157–178.

McKeen-Edwards, H. and Porter, T. (2013) *Transnational Financial Associations and the Governance of Global Finance*, London: Routledge.

McLoughlin, K. and Meredith, J. (2017) 'The rise of Chinese money market funds', *Bulletin of Reserve Bank of Australia*, March available at https://www.rba.gov.au/publications/bulletin/2017/mar/pdf/bu-0317-9-the-rise-of-chinese-money-market-funds.pdf

Medcraft, G. (2015) *IOSCO and the International Reform Agenda for Financial Markets - Speech*', IOSCO, 22 June, Madrid, available at http://download.asic.gov.au/media/3273669/speech-to-the-national-press-club-washington-dc-greg-medcraft-published-22-june-2015.pdf

Mersch, E. (2017) *Securitisation Revisited: Speech*, European Central Bank, 16 November, Frankfurt, available athttps://www.ecb.europa.eu/press/key/date/2017/html/ecb.sp171116.en.html

Montalbano, G. (2020) 'Policy entrepreneurship and the influence of the transnational financial industry in the EU reform of securitization', *Business and Politics* 22 (1): 85–112.

Morgan Lewis (2018) *Guide for Credit Risk Retention Rules for Securitization*, February, London, available at https://www.morganlewis.com/~/media/files/handouts/final_risk_retention_guide_handout.ashx

Morin, J-F. and Orsini, A. (2014) 'Policy coherency and regime complexes: The case of genetic resources', *Review of International Studies* 40 (2): 303–324.

Morse, J. C. and Keohane, R. O. (2014) 'Contested multilateralism', *Review of International Organisation* 9 (4): 385–412.

Moschella, M. and Tsingou, E. (2013a) 'Regulating finance after the crisis: Unveiling the different dynamics of the regulatory process', *Regulation & Governance* 7 (4): 407–416.

Moschella, M. and Tsingou, E. (eds) (2013b) *Great Expectations, Slow Transformations: Incremental Change in Financial Governance*, Colchester: ECPR Press.

Mosley, L. (2003). 'Attempting global standards: National governments, international finance, and the IMF's data regime', *Review of International Political Economy* 10 (2): 331–362.

Mosley, L. (2010) 'Regulating globally, implementing locally: The financial codes and standards effort', *Review of International Political Economy* 17 (4): 724–761.

Mügge, D. (2010) *Widen the Market, Narrow the Competition: Banker Interests and the Making of a European Capital Market*, ECPR Press.

Mügge, D. and Perry, J. (2014) 'The flaws of fragmented financial standard-setting: Why substantive economic debates matter for the architecture of global governance', *Politics & Society* 42 (2): 194–222.

Mügge, D. and Stellinga, B. (2015) 'The unstable core of global finance: Contingent valuation and governance of international accounting standards', *Regulation & Governance* 9 (1): 47–62.

Nassr, I. K. and Wehinger, G. (2015) 'Unlocking SME finance through market-based debt: Securitisation, private placements and bonds', *OECD Journal: Financial Market Trends*, available at https://www.oecd.org/finance/Unlocking-SME-finance-through-market-based-debt.pdf

Nesvatailova, A. (ed.) (2018) *Shadow Banking: Scope, Origins and Theories*, London: Routledge.

Nesvetailova, A. (2015) 'A crisis of the overcrowded future: Shadow banking and the political economy of financial innovation', *New Political Economy* 20 (3): 431–453.

Nesvetailova, A. and Palan, R. (2010) 'The end of liberal finance? The changing paradigm of global financial governance', *Millennium* 38 (3): 1–29.

Newman, A. L and Bach, D. (2014) 'The European Union as hardening agent: Soft law and the diffusion of global financial regulation', *Journal of European Public Policy* 21 (3): 430–452.

Newman, A. L. and Posner, E. (2016a) 'Transnational feedback, soft law, and preferences in global financial regulation', *Review of International Political Economy* 23 (1): 123–152.

Newman, A. L. and Posner, E. (2016b) 'Structuring transnational interests: the second-order effects of soft law in the politics of global finance', *Review of International Political Economy* 23 (5): 768–798.

Newman, A. L. and Posner, E. (2018) *Voluntary Disruptions. International Soft Law, Finance, and Power*, Oxford, UK: Oxford University Press.

Oatley, T. (2011) 'The reductionist gamble: open economy politics in the global economy', *International Organization* 65(2): 311–341.

Oatley, T. (2015) *A Political Economy of American Hegemony*, Cambridge: Cambridge University Press.

Oatley, T. (2019) 'Toward a political economy of complex interdependence', *European Journal of International Relations* 25 (4): 957–978.

Oatley, T. and Nabors, R. (1998) 'Redistributive cooperation: Market failures, wealth transfer and the Basle Accord', *International Organization* 52 (1): 35–54.

Occupy the SEC (2015) *Response to Consultation on Assessment Methodologies for G-SIFIs*, 29 May, Washington, available at https://www.iosco.org/library/pubdocs/479/pdf/Occupy%20the%20SEC%20(OSEC).pdf

Ophele, R. and D'Hoir, J. (2018) 'Moving beyond the shadow banking concept', in Banque de France, *Financial Stability Review*, April, Paris, available at http://209.236.64.83/fsr/fra_fsr_201804.pdf

Orsini, A., Morin, J-F., and Young, O. (2013) 'Regime complexes: A buzz, a boom, or a bust for global governance?', *Global Governance* 19 (1): 27–39.

Pagliari, S. (2012) 'Who governs finance? The shifting public-private divide in the regulation of derivatives, rating agencies and hedge funds', *European Law Journal* 18 (1): 44–61.

Pagliari, S. (2013a) 'Governing financial stability: The Financial Stability Board as the emerging pillar in global economic governance', in Moschella, M. and Weaver, K. (eds), *Handbook of Global Economic Governance*, London: Routledge, pp. 143–155.

Pagliari, S. (2013b) *Public Salience and International Financial Regulation. Explaining the International Regulation of OTC Derivatives, Rating Agencies, and Hedge Funds*, Doctoral dissertation, University of Waterloo

Pagliari, S. and Young, K. L. (2014) 'Leveraged interests: Financial industry power and the role of private sector coalitions', *Review of International Political Economy* 21 (3): 575–610.

Palan, R. and Nesvetailova, A. (2014) 'Elsewhere, ideally nowhere: Shadow banking and offshore finance', *Politik* 16 (4): 26–34.

Paredes, T. A. (2011) *Remarks*, Securities and Exchange Commission, 8 June, Washington.

Pauwelyn, J., Wessel, R., and Wouters, J. (eds) (2012) *Informal International Lawmaking*, Oxford: Oxford University Press.

Peirce, H. (2019) *Exchanging Views on Exchange-Traded Funds – Speech*, Securities and Exchange Commission, 10 June, Washington, available at https://www.sec.gov/news/public-statement/statement-peirce-061019

Perotti, E. (2020) 'The coronavirus shock to financial stability', *Vox*, 27 March, available at https://voxeu.org/article/coronavirus-shock-financial-stability

PIMCO (2014) *Response to Consultation on Assessment Methodologies for Identifying G-SIFIs*, 7 April, Newport, available at https://www.iosco.org/library/pubdocs/435/pdf/PIMCO.pdf

Piwowar, M. (2016a) *Opening Remarks*, Securities and Exchange Commission, 1 March, Washington, available at https://www.sec.gov/news/speech/speech-piwowar-03012016.html

Piwowar, M. (2016b) *Remarks Before the Quadrilateral Meeting*, 20 July, Washington, available at https://www.sec.gov/news/speech/speech-piwowar-2016-07-20.html#_ftnref7

Porter, T. (2014a) (ed.) *Transnational Financial Regulation after the Crisis*, London: Routledge.

Porter, T. (2014b) 'Technical systems and the architecture of transnational business governance interactions', *Regulation & Governance* 8 (1): 110–125.

Portes, R. (2019) *Shining a Light on Shadow Banking*, 17 January, London, available at https://www.london.edu/think/shining-a-light-on-shadow-banking

Posner, E. (2009) 'Making rules for global finance: Transatlantic regulatory cooperation at the turn of the Millennium', *International Organization* 63 (4): 665–699.

Posner, E. (2010) 'Sequence as explanation: The international politics of accounting standards', *Review of International Political Economy* 14 (4): 639–664.

Posner, E. (2015) 'International financial regulatory cooperation', in Zeitlin, J. (ed.), *Extending Experimentalist Governance? The European Union and Transnational Regulation*, Oxford: Oxford University Press, pp. 196-223.

Pozsar, Z. (2008) 'The rise and fall of the shadow banking system', *Regional Financial Review*, July: 13–25.

Pozsar, Z. et al. (2010) 'Shadow banking', *Federal Reserve Bank of New York Staff Report N.* 458, Federal Reserve, New York, available at http://www.newyorkfed.org/research/staff_reports/sr458.pdf

Pratt, T. (2018) 'Deference and hierarchy in international regime complexes', *International Organization* 72: 561–590.

Pratt, T. (2019) 'Vertically differentiated cooperation: Explaining policy change in international regime complexes', available at https://static1.squarespace.com/static/5c54747ad7819e06b909fb1f/t/5cb1e0ffee6eb001467d9c3c/1555161343948/Vertical_April2019.pdf

PricewaterhouseCoopers (2017) *Basel IV*, available at https://www.pwc.com/gx/en/advisory-services/basel-iv/toobox-booklet-basel-iv.pdf

Quaglia, L. (2011) 'The "old" and "new" political economy of hedge funds regulation in the European Union', *West European Politics* 34 (4): 665–682.

Quaglia, L. (2012) 'The "old" and "new" politics of financial services regulation in the European Union', *New Political Economy* 17 (4): 515–535.

Quaglia, L. (2014a) *The European Union and Global Financial Regulation*, Oxford: Oxford University Press.

Quaglia, L. (2014b) 'The European Union, the USA and international standard setting in finance', *New Political Economy* 19 (3), 427–444.

Quaglia, L. (2017a) 'The political economy of post-crisis international standards for resolving financial institution', *New Political Economy* 22 (5): 595–609.

Quaglia, L. (2019) 'The politics of state compliance with international financial standards', *Governance* 32 (1): 45–62.

Quaglia, L. (2020) *The Politics of Regime Complexity in International Derivatives Regulation*, Oxford University Press.

Quaglia, L. (2021) "It takes two to tango": The European Union and the International Governance of Securitisation', *Journal of Common Market Studies* 59 (6): 1364–1380.

Quaglia, L., Howarth, D., and Liebe, M. (2016) 'The political economy of European capital markets union', *Journal of Common Market Studies Annual Review* 54 (s1): 185–203.

Quaglia, L. and Spendzharova, A. (2017) 'Post-crisis reforms in banking: Regulators at the interface between domestic and international governance', *Regulation & Governance* 11 (4): 323–450.

Quaglia, L. and Spendzharova, A. (2019) 'Regulators and the quest for coherence in finance: The case of los absorbing capacity for banks', *Public Administration* 97 (3): 499–512.

Quaglia, L. and Spendzharova, A. (2021a) 'Regime complexity and managing financial data streams: The orchestration of trade reporting for derivatives', *Regulation & Governance*, https://doi.org/10.1111/rego.12377

Quaglia, L. and Spendzharova, A. (2021b) 'Disentangling derivatives: International policy reforms concerning central counterparties', *Journal of Economic Policy Reform*, doi/full/10.1080/17487870.2021.1942874

Raustiala, K. and Victor, D. G (2004) 'The regime complex for plant genetic resources', *International Organization* 58 (2): 277–309.

Ridding, S. (2020) 'Money market funds brace for rules overhaul after Covid shock', Financial Times, 30 October.

Ringe, W. G. (2015) 'Capital Markets Union for Europe: a commitment to the single market of 28', *Law and Financial Markets Review* 9 (1): 5–7.

Rixen, T. (2013) 'Why reregulation after the crisis is feeble: Shadow banking, offshore financial centers, and jurisdictional competition', *Regulation & Governance* 7 (4): 435–459.

Rubio, M. (2017) *Shadow Banking, Macroprudential Regulation and Financial Stability*, August, London, available at https://www.suerf.org/doc/doc_f033ab37c30201f73f142449d037028d_5989_suerf.pdf

Rule, D. (2014) *Regulatory Reform, Its Possible Market Consequences and the Case of Securities Financing – Speech*, Bank of England, 6 November, London, available at https://www.bankofengland.co.uk/-/media/boe/files/speech/2014/regulatory-reform-its-possible-market-consequences-and-the-case-of-securities.pdf?la=en&hash=ABD1236A5AB5A35B9A0F051C2E174C6EC129E402

Rule, D. (2015) *Simple, Transparent and Comparable Securitisation – Speech*, Bank of England, 17 June, London, available at https://www.bankofengland.co.uk/-/media/boe/files/speech/2015/simple-transport-and-comparable-securitisation.pdf?la=en&hash=239D0F48CEC56073E63E745533C2EB96FCCA6C1E

Ryan, P. J. and Ziegler, N. J. (2015) 'Patchwork pacesetter: The United States in the multi-level process of financial market regulation', in Maynz, R. (ed.), *Multilevel Governance of Financial Market Reform*, Cologne: Max Planck Institute, pp. 65–96.

Schapiro, M. (2010) *Opening Remarks*, Securities and Exchange Commission, 7 April, Washington, available https://www.sec.gov/news/speech/2010/spch040710mls.htm

Schapiro, M. (2011) *Opening Remarks*, 22 June, Securities and Exchange Commission, Washington, available at https://www.sec.gov/news/speech/2011/spch062211mls.htm

Schapiro, M. (2012) *Statement on Money Market Fund Reform*, Securities and Exchange Commission, 22 August, Washington, available at https://www.sec.gov/news/press-release/2012-2012-166htm

SchoenmakerD. (2013) *Governance of International Banking: The Financial Trilemma*, Oxford: Oxford University Press.

Seabrooke, L. and Henriksen, L. F. (eds) (2017) *Professional Networks in Transnational Governance*, Cambridge: Cambridge University Press.

Seabrooke, L. and Tsingou, E. (2014) 'Distinctions, affiliations, and professional knowledge in financial reform expert groups', *Journal of European Public Policy* 21(3): 389–407.

Seabrooke, L. and Wigan, D. (2016) 'Powering ideas through expertise: professionals in global tax battles', *Journal of European Public Policy* 23 (3): 357–374.

Seabrooke, L. and Wigan, D. (2017) 'The governance of global wealth chains', *Review of International Political Economy* 24 (1): 1–29.

Securities Industry and Financial Markets Association (SIFMA) (2012) *Responses to Consultative Interim Report on Securities Lending and Repos*, 25 May, Washington, available at https://www.fsb.org/wp-content/uploads/c_120806k.pdf

Sengupta, R. and Xue, F. (2020) 'The global pandemic and run on shadow banks', *Economic Bulletin*, Federal Reserve Bank of Kansas City, 11 May, available at https://www.kansascityfed.org/research/economic-bulletin/global-pandemic-run-shadow-banks-2020/

Shapiro, I. (2005) *The Flight from Reality in the Human Sciences*, Princeton: Princeton University Press.

Sil, K. and Katzenstein, P. (2010a) *Beyond Paradigms: Analytic Eclecticism in the Study of World Politics*, Palgrave: London.

Sil, K. and Katzenstein, P. (2010b) 'Analytic Eclecticism in the Study of World Politics: Reconfiguring Problems and Mechanisms across Research Traditions', *World Politics* 18 (2): 411–431.

Simmons, B.A. (2001) 'The international politics of harmonization: The case of capital market regulation', *International Organization* 55 (3): 589–620.

Singer, D. A. (2007) *Regulating Capital: Setting Standards for the International Financial System*. Ithaca: Cornell University Press.

Singer, D. A. (2004) 'Capital rules: The domestic politics of international regulatory harmonization', *International Organization* 58 (3): 531–565.

Slaughter, A-M. and Zaring, D. (2006) 'Networking goes international: an update', *Annual Review of Law and Social Science* 2: 211–229.

Spagna, I. (2019) *Dealer Bank Influence and the International Political Economy*, Doctoral Thesis, University of Waterloo.

Sun, G. (2019) '*China's Shadow Banking, and Traditional Shadow Banking*', BIS Working Paper N. 822, Bank for International Settlements, November, Basel.

Tarullo, D. (2011) *The International Agenda for Financial Regulation – Speech*, Federal Reserve, 4 November, Washington, available at https://www.bis.org/review/r111107b.pdf

Tarullo, D. (2012a) *Regulatory Reform since the Financial Crisis - Speech*, Federal reserve, 2 May, Washington, available at https://www.federalreserve.gov/newsevents/speech/tarullo20120502a.htm

Tarullo, D. (2012c) *Statement*, Federal Reserve, 7 June, Washington, available at https://www.federalreserve.gov/newsevents/press/bcreg/tarullo20120607a.htm

Tarullo, D. (2013) *Shadow Banking and Systemic Risk Regulation - Speech*, Federal Reserve, 22 November, Washington, https://www.federalreserve.gov/newsevents/speech/tarullo20131122a.htm

Tarullo, D. (2014a) *Statement before Committee on Banking, Housing and Urban Affairs*, US Senate, 6 February, Washington, available athttps://fraser.stlouisfed.org/files/docs/historical/federal%20reserve%20history/bog_members_statements/tarullo20140206a.pdf

Tarullo, D. (2015a) *Thinking Critically about Nonbank Financial Intermediation – Speech*, Federal Reserve, 17 November, Washington, available athttps://www.federalreserve.gov/newsevents/speech/tarullo20151117a.htm

Tarullo, D. (2015b) *Advancing Macroprudential Policy Objectives - Speech*, Federal Reserve, 30 January, Washington, available athttps://www.federalreserve.gov/newsevents/speech/tarullo20150130a.htm

Tarullo, D. (2016a) *Pedagogy and Scholarship in a Post-Crisis World – Speech*, Federal Reserve, 21 October, Washington, available at https://www.federalreserve.gov/newsevents/speech/tarullo20161021a.htm

Tarullo, D. (2016b) *Opening Remarks*, Federal Reserve, Washington, 12 July, available at https://www.federalreserve.gov/newsevents/speech/tarullo20160712a.htm

Thiemann, M. (2014) 'In the shadow of Basel: How competitive politics bred the crisis', *Review of International Political Economy* 21 (6): 1203–1239.

Thiemann, M. (2018) *The Growth of Shadow Banking: A Comparative Institutional Analysis*, Cambridge: Cambridge University Press.

Thiemann, M., Birk, M., and Friedrich, J. (2018) 'Much ado about nothing? Macroprudential ideas and the post-crisis regulation of shadow banking', *KZfSS Kölner Zeitschrift für Soziologie und Sozialpsychologie* 70 (1): 259–286

Thiemann, M., Raquel, C., and Ibrocevic, E. (2021) 'Measuring and mitigating systemic risks: How the forging of new alliances between central banks and academic economists legitimize the transnational macroprudential agenda', *Review of International Political Economy*, 28 (6): 1433-1458.

Tortola, P. D. (2020) 'The politicization of the European Central Bank: What is it, and how to study it?', *Journal of Common Market Studies* 58 (3): 501–513.

Tsingou, E. (2008) 'Transnational private governance and the Basel process: Banking regulation, private interests and Basel II', in Graz, J.-C. and Nölke, A. (eds), *Transnational Private Governance and its Limits*, London: Routledge, pp. 58–68.

Tsingou, E. (2015a) 'Club governance and the making of global financial rules', *Review of International Political Economy* 22 (2): 225–256.

Tsingou, E. (2015b) 'Transnational veto players and the practice of financial reform', *British Journal of Politics & International Relations* 17 (2): 318–334.

Tucker, P. (2010) *Shadow Banking, Financing Markets and Financial Stability - Speech*, Bank of England, 21 January, London, available at http://www.bis.org/review/r100126d.pdf

Tucker, P. (2012) *Shadow Banking: Thoughts for a Possible Policy Agenda - Speech*', Bank of England, 27 April, London.

Turk, M. (2014) 'Reframing international financial regulation after the global financial crisis: Rational states and interdependence, not regulatory networks and soft law', *Michigan Journal of International Law* 36 (1): 60–128.

Underhill, G. R. D. (2015) 'The emerging post-crisis financial architecture: The path-dependency of ideational adverse selection', *British Journal of Politics and International Relations* 17(3): 461–493.

Underhill, G. R. D. and Zhang, X. (2008) 'Setting the rules: Private power, political underpinnings, and legitimacy in global monetary and financial governance', *International Affairs* 84 (3): 535–554.

Urpelainen, J. and van de Graaf, T. (2015) 'Your place or mine? Institutional capture and the creation of overlapping international institutions', *British Journal of Political Science* 45 (4): 799–827.

Vestergaard, J. and Quorning, S. (2019) 'The ECBs half-baked supervision mandate or, how to get serious about shadow banking again', *FEPS Policy Paper*, September, Brussels, available at https://www.feps-europe.eu/attachments/publications/vestergaard%20and%20quorning%202019%20-%20eus%20halfbaked%20supervision%20mandate%20-%2009%2009%202019.pdf

Verdier, P-H. (2009) 'Transnational regulatory networks and their limits', *Yale Journal of International Law* 34 (1): 113–172.

Viola, L. A. (2014) 'The G-20 and global financial regulation', in Moschella, M. and Weaver, K. (eds), *Handbook of Global Economic Governance*, London: Routledge.

Viola, L. A. (2015) 'Orchestration by design: The G20 in international financial regulation', in Abbott, K.W., Genschel, P., Snidal, D., and Zangl, B. (eds), *International Organizations as Orchestrators*, Cambridge: Cambridge University Press, pp. 88–113.

Walter, A. (2008) *Governing Finance: East Asia's Adoption of International Standards*, Ithaca: Cornell University Press.

White, M. J. (2016a) *Keynote Address*, Securities and Exchange Commission, 20 May, Washington, available at https://www.sec.gov/news/speech/white-speech-keynote-address-ici-052016.html

White, M. J. (2016b) *Testimony before the Committee on Banking, Housing, and Urban Affairs*, US Senate, 14 June, Washington, available at https://www.sec.gov/news/testimony/testimony-white-oversight-sec-06-14-2016.html

Woll, C. (2013) 'Lobbying under pressure: The effect of salience on European hedge fund regulation', *Journal of Common Market Studies* 51 (3): 555–572.

Woll, C. (2014) *The Power of Inaction: Bank Bailouts in Comparison*, Ithaca: Cornell University Press.

Woll, C. (2016) 'Politics in the interest of capital: A not-so-organized combat', *Politics and Society* 44 (3): 373–391.

Wood, D. (2005) *Governing Global Banking: The Basel Committee and the Politics of Financial Globalisation*, Aldershot: Ashgate.

Woyames Dreher, V. (2019) 'Divergent effects of international regulatory institutions. Regulating global banks and shadow banking after the global financial crisis of 2007–2009', *Review of International Political Economy* 27 (3): 556–582.

Young, K. L. (2012) 'Transnational regulatory capture? An empirical examination of the transnational lobbying of the Basel Committee on Banking Supervision', *Review of International Political Economy* 19 (4): 663–688.

Young, K. L. (2013) 'Financial industry groups' adaptation to the post-crisis regulatory environment: Changing approaches to the policy cycle', *Regulation and Governance* 7 (4): 460–480.

Young, K. L. (2014) 'Losing abroad but winning at home: European financial industry groups in global financial governance since the crisis', *Journal of European Public Policy* 21 (3): 367–388.

Young, K. L. and Pagliari, S. (2015) 'Capital united? Business unity in regulatory politics and the special place of finance', *Regulation & Governance* 11 (1): 3–23.

Zaring, D. (2013) 'Sovereignty mismatch and the new administrative law', *Washington University Law Review* 91 (1): 59–112.

Zaring, D. (2020) *The Globalized Governance of Finance*, Cambridge: Cambridge University Press.

Zeitlin, J. (ed.) (2015) *Extending Experimentalist Governance? The European Union and Transnational Regulation*, Oxford: Oxford University Press.

Ziegler, J. N. and Woolley, J. T. (2016) 'After Dodd-Frank: Ideas and the post-enactment politics of financial reform in the United States', *Politics and Society* 44 (2): 249–280.

Zurn, M. (2019) 'Politicization compared: At national, European, and global levels', *Journal of European Public Policy*26 (7): 977–995.

Index

References to footnotes are indicated by the footnote number following the page number e.g. '2 n3'.
References to figures and tables are indicated by an *italic* letter *f* or *t* respectively after the page number.